careers *for your*
characters

careers *for your*
characters

A WRITER'S GUIDE
to 101 Professions *from* Architect *to* Zookeeper

Raymond Obstfeld *and*

Franz Neumann

WRITER'S DIGEST BOOKS
CINCINNATI, OHIO
www.writersdigest.com

Careers for Your Characters: A Writer's Guide to 101 Professions from Architect to Zookeeper. Copyright © 2002 by Raymond Obstfeld and Franz Neumann. Manufactured in the United States of America. All rights reserved. No part of this book may be reproduced in any form or by any electronic or mechanical means including information storage and retrieval systems without permission in writing from the publisher, except by a reviewer, who may quote brief passages in a review. Published by Writer's Digest Books, an imprint of F&W Publications, Inc., 4700 East Galbraith Road, Cincinnati, Ohio 45236. (800) 289-0963. First edition.

Visit our Web site at www.writersdigest.com for information on more resources for writers.

To receive a free weekly e-mail newsletter delivering tips and updates about writing and about Writer's Digest products, register directly at our Web site at http://newsletters.fwpublications.com.

06   05   04   03   02   5   4   3   2   1

Library of Congress Cataloging-in-Publication Data

Careers for your characters: a writer's guide to 101 professions from architect to zookeeper / by Raymond Obstfeld and Franz Neumann.
   p.   cm.
Includes index.
  ISBN 1-58297-153-6 (alk. paper) 1-58297-083-1 (pbk.: alk. paper)
  1. Characters and characteristics in literature. 2. Occupations in literature. I. Title.

PN56.4.O25   2002
809'.927—dc21   2002069005
                                                                      CIP

Edited by Meg Leder
Designed by Joanna Detz
Production coordinated by Kristen Heller
Cover design by Brian Roeth

Acknowledgments

This book would not have been as mind-numbingly comprehensive without the significant contribution of writer Jennifer ("You Must Add This") Rice. And certainly would not have been as clearly organized, let alone done on time, without the indispensible guidance of editor Meg ("Iron Fist") Leder. We thank them.

About the Authors

Raymond Obstfeld is the author of twenty-seven books including *The Novelist's Essential Guide to Crafting Scenes* and *Fiction First Aid*. He heads the writing program at Orange Coast College in Costa Mesa, California, and has taught at Cambridge University and the University of California at Irvine. He has written mysteries, suspense thrillers, and mainstream novels that have been published in eleven different languages. Four of his novels have been optioned for movies. Obstfeld lives in Tustin, California.

Franz Neumann has written two novels, numerous short stories, and has published nonfiction in Salon.com. He holds an MFA in Creative Writing and resides in Long Beach, California.

Table of Contents

How to Use This Book

AS THE AUTHOR of over thirty novels, I have spent many hours researching at libraries the professions of my characters. I do this for two reasons: (1) to make the characters more believable to the reader, and (2) to help me discover more about the personality of my characters. The more I learn about the work I've selected for my characters, the more I learn about why the characters might have selected that work. This exploration of professions helps me create more complex characters, richer settings, and more compelling plots.

Many beginning writers make the mistake of only researching the protagonist's profession. They simply mention the professions of the minor and peripheral characters; stick a gun, calculator, or piece of chalk in their hands; and shove them into the story where they stumble around like actors who barely remember their lines. The more knowledgeable the author is about the professions of these characters, the more authority he writes these characters with—and the more impact they have in the story.

The Importance of Professions

Selecting a character's profession is one of the most important decisions that a fiction writer makes for five reasons: (1) Credibility: To establish a "willing suspension of disbelief" as quickly as possible, the writer must convince the readers to check their skepticism at the door. You know how many times you've read a novel or seen a movie and said, "Cops [or lawyers or doctors, etc.] would never do *that!*" The moment that idea pops into readers' heads, they lose faith in the story and the author's ability.

The author need only begin his police procedural with an accurate presentation of a crime scene; after that the reader will trust the author's expertise and no longer doubt his choices. (2) Character: The profession implies a lot about the character and spares the reader a lot of pace-hindering narrative. Announcing that a character is a teacher instantly tells the reader that this person is dedicated to higher principles than just earning money. Even if the character turns out to be other than that—a mean-spirited dictator, a lazy slob—the contrast of what she is with what we'd expected has a greater impact on the reader than three pages of childhood background. This reversal works just as well if you start with a profession that the reader reacts negatively toward, but then tell the story of how the character goes against reader expectations. The thief who risks his life to save others. The prostitute with a heart of gold. (3) Setting: The protagonist's profession provides setting, which allows the writer to texture the story with interesting insider details about the profession. Readers appreciate becoming more educated about a subject as an indirect result of a compelling story. Learning the inner workings of a forensics department or the intricate details of the daily life of a politician or film star can be a fascinating bonus. (4) Plot: A character's profession may be the main catalyst for the story's plot. If she's a detective or a lawyer, then there will usually be a crime. If he's a teacher, there will usually be a conflict with a student. Certain genres require a lot of information about the professions of minor characters. The mystery novel generally follows the simple plot structure of finding a body and interviewing possible suspects. To make these interviews interesting, the mystery novel usually has the detective showing up at a character's workplace and asking questions while she performs her job. The familiar pattern of the interview becomes more interesting because we get distracted by learning details about a profession. (5) Theme: A story's theme is often directly related to the protagonist's profession. A lawyer may seek order in life because she fears the chaos that human emotions sometimes produce. As a result, she may repress her own emotions and therefore be closed off emotionally, unable to form relationships. However, a person cannot live a fulfilling life without acknowledging the part of herself that is emotionally chaotic. It fuels our passion and our compassion. A cop may be compelled to aggressively force order on society because each arrest is a way to control his own building violent rage.

What You'll Find in This Book

Consider this: You go into a giant library and see about a billion books. You use the computer for a subject search and narrow it down to a couple hundred choices. Now what? Sit there for two days going through all the books for just one profession, repeating this procedure for each character? Why not ask the reference librarian? Maybe she knows something about these books.

That's this book: the reference librarians.

This book is not the sum of all knowledge about each profession, but it's a pretty good start. With this book you should be able to reasonably depict any of the included professions. And, if you wish to go into greater detail, the book lists various resources for further research. Here's the breakdown of each chapter:

- **The Lowdown** provides an overview of the advantages of using the profession in fiction, so you can decide if it's right for your character.

- **Job Description** gives an overview of a job and its general responsibilities so you know the basics of your character's job.

- **Daily Life** walks you through the typical daily duties and covers buzzwords your characters may use and clothing they may wear.

- **Education** explains the educational requirements of a profession.

- **Job Conflicts** presents the main conflicts that people in the profession face. Here, you'll find helpful ideas for developing plots and character conflicts.

- **Myths About the Job** discusses stereotypes surrounding the profession so you can avoid them and, as a result, create more-authentic characters.

- **Jobs Within the Profession** is a detailed breakdown of specific jobs within the field. You'll find information on the basics of the subprofession, including duties, education, and more. You'll also find resources for further researching the individual job.

- **Additional Occupations** is a list of related occupations you may want to consider researching if you can't find just the right one in this book.

- **Nonfiction Resources** lists nonfiction books and documentary movies for further research.

- **Fiction Resources** lists novels, movies, and television shows that feature the profession, so you can immerse yourself in other portrayals of the field.

- **Web Sites** offers the best Web sites for general research of the profession.

- **Book Excerpts** presents short excerpts from novels and stories that feature the profession.

Beyond This Book

This book will help you expertly represent professions. For many stories you won't need any other source. But if you do, use the various lists to go directly to the best sources without having to sift through thousands of selections (I've already done that!). Once you do your research, you may want to go directly to the source: Interview a cop, visit a toy factory, sit in a courtroom. Besides providing you with information you can use, this will build your confidence in your ability to portray these professions well.

CHAPTER 1

Advertising

Director, Creative Director, Art Director, Copywriter, Graphic Designer, Web Designer, Production Artist, Programmer, Production Manager, Traffic Coordinator, Media Director, Media Buyer, Research Executive, Independent Contractor, Account Executive, Client

The Lowdown

The world of advertising has been a popular fiction setting for several reasons: (1) It's cutthroat, so there's lots of plot and character conflict, (2) many writers (such as Elmore Leonard and James Patterson) received their training in advertising, so it's a world they know a lot about, (3) there's much creative activity, which makes it natural to reveal the creative side of a character, (4) the stakes, in terms of money and career, are high, and (5) built into the business is the age-old theme of commerce vs. art. That final feature is crucial because often it is the focal point of the protagonist's personal struggle: creating art that is his own personal expression to enlighten and entertain an audience vs. doing hackwork that misleads, manipulates, and misinforms the audience in order to please a client, sell a product, and promote his own career.

These elements provide characters in the advertising world with a lot of drama. The frequent deadlines of the profession provide built-in "ticking bombs" to intensify the suspense (Can the protagonist come up with a whole new ad campaign by tomorrow morning, or will she lose the client and her career?). In addition, the wacky nature of ad campaigns can provide a lot of broad comedy. Goofy ad campaigns can be a source of a lot of humor and plot fun. Also, throwing two characters with vastly different ideas and approaches together to work on the same ad campaign can create an atmosphere of hostility, backstabbing, or even romance.

Job Description

Advertising is the act of bringing a product or service to people's attention through print, television, radio, or other media in order to generate and maintain name recognition, boost brand awareness, and increase market share.

From television commercials to print ads, from direct mail (aka junk mail) to billboards, the handiwork of advertisers surrounds us. The average person is exposed to thirty thousand TV commercials a year and countless ads in newspapers and magazines. Advertising also takes advantage of new technologies—using methods such as banner ads, direct mail e-mail, and pop-up windows on the Web—while still utilizing traditional forms, like paper direct mail. Half of the mail handled by the U.S. Postal Service is direct mail, approaching a hundred billion pieces a year. With this bombardment, it takes a large group of talented individuals to make advertising retain freshness and effectiveness.

A 120 billion-dollar industry, advertising attracts professionals from a wide range of backgrounds. These professionals are responsible for varied tasks, including market research, graphic design, writing, and client relations. In 2000, advertising employed 302,000 people, mostly in large metropolitan areas, including New York, Chicago, Detroit, and Los Angeles. Of the twenty-one thousand firms, 80 percent had fewer than ten employees, with the majority of staff working on the creative side of the business. Eight percent of advertising professionals are self-employed. Many firms consist of only one or two persons.

In-House Advertising Department

Most advertising comes from independent advertising agencies and the in-house advertising departments of large corporations. For companies in need of advertising, an in-house staff of creative people can quickly create advertisements for products and services at a reasonably low expense. Companies whose advertising takes the form of enormous catalogs might benefit from having their own advertising resource close at hand. Though keeping advertising in-house may sometimes be appealing, creative directors, art directors, copywriters, graphic designers, and production artists can quickly tire of presenting the same products and services year after year. This can lead to lackluster advertisements and high turnover.

The Advertising Agency

One factor vitalizing the work of independent advertising agencies is competition. Companies who make known that they want to use a different agency are greeted with elaborate campaign ideas from numerous advertising agencies vying for new business. To win accounts, advertising agencies have to display their finest efforts.

Independent advertising agencies may offer a wide range of services, from marketing research to ad creation to placement and purchase of media space for an ad campaign. Smaller agencies, known as boutique agencies, may limit their offerings to their core competencies, such as concept and design. Thirty percent of all agencies specialize in a certain type of advertising, such as a product (e.g., soft drinks, automotive, billboards) or a medium (e.g., mass transit or interactive).

The Two Sides of an Agency

Those who work in advertising can be categorized under two groups: account services and creative services. Directors, media directors, media buyers, marketing executives, and account executives run the business side of an advertising agency, while those who create the actual advertisements are known as the "creatives." Some crossover occurs between the two groups. Those at the top of one group may have worked their way up. The creative director, for example, may have gone from production artist to graphic artist to art director to creative director, and she may also have experience in marketing.

Daily Life

Work Schedule
Running an advertising agency is stressful work. Directors work twelve-hour days, eschew free time and, like account executives, hopscotch across the country for campaign pitches and meetings. In general, the noncreative individuals who don't need to travel extensively, including media directors and traffic coordinators, have the most consistent hours. The creatives are prone to large swings in schedule, finding one week light and easy and the next filled with multiple twenty-four-hour shifts in an effort to create an elaborate advertisement, apply client changes, or make a print deadline. Roles and systems exist to attempt to level these extremes, but hard hours are more or less the nature of the business. It's not surprising, therefore, that many employees are young: A full 59 percent are between the ages of twenty-five and forty-four. Many young employees either work their way up the ranks or burn out from the frenetic pace and move to other professions.

Dressing the Part
Perhaps like no other workplace, the advertising agency hosts extremes of fashion. Account executives and anyone meeting with a client dressed in pressed, lint-free suits. At the other extreme, production and graphic artists may be pierced, shaved, and wearing headphones as they sit behind their twenty-one-inch monitors. In general, attire for those who never see a client is relaxed and casual.

Buzzwords
accordion insert: A magazine ad presented with an accordion-like fold.

adjacencies: Commercial time between television shows.

advertising budget: The amount of money an advertiser sets aside for advertising.

advertising page exposure: Measures the degree of opportunity people have to see an ad, regardless of whether they actually view or read it.

advertorial: An advertisement disguised as a press release or an editorial.

agency commission: Payment an advertising agency receives from media outlets, such as publications, TV shows, etc., in which they place a client's ad.

art proof: The version of an advertisement to be approved by a client.

artwork: The layout and graphics in an ad.

bait advertising: Pulling people into a store by advertising items that are difficult to find and often in short supply.

bleed: Ads in which graphic imagery extends to the very edge of a page.

body copy: The text in an ad. Text is further classified as *headline, tag line, pull quotes,* and *callouts.*

boutique: A small advertising agency offering limited services.

brand manager: The person in charge of marketing and maintaining the image of a product or company.

business-to-business advertising: Also known as B2B, this form of advertising targets an audience of business customers rather than individual consumers.

collateral materials: Advertising items such as catalogs, brochures, and data sheets.

consumer advertising: Advertising that targets end consumers.

cost per inquiry: The amount it costs to make one person interested enough to ask for more information about a product.

cost per thousand (CPM): The cost of purchasing ad space or airtime to reach an audience in increments of one thousand people.

creatives: The creative side of an ad agency; it is usually made up of art directors, designers, and copywriters.

direct mail: A polite term for junk mail; printed material sent through the mail to solicit business.

direct marketing: Marketing to consumers through telemarketing or direct mail.

direct response: Ads that ask viewers to respond, often through a promotion.

fulfillment house: A company that manages promotions and coupons.

full-service agency: An advertising agency that offers a wide selection of services, including marketing, planning, and media placement.

galley proof: A proof of an ad, including copy.

house agency: Referred to as an in-house ad department, this is an ad agency within a large company.

independent contractor: A freelancer hired by an ad agency to work on a project. Such freelancers may include art directors, copywriters, and designers and are often used to meet deadlines on large accounts.

insert: A printed ad, either unbound or bound, that appears in a publication.

media buying: An agency service that finds placement for ads.

media plan: Selecting media for an advertisement based on market and demographic research.

point-of-purchase displays: Also known as POP displays, these are often found at checkout counters.

storyboard: A complete outline, including dialogue and visuals, for a commercial.

Education

While some schools offer degrees in advertising, most ad agencies are made up of employees with backgrounds in marketing, business, liberal arts, and psychology. More important than any particular degree is the ability to consistently think creatively, keep clients happy, and feel fulfilled. Climbing the corporate ladder is much less a matter of holding academic degrees as it is practical experience and creative and business acumen.

Job Conflicts

Workload

While advertising is an attractive field allowing for upward mobility and paying solid, and sometimes generous, salaries, the work can be demanding. Often, advertising professionals find themselves in a never-ending cycle of deadlines, meetings, crises, and last-minute changes of plan. Travel, too, can quickly consume an advertising professional's schedule, so evenings and weekends must be spent working on clients' campaigns. Account executives must often juggle numerous clients and their whims while also vying for new business. Production staff can spend interminably long shifts in front of the computer.

Part of the reason for the heavy workload is the use of technology. Computers are now used for tasks that graphic artists and illustrators once did completely by hand. Creating illustrations, laying out images, and adjusting text are all done by computer, and formerly time-consuming tasks such as creating color proofs now often happen in-house on high-quality printers. On one hand, the move to computers has meant more creative opportunity, but the cost has been an increase in workload. Today's graphic designer is able to accomplish what would have taken a handful twenty years ago. The result is an increased pace of production and increased workload for all involved, including copywriters, creative directors, and even account executives.

On the other hand, work can disappear. Mergers, lost accounts, or economic downturns can cause agencies to lay off large numbers of employees. Those companies specializing in niche markets—for instance, the Web-only agencies of late—

can be devastated. In these cases, it may be difficult for former employees to find work.

Burnout

With the frenetic pace of advertising, many professionals can be easily drained of their creative energy. Some tire of working on the same accounts. Others simply suffer from sheer boredom in creating layouts for a catalog. For still others, advertising may no longer seem to be meaningful work. The result for agencies is frequent turnover of employees. Some people leave the business altogether; others move from agency to agency, propelled by the prospect of interesting projects or better salaries ahead. Even in good times, it's not uncommon for an employee to spend only a few years at an agency. It's almost expected. Management's challenge is to strike a balance between achieving successful accounts and keeping the job interesting and rewarding enough to keep the talent they've been fortunate enough to cull. This may mean increasing benefits for employees by providing better offices, company cars, or profit sharing.

Creatives vs. Account Services

Times of crisis caused by tight deadlines can set an agency's account services personnel and creatives at odds. Account executives may find that production on an advertisement isn't moving fast enough to appease a client's growing unease. Creatives, on the other hand, may feel that account executives aren't giving clear or timely enough direction on client changes; the timing for communicating change information determines whether the creatives have several days to finish an ad or must spend an entire weekend working on it.

Myths About the Job

Advertising Firms Will Do Anything to Steal a Client

This isn't so much a myth as an exaggeration. Major advertising clients, such as car or food companies, can generate many millions of dollars in revenue each year for advertising professionals. These clients are well aware of their power and often allow themselves to be courted by other agencies in order to create a more competitive edge within their current agency. In other words, the client, not the advertiser, usually dangles the carrot.

They Will Say Anything to Sell a Product

Again, this is an exaggeration. We hear about ads that blatantly lie about a product, but this doesn't happen as often as you may think. Yes, a car's ad agency ran an ad showing how well the car withstood a crash, neglecting to inform the public that the car in the ad was reinforced with steel. And there's the movie studio whose marketing department wrote for its movies fake positive reviews and ran them in ads. The fallout from getting caught lying usually isn't worth the risk. More effective and safe is to simply mislead in ads. For example, "I'm not a doctor but I play one on TV," promotes a painkiller. Or a dramatization shows someone claiming a doctor riding next to him on the plane gave him a particular painkiller. There was no plane ride, there was no doctor, yet the audience will associate that pain reliever with doctors.

Jobs Within the Profession

Director

Job Description: Climbing to the top of an advertising agency, either as a sole owner or as a partner, requires talent, dedication, and tenacity. Those at the top often have a balanced view of both the business and creative sides of the advertising process. Some start as copywriters or graphic designers, learn the craft on their way up the ranks, and gain managerial insight from their experience at one or more agencies.

Directors at smaller agencies may spend some of their time running the business and the rest as a creative director. In larger agencies, directors may be able to devote more time to developing their business. They may look for smaller agencies to buy in order to supplement their staff and expand their client list. Some directors may work tirelessly to get the business ready to go public. Others may prime their business for a buyout by a larger agency. Directors also try to attract new talent to their agencies while retaining their best employees.

Education: Degrees in business, communication, and graphic arts form a foundation; the practical education that comes from years in the advertising business is crucial.

Clothes and Tools: Directors dress to win their client's favor: a suit for a formal meeting; golf pants for a meeting on the links. A director is likely to keep a personal organizer in the glove compartment of her import luxury car and carry in her wallet an airline credit card with enough accumulated frequent flier miles to circle the moon.

Earnings: In a successful agency, a director can expect to earn $200,000 or more per year, though not without considerable cost in terms of his own free time. Keeping an agency successful requires the ability to work under pressure at all times. The occurrence of stress-related deaths among top advertising executives is 14 percent higher than that for executives outside advertising.

Further Info:
- Read an advertising executive's resume at www.advantageres umes.com/sample_of_avert_exec_res1.htm.

Further Reading:
- *Ogilvy on Advertising*, David Ogilvy.

Creative Director

Job Description: The creative director is responsible for the overall creative concept for an ad campaign. She isn't responsible for creating the design itself, but she must develop a campaign that conforms to an established strategy for the client. A creative director usually serves first as an art director or senior copywriter and should understand and be proficient in both the written and visual aspects of advertising. The creative director often works closely with the client's branding department in developing a campaign. He is responsible for the entire scope of the campaign and must supervise and give direction to the project's art director and copywriter. To achieve success in a campaign, a creative director must be a diligent administrator who is open to the ideas and complaints of both the copy and design sides creating an advertisement.

Education: A degree in design, communications, or business is most common.

Clothes and Tools: Creative directors tend to dress conservatively as a reflection of their position. They should be comfortable with the equipment involved in layout, film, photography, and typography.

Earnings: A creative director can earn up to $200,000 a year. As a reward for past work or an incentive to stay at an agency, creative directors may receive a share of the agency's profits.

Further Reading:
- *Up the Agency*, Peter Mayle.

Art Director

Job Description: Working under the creative director's supervision, the art director creates the graphics and layouts for print ads. The campaign may also involve video and photo shoots, which the art director commonly supervises. Mock-ups of an ad are created using the creative director's layout and the copywriter's text and then shown to the client for approval or revision. Once the client approves the layout and copy, the art director's role in the creation of that ad is mostly finished. Graphic designers and production staff handle the final production.

Education: A degree in graphic or visual arts is most common.

Tools: Art directors should be highly capable in creating mock-ups for the client and should be well versed in all software applications used by the production staff.

Earnings: The salary range is generally $30,000 to $80,000, or more, depending on the success of the agency.

Copywriter

Job Description: The creative director, art director, and copywriter make up the creative team that brainstorms and creates an ad campaign. In the heyday of copywriting, the text was the most important part of an ad. The art director used the copywriter's work to create visuals to reinforce the words. Today, copywriters and art directors are on roughly equal ground, working together to meld images and words into an effective message.

Copywriters may interview, research, and write everything from television ads to print pieces, from collateral materials (such as brochures) to direct mail. They may also edit copy provided by a client for a project and write articles and press releases for journals and newspapers. A copywriter's success lies in feeling comfortable enough with a vast array of products and services to write about them succinctly. Successful copywriters appreciate that effective advertising relies on a combination of text and graphic design; copywriters should, therefore, be comfortable with layout, design, and typography and know the advantages and limitations of different forms of media.

Most agencies hire copywriters with a minimum of three years of experience. Many copywriters start their advertising careers as interns or junior copywriters, or they cross over from another writing-related field.

Education: Typically, a copywriter has at least a degree in english or communication.

Tools: A copywriter spends much of her time in front of a word processor.

Employment Opportunities: Most copywriters work in large metropolitan areas. Small boutique agencies may rely on freelance copywriters. Most agencies have at least one full-time copywriter on staff. Agencies handling substantial accounts may appoint a copywriter to a specific account. Copywriters may be promoted to senior copywriter, creative director, and eventually partner.

Earnings: Junior copywriters can expect to start in the $30,000 range. Copywriters, especially senior copywriters, may be able to earn six-digit salaries if the result of their ideas is a boost in the fortunes of the agency. The average copywriter pulls in about $40,000 a year.

Further Info:
- American Association of Advertising Agencies
  130 Battery St., Suite 330
  San Francisco, CA 94111

Further Reading:
- *The Elements of Copywriting*, Gary Blake.
- *The Copywriter's Bible*, Designers and Art Directors Association of the U.K., ed.

Graphic Designer, Web Designer

Job Description: Designers typically specialize in one of three media: print, video, or interactive. Designers develop or refine on the computer the creation of the art director and copywriter. Graphic designers need to be proficient in visual design, typography, and color. A strong background in illustration or art history is also beneficial. To avoid creating impossible or over-budget designs, designers who work in interactive design need a thorough knowledge of programmers' capabilities. A strong understanding of interface design (the creation of navigation systems, such as menus and buttons) is another prerequisite.

Education: While a bachelor's degree isn't always required, most designers hold at least some degree in graphic arts. Web designers may come from a graphic design background or be self-taught.

Tools: Working in an extensively digital world requires designers to keep abreast of the latest in software improvements and exhibit comprehension of a wide range of software tools. These include industry-standard programs for image manipulation and creation, such as Adobe Photoshop, and layout, such as QuarkXPress. In addition, a graphic designer may need to use illustration programs, typography applications, and prepress and color calibration software. Web designers must be proficient in graphic compression and thoroughly understand the programming used for Web page creation. Some Web designers may code their own pages; others pass the finished graphics to production staff, who slice, compress, and place the graphics into coded Web pages.

Earnings: Designers earn annual salaries of $25,000 and up.

Further Info:
• Communication Arts Network (www.commarts.com). Site includes design sites of the week, along with columns on design issues, advertising, freelance work, legal affairs, and design technology.

Further Reading:
• *Becoming a Graphic Designer: A Guide to Careers in Design*, Steven Heller.

Production Artist, Programmer

Job Description: At the bottom of the creative heap lie production artists and programmers. They turn the designs of the graphic designers and art directors into finished products that can be sent to printers or uploaded onto the Web. Hours can be long and arduous; the work schedule is dictated by the speed of work coming from the higher-ups. For agencies with large retail accounts, holiday seasons start early, and work can be nonstop in the months preceding a major holiday.

Production artists must be able to carry a heavy workload of producing finished pieces based on someone else's creativity. This is the first step for someone working up to a position as graphic designer, and it's the perfect role for those who enjoy working with computers and want to build up a portfolio. Interns may work in these capacities.

Education: Production artists and programmers have a degree or have completed courses in graphic design or programming.

Clothes and Tools: Production artists are the lifeblood of an ad agency, but they're also kept far from clients' eyes—most production artists wouldn't have it any other way. As long as they are talented and work fast, they're left to their own devices and have such "luxuries" as quirky cubicles and personal music devices not enjoyed by other members of an agency.

Earnings: Salaries range from $20,000 to the low $30,000s. Programmers with specialized skills may earn much more. Compensation may include insurance plans and other benefits.

Production Manager, Traffic Coordinator

Job Description: During any given week, a successful agency has a score of ads that need to be finished and sent to the printer. While the creative team must communicate with the account executives regarding client changes and approval, the creative team also must coordinate with the production staff as well as outside agencies, such as printers. Making these professionals handle these logistics *and* create effective campaigns would be like asking planes to land at LaGuardia without assistance from a control tower. Production managers and traffic coordinators schedule the production of advertisements; allocate creatives to jobs; and track job numbers, deadlines, and revisions. Their most important role is to see that all employees get the information they need, thereby bringing projects to a close as quickly as possible and using the talents and time of the employees as efficiently as possible.

Production managers and traffic coordinators maintain records of approval and revisions and follow up on the status of ads sent to printers or clients. They may also create the schedule for the following week's work and give it to the creative department during production meetings.

Education: A degree in business is helpful, but the keys to success lie in impeccable organizational and communication skills.

Earnings: Annually these professionals earn $40,000 and up.

Media Director, Media Buyer

Job Description: Newly created advertisements must reach beyond the client and agency to be of any use. Ads must be placed in media such as magazines, newspapers, television, radio, and the Web. No client will spend millions of dollars on an ad campaign without also developing a solid marketing analysis to dictate where and when the ads go in front of the public. A media director develops media schedules based on this marketing, finding magazines and television shows, for example, that match the target demographic of the product or service being pitched. Media buyers contact media outlets' advertising sales agents and purchase print or airtime for the advertisements while following the budget set by the client. They keep tabs on outlets for future ads and need to be able to stretch the clients' advertising dollars.

Education: A marketing and/or business degree is useful for media directors and buyers.

Earnings: Media directors and media buyers can expect to earn $25,000 and up each year.

Research Executive

Job Description: For an ad campaign to be successful, its creators must thoroughly understand the market, including competitors, buyer demographics, and other data. Large advertising agencies may have their own research departments to gather this information. By collecting, analyzing, and explaining reams of data, a research executive can provide both the agency and the client with the basis for starting a campaign. Research executives must be adept at locating, mining, and presenting data from a wide range of sources, including text, databases, and the field. Research executives usually have at their disposal junior researchers who aid in the collection and analysis of data.

Education: Marketing or statistics degree.

Earnings: Annual pay for a research executive is generally $35,000 and up.

Independent Contractor

Job Description: Advertising agencies frequently use independent contractors, or freelancers, to help handle the workload. Agencies may hire freelancers to help with the enormous amount of work posed by a new account. Freelancers provide immediate help to agencies and reduce the need for the tedious process of recruiting and hiring new employees. For most agencies, the benefit of independent contractors' immediate availability outweighs their cost—most freelancers earn more per hour than full-time professionals do. However, freelancers miss out on fringe benefits and the promise of steady work; some work less than full schedules. Flexible hours as well as the prospect of working with a large group of people on many accounts are the main attractions for many freelancers. Others moonlight in this manner to supplement their regular income. The most common independent contractors include photographers, illustrators, graphic artists, copywriters, production staff, and art directors.

Earnings: Most freelancers bill their clients—the agencies—at a daily or hourly rate. Some agencies prefer to be invoiced at a fixed sum per project. Freelancers invoice their clients at the end of a job or at agreed-upon intervals during a long project. Independent contractors must typically wait a month or more for payment, and they sometimes need to make additional efforts to collect it.

Account Executive

Job Description: Account executives find new accounts, maintain and grow existing relationships with clients, and see to the fulfillment and deployment of ad campaigns to the client's satisfaction. Junior account executives may be assigned to less-lucrative clients or to attract new business—making cold calls, responding to inquiries, and meeting with potential clients. An account executive serves as the client's key contact at the agency.

Account executives must be confident, resilient, and relentless in their pursuit of clients. As a salesperson peddling an ad agency's services, an account executive must pitch his agency in such a way as to differentiate it from other agencies. Attentiveness to a client, coupled with the ability to succinctly communicate a client's desires to the creative team, makes for a successful account executive.

Education: Degree in marketing, advertising, or business.

Clothes and Tools: Account executives, who spend much time with clients, dress to impress. Word processors, databases, and personal digital assistants are never far from their fingertips, which are almost always holding telephones.

Earnings: Account executives can earn $30,000 to $60,000 or more per year.

Client

Job Description: An advertising agency's livelihood consists solely of its cut of its clients' advertising budgets. Oftentimes, clients with large budgets allow an established agency's creatives to flex their talents, which can lead to award-winning campaigns. A client can be an ad agency's greatest proponent, bandying the agency name about much like one would the name of a powerful Hollywood agent, but a client also can be a great source of frustration. Clients who lack faith in an agency, demand last-minute changes, and make late payments to the agency can seem like more trouble than they're worth. Agencies living on the edge typically must accept these types of clients—or go under.

A business starts the process of advertising a product or service by soliciting ideas from competing ad agencies. If the business is a lucrative one, agencies may spend small fortunes on mock-ups, elaborate presentations, and reams of research in order to earn favor and win the account. Each agency tries to sway the company to use its services. Once a business chooses an agency, that agency must develop an ad campaign. The business is now a client who may be wined, dined, and wooed to approve both campaign ideas and large budgets. For the client who is willing to let the agency utilize its talents in marketing and design, the experience can be fulfilling. Patience is also key—developing a campaign may take more than three months. For the client who dictates and attempts to excessively control a campaign, the experience can be frustrating. If a client and agency no longer work well together, the client may decide to start fresh with another agency (and the agency may be happy to see the client leave). Only 4 percent of advertising accounts switch to another agency each year. This low rate is probably due to the amount of work involved (the company must solicit bids then wait months for the new campaign) and the risk of signing on with an agency that is not an improvement over its predecessor.

Additional Occupations

Advertising is an enormous field encompassing a number of networked occupations, all of which contribute to either the creative process or the formulation and distribution of the message of an advertising campaign. Some of these other occupations include

- illustrator
- photographer
- video director
- video editor
- telemarketer
- media seller
- statistician
- public relations manager
- product demonstrator
- printer
- IT support
- advertising sales agent

Potential employers for the above positions include the following:

- corporations
- marketing firms
- magazines
- television networks
- billboard companies
- video production companies

Advertisers in Nonfiction

Books
- *Advertising Today*, Warren Berger. Guide to ad business.

- *Ogilvy on Advertising*, David Ogilvy. An insider account of the advertising business.
- *Up the Agency*, Peter Mayle. An invaluable collection of experience and insider knowledge of the advertising industry from a former copywriter and creative director.

Documentaries
- "The Ad and the Ego" (1997). Documentary on the cultural impact of advertising in America.
- "The Merchants of Cool" (2001). TV documentary about ads aimed at teens.

Advertisers in Fiction

Books
- *Big Trouble*, Dave Barry. Contains valuable insight into the daily grind and frustrations of a one-person advertising shop.
- *The Ladies' Man*, Elinor Lipman. Jingle writer affects three women's lives.
- *The Savage Girl*, Alex Shakar. Advertising, marketing, and trend spotting predominate this novel.

Movies
- *North by Northwest* (1959). Cary Grant is an ad exec in this Hitchcock suspense film.
- *Putney Swope* (1969). Underground classic about a black man's accidental rise in an ad agency.
- *Nothing in Common* (1986). Tom Hanks is an ad exec attempting to climb the corporate ladder while mending his relationship with his estranged father. Later adapted into a short-lived TV show.
- *Baby Boom* (1987). Advertising executive tries to balance work and raising a baby.
- *The Dream Team* (1989). An ad executive who thinks Jesus speaks to him joins a group of sanitarium patients on the streets of New York.
- *How to Get Ahead in Advertising* (1989). Stress takes a bizarre toll on a worrying advertising executive.

- *A Shock to the System* (1990). Ad exec portrayed by Michael Caine strikes back when he doesn't get a promotion.
- *Indecency* (1992). TV movie about three friends working in an ad agency.
- *Drop Squad* (1994). Kidnapping of a black ad exec whose ads belittle blacks.
- *What Women Want* (2000). Advertising executive gets the "gift" of hearing women's thoughts.
- *Kate & Leopold* (2001). Romantic comedy with Meg Ryan as Kate, who works in an ad agency.

Television
- *Bewitched* (1964–1972). Ad man Darrin Stephens is married to his job and to a witch. Sitcom is still in syndication.
- *Bosom Buddies* (1980–1982). Sitcom featuring Tom Hanks and Peter Scolari as advertising designers who must dress as women to get cheap rent.
- *Campaign* (1988). Television miniseries about an ad agency.
- *thirtysomething* (1987–1991). Extensive depictions of running a small independent ad agency and, in later episodes, working at a large firm.

Web Sites

- **Adweek** (www.adweek.com). The industry-standard publication for news about the goings-on of agencies, major clients, and the general state of advertising.

- **American Association of Advertising Agencies** (www.aaaa.org). Trade association for advertisers.

Book Excerpts

''Kyle Dice from Nestlé called this morning. He let me have it about the carob-egg breakfast cake.''

Javier looks up worriedly. ''It's not selling,'' he ventures.

''That was *your* thing, Javier, cake for breakfast. They followed you on that.''

Javier's fingers grope around in his unruly hair. ''Damn. It's their own fault. They did it wrong . . . It's too dark. People want bright foods in the morning: fruits, juice, eggs, cottage cheese, yogurt.''

—The Savage Girl, Alex Shakar

''Market researchers are public advocates,'' he says. ''We bring consumers' desires to the attention of private companies. We're like congressmen: we represent the public.''

Cabaj nods, thoughtful, then looks to Ursula. ''You think of yourself this way, too?'' he asks.

''Not so much like a congressman,'' she says. ''More like . . . a missionary. Or maybe a saint. Like Mother Teresa, kind of, but with an expense account.''

—The Savage Girl, Alex Shakar

''I look at this ad,'' the Big Fat Stupid Client From Hell was saying, ''and it doesn't say to me, 'Hammerhead Beer.' ''

Eliot Arnold, of Eliot Arnold Advertising and Public Relations (which consisted entirely of Eliot Arnold), nodded thoughtfully, as though he thought the Client From Hell was making a valid point. In fact, Eliot was thinking it was a good thing that he was one of the maybe fifteen people in Miami who did not carry a loaded firearm, because he would definitely shoot the Client From Hell in his fat, glistening forehead.

—Big Trouble, Dave Barry

At the beginning, he spent most of his time going around begging people to become his clients. But after a couple of years of hard work, he'd reached the point where he spent most of his time going around begging for his clients to pay the money they owed him.

—Big Trouble, Dave Barry

Advertising has been variously described as an art, a profession, a sinister instrument of mass persuasion, and a ludicrous waste of money. It hovers on the fringes of big business and show business, of sports and politics, of sleaze and respectability all at once. It is impossible to ignore, and yet most people deny that they are influenced by it. Sometimes it works and sometimes it doesn't. In either case, conclusive proof is hard to come by because of all the other elements involved in persuading millions of people to make a particular choice. It is this—the delightfully imprecise nature of advertising—that makes it such a happy hunting ground for the articulate young person who is convinced he or she has a great idea.

—Up the Agency, Peter Mayle

By the end of his first day on the job Harry had a friend and an enemy. The friend was Morton Radford, senior fashion artist of the department, a man who had survived four advertising managers and twenty years of alcoholism. He was now enjoying—or enduring—a dry cycle of five years, a new record in his colorful history. . . .

Harry was given a space at a battered desk in a cubicle with a young copywriter named Grady Woods, who casually sat on Harry's desk while introducing himself, as a way of establishing rank, but Harry was too dense to understand. Half an hour later he unthinkingly sat on Grady's desk to ask him some questions, and Grady startled him by saying, with remarkable ferocity, ''Get

your ignorant posterior off *my* hardwood.''
To a young man on the way up, his desk is a
vital extension of his personality, and can
be sat upon only by superiors exercising
their authority.

—Getting Straight, Ken Kolb

CHAPTER 2

Architecture

Architect, Intern Architect, Architectural Drafter,
Building Contractor, Interior Designer, Landscape
Architect, Civil Engineer, Urban Planner

The Lowdown

Fiction often contrasts the orderly world that an architect creates on paper with the chaotic life that he leads away from the drafting desk. Like writers who make every character say and do what they want them to say or do, architects create an efficient yet attractive use of space. Thematically, the profession of architect is sometimes used as a commentary on the danger of trying to control everything in one's life. It's one thing to dominate a space by drawing neat lines on paper; it's another to deal with people who live in that space.

Architecture provides an opportunity to reveal a character through the grandeur of his creative vision. A reader is impressed by someone who can envision an entire building, perhaps many stories high, then make it a reality. However, as with many other professions, this one also involves the conflict between commerce and art. The architect's grand vision is at risk of being compromised by the less knowledgeable client.

Another appealing aspect of writing architect characters is the opportunity to use their setting. The sheer size of buildings being constructed and amount of money that must be committed provides large stakes. A large cast may be written because so many people are involved in the planning, financing, and construction. Each step along the way is filled with potential conflicts that can spice up a plot and help flesh out characters.

Job Description

Architects design a wide range of buildings and plan and oversee their creation. Architects may specialize in residences, office buildings, shopping centers, schools, hospitals, or other buildings. Architectural drafters, interior designers, landscape architects, and lighting designers are some of the related professionals who bring an architect's vision to life.

Over 100,000 architects are employed in the U.S., and many architecture school graduates work as interns. Approximately 30 percent of architects are self-employed. Others work in architectural firms, the majority of which employ fewer than five architects. Eight percent of architects are women, but that number will change because 18 percent of new architecture degrees are earned by women.

Architects work as salaried employees at architectural firms or practice independently, most often in large metropolitan areas, including Boston; Chicago; Los Angeles; New York City; and Washington, DC. Most of those who are self-employed have worked at a firm. Self-employed architects may have the opportunity to work from home as well as to work part-time. However, since the number of new buildings is tied to the state of the economy, architects can expect fluctuations in the number of clients and ongoing projects. Architects may also be employed by building contractors or by the government. The Department of Defense, General Services Administration, and Housing and Urban Development employ 1,300 architects.

The successful architect exhibits the talent as a designer to create an internal sense of satisfaction, meets budget constraints, and consistently delivers pleasing buildings. Key among a successful architect's most desirable qualities is the ability to communicate concepts with a client and, in turn, win the client's trust and a higher degree of design independence. For architects designing suburban residential structures, success may be measured more by how well they manage to work within a budget. For architects designing schools or hospitals, success may be found in their ability to create environments conducive to learning and healing. For the top echelon of architects whose work graces the pages of coffee table volumes, success may be measured by the scale, complexity, and artistic quality of their work, as well as the legacy of buildings they leave behind.

Daily Life

Some 40 percent of architects work more than forty hours a week. Those who are self-employed may have lulls between projects, but all architects may work many overtime hours as critical design and construction deadlines approach.

Work Schedule
Here are some tasks that an architect may tackle during the course of a work day.

- Create plans or oversee the drafting of plans for a shopping center.
- Assist another client in choosing a site for construction.
- Aid a client in choosing a contractor for a building project.
- Discuss design ideas with a new client.
- Review new developments in heating, electrical, and plumbing systems as they pertain to a project.
- Visit the construction site to make sure work is progressing at a pace that will meet the deadline.
- Work on remodeling an office block to accommodate the disabled.
- Meet with the landscape architect on the shopping center project.
- Telecommute from home office and use Web-based tools to exchange information with the firm.

Dressing the Part

Business casual is the norm for most architects, and they may dress more conservatively when meeting with clients.

Keys to the Kingdom

Architects have access to construction sites, building plans, and computer drafting systems and networks.

Tools of the Trade

An architect's drafting tools traditionally include

- brush
- diazo copier
- dividers
- drafting eraser
- drawing board
- drawing pencils and leads
- drawing sheets
- engineering copier
- erasing shield
- irregular curves
- lettering guide
- lettering set
- protractor
- scale units
- stick eraser
- T square
- technical inking pens
- triangles

The current arsenal of drafting tools can be found in electronic form in computer-aided design (CAD) software such as Autodesk AutoCAD. In addition to using CAD software to print traditional paper designs, architects can export their designs to three-dimensional rendering programs that can create models and animations of their designs.

Elbow Rubbing

Architects deal with a variety of building professionals, including intern architects, who are learning the craft; architectural

drafters, who work on plans for buildings; building contractors, who erect architects' designs; interior designers, who
work in tandem with the architect to achieve useful and aesthetic space; landscape architects, who work to complement
a structure's surroundings; lighting designers; building inspec-
tors; and, of course, clients.

Buzzwords

aquifer depletion: Dwindling underground water supplies;
usually caused by usage that exceeds the rate for an aquifer to
be replenished.

green architecture: Encompasses a class of architecture emphasizing sustainability and energy efficiency achieved through the
use of such resources as solar power and renewable materials.

space planning: The creation of living and working spaces
with emphasis on the user.

streetscaping: Architectural and landscaping principles applied
to roadways, medians, and sidewalks.

telecommuting: Working away from an architect's main
office—usually from home or while on the road—through
the use of phone, fax, and the Internet.

Education

Architects hold at least a bachelor's degree in architecture from
one of the over one hundred schools of architecture accredited
by the National Architectural Accrediting Board. The degree
requires five to six years of study, which for some includes a
two-year program for a master's degree in architecture. Among
subjects architecture students study are design, architectural
history, graphics, architectural theory, engineering, math, sociology, economics, chemistry, building design, professional
practice, and urban planning. Skills are put into practice in a
design studio where they also learn drafting and CAD skills.
The final semester of an architecture program consists of creating a full-blown building project, including a three-

dimensional model. Skills are further honed and expanded in master's degree programs, and graduate degrees are an option for architects more heavily involved with teaching or research.

Licensing

Although an architect doesn't need to be licensed in order to design a building, a project needs a licensed architect to take legal responsibility. Most government projects and general building contractors do require licensed architects. Before taking the architect registration examination (ARE), an architect must hold a bachelor's degree and accumulate three years of experience as an intern architect; those holding master's degrees need only two years of experience. In some states, a candidate with at least twelve years of experience (in lieu of a degree) may be allowed to take the licensing exam after first passing a qualifying exam. Once a candidate has passed the ARE and has met the requirements set by the architectural licensing board in her state, she can practice and take responsibility for her designs. Architects licensed in one state are not necessarily licensed to practice in another. To maintain their licenses, architects in some states are required to continue their architecture education through seminars, independent study, or workshops.

Job Conflicts

Client's Budget

Two factors have the potential to stand in every architect's path: (1) the budget and (2) the client, who sets the budget. An architect has to be as much a salesperson as a designer when it comes to attracting clients. Once an architect lands an account, he must continue to serve the client's desires. At the same time, clients' uninformed opinions can't be allowed to sway the integrity of an architect's vision. The ultimate decision maker is the budget. Whether coaxing more money out of a client or cutting back on the scope of a design, an architect must be able to work within budget constraints without sacrificing the essential elements of her design. Sometimes finding alternative materials or methods is crucial to keep budget constraints from choking a project. In addition, an architect must be able to communicate actual costs to a client who may be unwilling to spend.

Vulnerability

In light of terrorist attacks on skyscrapers, architects now have to expand their view of the vulnerability of the buildings they design. In addition to natural disasters, acts by humans must be considered for such elements as emergency escapes, fire protection, and structural integrity. Debate on the future of skyscrapers themselves has arisen; some architects see the structure as persevering, while others have begun to focus on building equally efficient, more-horizontal structures.

Myths About the Job

Architects Are Wealthy

While associates in a successful architectural firm have a good chance of being well rewarded, competition for these positions can be intense. Starting salaries are modest, considering the amount of education and years of internship it takes to become a fully licensed architect.

Architecture Is All About Creativity

Many architects wish this were so. In truth, much of an architect's daily routine consists of poring over technical drawings and charts, as well as playing salesperson to try to gain new clients and projects.

Architects Are Expensive to Use

Unless you ask Gehry or Pei to design an addition for your house, an architect's services can be affordable. Different materials can be used in order to fit a budget, and an architect's insight can help make a building more energy efficient, which saves money over the life of the building. In addition, architects who bid out a construction project have the experience to judge whether a client is getting a good deal. Furthermore, by keeping a close eye on a project and visiting the construction site, architects can keep expensive construction delays to a minimum.

Jobs Within the Profession

Architect

Job Description: Architects design and oversee the construction of homes, offices, and other buildings. Architects who manage to retain their enthusiasm for architecture in the face of difficult clients and budget constraints enjoy a tremendous sense of accomplishment. Unlike almost any other profession, architects' work is manifested in huge physical structures, reminders of not only the efforts involved but also the success of providing a place to live, work, or play. Architects typically enjoy a wide range of other perks, including solid salaries, schedule flexibility (if self-employed), prestige in adding new buildings to their portfolios, increased contracts, and such luxuries as living in a home they designed. Architects also can garner the respect of the community through such activities as restoration projects or school or hospital construction.

Earnings: The median annual income for architects is over $50,000, and associates in successful architectural firms earn $100,000 or more. Self-employed architects may face more unsteady work, but those who are successfully established typically earn more than their salaried counterparts at firms. Going it alone can be an expensive endeavor for an architect. Self-employed architects must secure their own retirement plans and medical insurance, while most architectural firms offer both. While firms reimburse their architects' expenses, self-employed architects pay for their own travel, expensive drafting equipment, computer hardware, costly CAD software programs, and other business expenses.

Further Info:
- The American Institute of Architects
  1735 New York Ave., NW
  Washington, DC 20006

- The Association of Collegiate Schools of Architecture, Inc.
  1735 New York Ave., NW
  Washington, DC 20006
- The National Council of Architectural Registration Boards
  1735 New York Ave., NW, Suite 700
  Washington, DC 20006

Intern Architect

Job Description: After graduating from an architectural program, most, if not all, architects serve as interns at architectural firms. During a period of usually three years, they shape their knowledge of architecture with hands-on, real-world practice. Interns learn the complexities of design and planning by researching building codes and materials as well as serving as drafters who create architectural drawings. Interns may supervise a phase of design or construction, or they may create installation and building criteria based on a senior architect's designs. They can gain insight into the business operations by dealing with clients and securing plan approval from city and neighborhood organizations. Learning the practical aspects of an architect's career prepares them for the ARE.

Education: Interns hold a five- to six-year bachelor's degree in architecture and have studied design, theory, engineering, math, and other relevant subjects.

Earnings: The average intern architect can expect to earn about $35,000 a year, depending on the size and success of the architectural firm.

Further Info:
- The Intern Architect Program (www.raic.org/IAP-E.htm) provides guidelines for interns, employers, and mentors to help in the training of future architects.
- E-Architect (www.e-architect.com) provides forums for discussions on becoming an architect.

Architectural Drafter

Job Description: Architectural drafters carry out much of the production of architectural plans per the architects' specifications. While drawings used to be created by hand, most drafters now rely heavily on CAD software to generate diagrams, blueprints, and renderings. To help clients visualize projects, drafters create scale plans of structures, foundations, exterior landscaping, and interior designs. Other tasks include creating forms, charts, and diagrams for construction; developing schematic diagrams for wiring, cable, and electrical systems; and analyzing heat loss. Drafters may also be called upon to match a proposed building with the existing topography of a site, paying careful attention to existing pipelines and underground cable.

Education: Architectural drafters have usually attended a four-year college or technical school to receive technical training and knowledge in mathematics, science, engineering, and drafting standards. In addition to learning CAD drafting systems, many drafters have taken courses in freehand drawing. With experience and additional education, drafters can pursue careers in architecture or engineering. Although most firms don't require that drafters be certified, certification is provided by the American Design Drafting Association (ADDA).

Number of Architectural Drafters: The two fields (engineering and architecture) combined have about 100,000 drafters.

Earnings: The average drafter earns roughly $20 per hour, and senior drafters at successful firms earn more.

Further Info:
- American Design Drafting Association
  P.O. Box 11937
  Columbia, SC 29211
  www.adda.org
- American Institute for Design and Drafting
  966 Hungerford Dr., Suite 10-B
  Rockville, MD 20854

Further Reading:
- Architecture Magazine
  770 Broadway
  New York, NY 10003

- Architectural Record
  Two Penn Plaza
  New York, NY 10121
- Architectural Review
  151 Rosebery Ave.
  London EC1R 4GB
  United Kingdom
- Design-Build
  One Prudential Plaza, Suite 400
  Chicago, IL 60601

Building Contractor

Job Description: Building contractors coordinate the construction of new buildings per architects' plans. They order building materials based on architects' specifications and plan delivery of the materials to match construction stages. Building contractors deal with construction issues that need to be solved on the site and with an architect. Contractors may hire subcontractors to aid in construction and keep work on schedule and within set standards. In addition to building a structure, contractors coordinate inspections required for occupancy and performed by local authorities. Contractors hold state-issued licenses in a variety of trade areas.

Education: A contractor may have a degree in construction management, significant experience in a construction trade and business management, or both.

Earnings: A building contractor's income is dependent on the size and number of construction projects. The average income is approximately $50,000 a year.

Further Info:
- Associated General Contractors of America
  333 John Carlyle St., Suite 200
  Alexandria, VA 22314
  www.agc.org

Interior Designer

Job Description: Interior designers work independently or with an architect to furnish and enhance interior spaces to best suit a building's function and a client's needs. They may design interior spaces as part of a building's construction or during remodeling and redevelopment. Emphasizing aesthetics and functionality, interior designers may design custom furniture and lighting systems. They create drawings and three-dimensional models of interior spaces when necessary to facilitate visualization. They must use materials that meet code specifications, and they must work with an architect's vision. Working long, often odd, hours with a high degree of travel, interior designers can expect to work an average of forty-five hours a week. The workday may be extended in order to accommodate a client's schedule.

Education: Many interior designers hold a bachelor's degree in interior design from a school accredited by the National Council for Interior Design.

Number of Interior Designers: As of 2000, about forty-six thousand people worked as interior designers.

Earnings: Interior designers can expect to earn between $20,000 and $50,000 a year as consultants or as employees of engineering firms.

Further Info:
- American Society for Interior Designers
  608 Massachusetts Ave., NE
  Washington, DC 20002

Landscape Architect
Job Description: Landscape architects work with clients and architects to assess needs for outdoor spaces. Dividing their time between the field and the office, they may be consulted or hired to design spaces for parks, highways, shopping centers, residential and commercial properties, golf courses, hotels, and resorts. They survey grounds to determine such features as soil quality, drainage, and areas of sun and shade, then they decide where to create or place retaining structures, trees, plants, or water features such as pools or ponds. They may use three-dimensional modeling to visualize plans for grounds. In addi-

tion to designing and implementing drainage and water supply systems, they assess the needed function of a space, considering vehicle and pedestrian traffic, conservation, water supply, and any limitations per community rules.

Education: A landscape architect has a bachelor's degree in landscape architecture and experience as a postgraduate intern. Landscape architects are licensed by passing the Landscape Architect Registration Examination.

Number of Landscape Architects: As of 2000, landscape architects held about twenty-two thousand jobs, and over 25 percent of them were self-employed.

Earnings: Landscape architects earn between $25,000 and $80,000 a year.

Further Info:
- American Society of Landscape Architects
  636 Eye St., NW
  Washington, DC 20001
  www.asla.org

Civil Engineer

Job Description: Civil engineers design and construct infrastructure systems, including roads, dams, bridges, sewage systems, canals, airports, rail systems, and factories. In addition, they must study risks from disasters and design structures and infrastructures accordingly.

Education: Civil engineers hold bachelor's, master's, or doctor's degrees in engineering.

Number of Civil Engineers: There are over 230,000 practicing civil engineers, half of whom work for firms. About 12,000 are self-employed, working in a consultant capacity. The rest are employed by the government.

Earnings: The median annual income for civil engineers is $55,000. Salaries may be higher for civil engineers with additional degrees.

Further Info:
- American Society of Civil Engineers
  1801 Alexander Bell Dr.
  Reston, VA 20191
  www.asce.org

Urban Planner

Job Description: Urban planners create plans for the use of land, with particular regard to growth and revitalization of urban areas. An urban planner may specialize in one facet of urban planning, such as housing, transportation, urban design, environmental issues, or preservation. Their input helps developers, local governments, and residents decide if and how land should be developed based on a development's influence on the rate of urban growth and impact on the environment. Urban planners typically work forty hours a week plus additional evening and weekend hours to meet with local governments and communities.

Education: A master's degree in urban planning is usually required.

Number of Urban Planners: There are over thirty-five thousand practicing urban planners. Sixty percent work for local governments, often as advisors.

Earnings: The median income for an urban planner is $46,000 a year.

Further Info:
- American Planning Association
  122 South Michigan Ave., Suite 1600
  Chicago, IL 60603
  www.planning.org

Additional Occupations

Designing, constructing, and furnishing buildings require the craft and experience of a wide range of professionals. Some of these are

- building inspector
- carpenter
- craftsman
- foreman
- furniture designer
- heavy-equipment operator
- interior decorator
- landscaper
- lighting designer
- roofer
- security specialist
- space planner
- tiler
- welder
- woodworker

Employers for those positions include the following:

- architectural firm
- building contractor
- city inspector's office
- interior design firm
- security firm
- specialty trade firm

Architects in Nonfiction

Books
- *The Architect's Guide to Running a Job*, Ronald Green. Checklists and diagrams display an architect's role.
- *The Architect's Handbook of Professional Practice*, Joseph A. Demkin, ed. An exhaustive and thorough guide to the practice of being an architect.
- *Architects on Architects*, Susan Gray, ed., and Paul Goldberger. Architects discuss their influences and achievements.
- *The Architecture Pack: A Unique, Three-Dimensional Tour of Architecture Over the Centuries*, Ron Van der Meer. Pop-up book for adults allows unique exploration of architecture.
- *The Fountainheadache: The Politics of Architect-Client Rela-*

tions, Andy Pressman. Discussion of the keys to successful business relationships.

- *Landscape Architect's Portable Handbook*, Nicholas T. Dines and Kyle D. Brown. A concise resource for the practice of landscape architecture.

Architects in Fiction

Books

- *The Fountainhead*, Ayn Rand. The struggles of an architect in the 1920s and 1930s.
- *Outside the Dog Museum*, Jonathan Carroll. Architect suffers nervous breakdown in this magic realism portrayal.
- *The Physics of Sunset*, Jane Vandenburgh. An architect's affair set against San Francisco earthquake.

Movies

- *The Fountainhead* (1949). An architect bucks trends.
- *Strangers When We Meet* (1960). Kirk Douglas stars as an architect in love with a client's wife.
- *The Towering Inferno* (1974). An architect's skyscraper catches fire.
- *The Belly of an Architect* (1987). An architect becomes obsessed with his stomach.
- *Three Men and a Baby* (1987). An architect is one of three men juggling careers with caring for a baby.
- *Indecent Proposal* (1993). An architect and his wife want their dream home so badly they accept a millionaire's proposal.
- *Town & Country* (2001). An architect finds himself at one of life's junctures.

Television

- *The Brady Bunch* (1969–1974). This series features sitcom TV's most famous architect.
- *Once and Again* (1999–2002). While struggling with his failing business, an architect balances a new marriage, an ex-wife, fatherhood, and his role as a stepfather.

Web Sites

- Architext Links (www.morrisqc.com/architext). Comprehensive listing of links to architecture-related sites.

- Illustrated Architecture Dictionary (http://bfn.org/preservationworks/bam/vocab/vocab.html). Pictures of architectural elements in actual buildings.

- Yahoo! Commercial Directory: Architecture Firms (http://dir.yahoo.com/Business_and_Economy/Business_to_Business/Architecture/Firms/Complete_Listing/). Web sites of architectural firms.

Book Excerpts

When structures began to rise not in tier on ponderous tier of masonry, but as arrows of steel shooting upward without weight or limit, Henry Cameron was among the first to understand this new miracle and give it form. He was among the first and the few who accepted the truth that a tall building must look tall. While architects cursed, wondering how to make a twenty-story building look like an old brick mansion, while they used every horizontal device available in order to cheat it of its height, shrink it down to tradition, hide the shame of its steel, make it small, safe and ancient—Henry Cameron designed skyscrapers in straight, vertical lines, flaunting their steel and height. While architects drew friezes and pediments, Henry Cameron decided that the skyscraper must not copy the Greeks. Henry Cameron decided that no building must copy any other.

—The Fountainhead, Ayn Rand

''When did you decide to become an architect?''

''When I was ten years old. [. . .] I love this earth. That's all I love. I don't like the shape of things on this earth. I want to change them.''

''For whom?''

''For myself.''

—The Fountainhead, Ayn Rand

John Erik Snyte shot to his feet, flung a door open into a huge drafting room, flew in, skidded against a table [and] stopped. Within twenty minutes, he left Roark at a drafting table with paper, pencils, instruments, a set of plans and photographs of the department store, a set of charts and a long list of instructions.

—The Fountainhead, Ayn Rand

He saw the house to be as elemental as the perfect chair he had not yet designed but might one day, the old joke being that the most brilliant of architects was incapable of making a chair that not only looked good in a room but was actually comfortable for a human being to sit in. A chair had every physical and aesthetic problem pared down, reduced to simple form: context, balance,

materials, scale, all the problems in the
physics of stress and of fabrication.

—The Physics of Sunset, Jane Vandenburgh

≈

There were . . . no new buildings he honestly
admired. The best work in the Bay Area was
modest and residential and had all been done
so long before. The best work by modernists
was in Los Angeles, was being done by those
who followed Neutra and Wright, but that was
a city Alec actively hated.

—The Physics of Sunset, Jane Vandenburgh

Clergy

Roman Catholic Priest, Roman Catholic Nun, Protestant Minister, Jewish Rabbi, Jewish Cantor, Correctional Chaplain, Military Chaplain, Instant Minister

The Lowdown

Clergy members are popular characters in fiction because they live their daily lives amidst the turmoil and chaos of human weaknesses and personal failings, yet they are expected to remain pure. This conflict mirrors everyone's struggle to live nobly despite the temptations they face all the time. Recent news accounts of clergy members, especially Catholic priests, who face prosecution for molestation reveal just how difficult this conflict is. Yet clergy members symbolize human beings at their noblest, living self-sacrificing lives to better society.

Clergy as characters gives the writer an opportunity to explore the inner turmoil of the clergy and provides a rich array of characters and conflicts to create dramatic tension. Members of the clergy must help their followers through trying personal challenges: sickness, death, marriage, divorce, etc. Prison chaplains must deal with the problems of imprisoned criminals; military chaplains encounter the problems of people in a restrictive profession that might present life-threatening situations. The stakes are usually high.

Writers using clerics as protagonists can use the rich histories and teachings of specific religions to add texture to their characters' stories. Learning about traditions and beliefs that might not be familiar can enhance reader's experience by making the story more compelling.

Job Description

Clerics are spiritual leaders of religious congregations. This profession requires confidence, self-motivation, high levels of tolerance and compassion, and the ability to work well with others. Self-discipline is required: Most congregations expect their clergymen to live a life exemplifying the ideals of their religion. Despite these rigorous requirements, those who join the clergy generally stay in the profession for the rest of their lives. In 1998, 12 percent of clergy were age sixty-five or older; only 3 percent of workers in all professional specialty occupations fell into this age bracket.

Clerics' main religious duty is to interpret the beliefs and traditions of their faith and teach them to the members of their congregations. This includes organizing and leading regular religious services as well as officiating at special ceremonies such as confirmations, weddings, and funerals. Leading a religious service usually involves initiating group prayer, administering sacraments, delivering a sermon, and reading from a sacred text (e.g., the Bible for Christians, the Torah for Jews, the Qur'an for Muslims). Spiritual duties may also extend to activities outside the religious ceremonies: visiting the sick; comforting those who are grief stricken; and counseling troubled congregants on personal, spiritual, and moral problems.

Most clerics also have numerous administrative duties related to maintaining the place of worship and running various programs for the congregrants and the community. This includes soliciting donations, increasing membership, and organizing programs that range from education to youth sports to senior activities. Depending upon the type of congregation, some clergymen also work with committees and officials, elected by and from the congregation, who oversee the finances of the congregation.

Large congregations may have more than one clergyman. Sometimes one is the senior cleric while the other serves as an associate. Senior clerics tend to deal with the administrative duties of overseeing building maintenance, ordering supplies, raising funds, and supervising staff and volunteers. Associates sometimes specialize in one or more areas such as music, education, or youth ministry.

Daily Life

Work Schedule
Typically, clerics who lead congregations work long hours and have irregular schedules. Those who work outside the congregational setting, such as teachers or chaplains, tend to have more-regular schedules. In 1998, nearly one-fifth of full-time clergy members—three times the proportion of all workers in professional specialty occupations—put in more than sixty hours per week. Although their duties tend to be intellectual, they are called upon at short notice to help congregants in need of comforting or counseling. The community, administrative, and educational responsibilities of clerics often demand that they work early mornings, evenings, holidays, and weekends.

Dressing the Part
Clerics may dress in suits or casual clothes, depending on the duties they are performing. Some religions (such as Roman Catholicism and Orthodox Judaism) require that special robes and other adornments be worn for performing certain ceremonies. Roman Catholic priests wear white clerical collars, as do some ministers. See "Jobs Within the Profession" later in the chapter for additional information.

Buzzwords
deacon: In Episcopal churches, minister of the third order, below bishop and priest. In various Protestant churches, a lay officer who deals with secular concerns of the church.

Eucharist: The Christian sacrament commemorating the Last Supper. Consecrated bread and wine symbolizing the body and blood of Christ are consumed.

God squad: A slang term referring to members of the clergy or any zealous religious group.

liturgy: A form of public worship that may have certain formalities regarding how it is performed.

Mass: In the Roman Catholic Church, the ceremony of the Eucharist. *High Mass* includes the use of incense and music and usually the assistance of a deacon or subdeacon. *Low Mass* is performed with no music and a minimum of ceremony.

parish: An area having its own church and clergy.

parishioner: A member of a parish.

parochial: Of or concerning a parish.

parochial school: A private elementary or high school maintained by a religious organization, especially the Roman Catholic Church.

parson: A member of the Protestant clergy.

pastor: A priest or minister in charge of a church or congregation.

rector: In the Church of England, the incumbent of a parish. In the Roman Catholic Church or Episcopal Church, a priest in charge of a church or religious institution.

rectory: The priest's house.

sinhound: A slang term for *minister.*

synagogue: A Jewish place of worship. Some are called *temples,* depending upon the denomination.

Torah: The sacred text containing the Pentateuch (the first five books of Jewish and Christian scriptures). Written in Hebrew, the Torah is a scroll kept in an ark.

yarmulke: A skullcap worn by Jewish males.

Education

Educational requirements for clerics vary greatly by denomination. Currently, three out of four members of the clergy have earned at least a bachelor's degree. Some denominations accept into the clergy anyone, regardless of education, who has been "called" by God to the profession. However, many denominations insist on not only a bachelor's degree but also graduate studies in theology.

Job Conflicts

Women in the Clergy

Some denominations do not allow women to serve in the clergy. For example, the Roman Catholic Church does not permit women to serve as priests. This hotly debated issue has given rise to action. Breakaway congregations have formed in several denominations. Women can serve as clerics, but these congregations are not officially recognized by their main church. Rules are changing regularly. As various denominations hold their conferences, new rules regarding women in the clergy are put to a vote. Each year more denominations endorse women in the clergy. Check with a particular denomination for the current status of this issue.

Loss of Faith

Like any other professional, a clergyman may experience job burnout. This can manifest itself as a loss of faith, either in God or in the cleric's own ability to perform required duties. Members of the clergy, often called upon to help people through the darkest times, are exposed to an excess of emotional turmoil. Over time, this can cause them to question their faith in God's plan.

Confessions

Many stories have been written regarding the sanctity of a confession. Typically in such stories a criminal confesses to a crime he's committed or is about to commit, and the priest agonizes over whether to inform the authorities or honor his duty to remain silent. Legally, a priest cannot be compelled to reveal the content of a confession. The conflict lies between the priest's duty to the confessor and the priest's obligation to protect the community. This dilemma applies only to Roman Catholic priests. Other denominations' and religions' clergy have no legal expectation of complete confidence.

Celibacy

Roman Catholic priests and nuns take a vow of celibacy. The past few decades have seen much debate regarding this requirement within the Church, especially in view of the decreasing number of priests. This conflict is also a favorite of writers since it deals with the powerful theme of bodily passions vs. spiritual commitments.

Sexual Misconduct

Society has been plagued with revelations of sexual misconduct by members of the clergy, especially that of the Roman Catholic Church. This issue has provided the story line for many movies, TV shows, and novels. These stories address not just the sexual act but the clerics' drives vs. duties and the congregants' trust of those in authority. In addition, such stories often examine how churches deal with such accusations. Some turn a blind eye to such activity or even cover up the incidents.

Homosexuality

A hot topic among many congregations is how to treat homosexuals. The issue is raised on an annual basis at most conferences. Some groups condemn the act but not the person; these groups accept homosexuals as part of the congregation and try to convince them not to act on their desires. Some people even claim they can "cure" homosexuality through prayer and counseling. Other congregations reject the act and the participant as evil; this has led to breakaway congregations that welcome homosexuals and may be ministered by openly homosexual clerics.

Church Hierarchy

Members of the clergy often may be at odds with those with whom they work. Conflict may arise with someone higher up in the religion's organization or with a board of laypersons who disagree with the clergyman's methods. In many stories that deal with this conflict, the clergy member is often more progressive or liberal than her superiors. This is especially true in stories dealing with prison and military chaplains.

Myths About the Job

Clergy Members Have Overcome Temptation and Live Serene, Contemplative Lives

Recent news accounts of priests who have molested youth, a rabbi who hired a hit man to kill his wife, and Buddhist monks who have been in fistfights with each other confirm that clerics constantly struggle with the same desires as the rest of us. When one "falls" it makes the news and serves as a warning to all of us. However, despite the occasional sensational story, the vast majority of clergy are respected because they face temptations and resist them.

Clergy Members Live in Harmony With Their Congregations

A main conflict in a clergy member's life is his relationship with the congregation. Sometimes clerics must strike a balance between what the religion teaches and what the congregation wants to hear. For example, being too dogmatic and strict can alienate the congregation and lead to the cleric's dismissal. Delivering boring sermons can lead to the same fate. Being an effective clergy member requires an entertainer's awareness of how to affect the audience.

Jobs Within the Profession

Roman Catholic Priest

Job Description: Catholic clergy members are male and called priests (see "Women in the Clergy"). They take oaths of celibacy and obedience. A priest, especially of a religious order, is often addressed as Father (e.g., Father Ryan).

There are two types of priests: diocesan and religious. All priests are ordained by a bishop and have the same powers within the church. The two types differ in terms of lifestyle, work, and the church authority to which they answer.

Diocesan priests serve the people of a diocese, which is a church region. The bishop of a diocese usually assigns a diocesan priest to a parish, and a newly ordained diocesan priest may begin his career as an assistant pastor. A priest's day usually begins with morning meditation and Mass and may end with either parishioners' counseling sessions or an evening visit to a home or hospital. Diocesan priests counsel couples preparing to marry or parishioners dealing with personal or spiritual problems. The priest may also be involved with charitable organizations and community projects.

Leaders of a religious order assign duties to religious priests. Some religious priests specialize in areas such as teaching or counseling. Others serve as missionaries in foreign countries and often live in extremely primitive conditions. Still others live in monasteries (secluded religious communities) where they spend their time in prayer, study, and monastery chores such as gardening.

Both religious and diocesan priests may work as teachers and administrators in Catholic seminaries, colleges, universities, and high schools. Religious priests tend to staff institutions of higher learning, while a diocesan priest usually focuses on the parochial school associated with his church.

The hierarchy of the Catholic clergy is as follows:

- **Pope**. Head of church, infallible in matters of faith and morals.

- **Cardinal**. Appointed by the Pope. There are 178 Cardinals worldwide, including 13 in the U.S. They form the College of Cardinals, advising the Pope and, upon his death, choosing his successor.

- **Archbishop**. A Bishop of a large diocese, called an archdiocese. A Cardinal can also be an Archbishop. There are 45 Archbishops in the U.S.

- **Bishop**. Teacher of church doctrine, a priest of sacred worship, a minister of church government. The U.S. has 290 active Bishops, of which 194 head a diocese.

- **Priest**. Ordained minister with the power to administer most sacraments. He can be a member of a particular religious order or serve a congregation.

- **Deacon**. A transitional deacon is a seminarian studying for priesthood. A permanent deacon assists a priest in performing some sacraments. He can be married.

Education: Becoming a priest usually requires a bachelor's degree plus four years of theology study at a seminary. Training can begin as early as high school. As of 1998, nine high school seminaries offered college-preparatory programs, which usually focus on English grammar, speech, literature, social studies, and religion. Latin is sometimes required, and the study of modern languages is encouraged. Hispanic communities require a thorough knowledge of Spanish.

College training for the priesthood takes place at eighty-seven priesthood formation programs offered through Catholic colleges or universities or college seminaries. Studies usually include philosophy, religion, and prayer.

After receiving a four-year college degree, the aspiring priest earns his master of divinity or master of arts degree at one of the forty-seven theological seminaries (also called theologates). Theological courses usually include sacred scripture; dogmatic, moral, and pastoral theology; homiletics (the art of preaching); Catholic church history; liturgy (sacraments); and canon law. Fieldwork is generally required.

Postgraduate (beyond ordination) work is encouraged by the church. Many priests specialize in fields other than theology, particularly in social sciences such as psychology and sociology.

Clothes: A priest wears a clerical collar. During religious ceremonies, he may also wear a small square cap with three ridges on top called a *biretta*. Ropes, belts, and sashes used to close the vestments are called *cinctures*. The vestments of bishops and cardinals are more elaborate and differ from one another.

Number of Priests: In 1998, about forty-seven thousand men were priests, two-thirds of whom were diocesan priests. Although priests are in nearly every town and rural community, the majority are in large cities, where most Catholics live.

The last few decades have seen increasing shortages in the number of priests. As of 2002, there are not enough priests to fill the needs of the church, and seminary enrollment is currently insufficient to solve the shortage. The church has responded to this shortage by allowing permanent deacons and laypersons to perform certain functions within the church. Ordained deacons, whose number has increased significantly over the past twenty years, are permitted to preach and perform liturgical functions such as baptisms, marriages, and funerals. However, deacons may neither celebrate Mass nor administer the sacraments of reconciliation and anointing of the sick.

Earnings: Diocesan priests' salaries vary by diocese. In 1998, the annual salary range was $12,936 to $15,483. Diocesan priests also may receive benefits such as a car allowance, room and board in the parish rectory, health insurance, and a retirement plan. The diocesan priest who performs church-related work such as teaching is likely to receive less pay than a layperson who does the same job. A priest may receive "contributed services," including housing and related living expenses, as compensation.

Because religious priests take a vow of poverty, their expenses are paid by the religious order. Religious priests donate all personal earnings to the order. The Internal Revenue Service recognizes their vow of poverty and exempts them from paying federal income tax.

Further Info:
- Center for Applied Research in the Apostolate (CARA)
  Georgetown University
  Washington, DC 20057
- Vocations and Priestly Formation: United States Conference of Catholic Bishops (www.nccbuscc.org/vocations/index .htm). Provides information on becoming an ordained priest.

Further Reading:
- *Sex, Priests, and Power: Anatomy of a Crisis*, A.W. Richard Sipe.
- *The Spirituality of the Diocesan Priest*, Donald B. Cozzens.
- *Far From Rome, Near to God: Testimonies of Fifty Converted Roman Catholic Priests*, Richard Bennett, ed.
- *Extraordinary Lives: Thirty-Four Priests Tell Their Stories*, Francis P. Friedl and Rex Reynolds.

Roman Catholic Nun

Job Description: Although nuns are prohibited from performing the sacraments, they share most of the duties of priests. Nuns teach kindergarten through university level classes and serve as school administrators as well. They perform missionary work at home and abroad, often in dangerous and hostile environments. Some nuns serve as nurses and doctors, and some others run community service organizations.

Education: The Passionate Nuns of St. Joseph's Monastery provide the following prerequisites for becoming a nun: A woman must (1) be a Roman Catholic for at least three years, (2) be between the ages of eighteen and forty, (3) be a high school graduate capable of some college-level study, (4) have at least two years' experience in some social life, and (5) be physically and psychologically healthy. To become a nun a woman must (1) contact a monastery, (2) serve as an aspirant for at least seven weeks, (3) serve as a postulant for one year, (4) serve as a novice for one year, (5) serve as a junior professed nun for six years, and (6) make a final profession. This process may vary depending upon the order that one wishes to join.

Clothes: Many nuns today wear casual clothes like everyone else does. Few wear the traditional *habits* we're used to seeing on nuns in the movies. The traditional white band that encircles a nun's face is called a *wimple*. The wide cloth that covers the neck and shoulders is a *guimpe*. The cloth hanging down from the back of the head is called a *veil*. A nun usually wears a cross that hangs around her neck.

Further Info:
- Poor Clares of Perpetual Adoration (www.poorclares.org/dis

cern.html). Provides information on how to become a nun at the Sancta Clara Monastery. (Contact them at 4200 N. Market Ave., Canton, OH 44714; (330) 492-1171; or sismomzelt@ yahoo.com.)

Further Reading:
• *For the Love of God: The Faith and Future of the American Nun*, Lucy Kaylin.

Protestant Minister

Job Description: Most Protestant ministers serve the five largest Protestant denominations: Baptist, Episcopalian, Lutheran, Methodist, and Presbyterian. The duties of ministers vary greatly among the denominations and even within a denomination. In general, the minister leads the congregation in worship services and administers certain rites, including baptism, confirmation, and Holy Communion. The worship services vary widely. Some ministers follow a strict traditional order while others make changes to fit the needs of the congregation. In general, worship services include Bible readings, hymn singing, prayer, and a sermon. Ministers also officiate at weddings, funerals, and other occasions. Ministers of small congregations generally take a hands-on approach to running the church and working with members of the congregation. However, churches with large congregations may have several ministers who cover specific areas, such as education and music.

Newly ordained ministers often begin their careers in small churches or as assistant pastors in churches with experienced ministers and large congregations. Pastoring a church with a large congregation usually requires many years of experience. Most ministers serve in urban areas, but in less-populated areas, a minister may serve two or more congregations. Some small churches hire part-time ministers, usually seminary students, retired ministers, or even specially trained laypersons.

The hierarchy of a church depends upon its denomination. In some denominations, ministers are hired by and responsible only to the congregation they serve. In others, ministers work under elder ministers or at the direction of the diocese bishop. Some denominations transfer ministers to new pastorates every few years.

Some denominations permit women to serve as ministers; others do not. Check with a particular denomination for its current status on this issue.

Education: Each denomination has its own educational and training requirements. Many demand a bachelor's degree as well as some theological studies at a seminary. Yet some denominations require no formal training or religious education and may ordain as a minister a recent high school graduate.

Large denominations have their own schools of theology, but some of these schools are open to members of other denominations. In 1998 and 1999, the Association of Theological Schools in the U.S. and Canada accredited 135 Protestant theo logical schools. Students admitted must already have earned a bachelor's degree or its equivalent. Many denominations require for the master of divinity degree a three-year course following the completion of the bachelor's degree. Curriculum consists of Bible studies, history, theology, practical theology, pastoral care, preaching, religious education, and administration. A doctor of ministry degree usually requires an additional two years of study and two years of service as a minister.

Clothes: In general, a minister wears a suit or casual clothing as appropriate for the occasion. During worship services or other religious ceremonies, ministers may wear special garments. These include a clerical collar, a robe or a *cassock,* a shorter robe (*surplice*) worn over the cassock, an academic hood that hangs down the back, and a shawl (*tippet*).

Number of Ministers: In 1998, over 400,000 people were Protestant ministers. This number includes such related clergy members as chaplains in hospitals, the armed forces, universities, and correctional facilities.

Earnings: Annual earnings vary depending upon the education and experience of the minister as well as the size and wealth of the congregation. Some denominations pay their ministers according to the average income of members of the congregation. These ministers who serve urban, wealthy areas can earn high salaries. Ministers who work with less-affluent congregations sometimes take part-time secular second jobs to make ends meet.

Further Info:
- Religious Pastoral Ministry (www.msj.edu/career/rel_pm.ht m). Provides information about education, training, and jobs for ministers.

Further Reading:
- *A Guide to Religious Ministries*, Victor L. Riddler. Helpful information on choosing a career as a minister.

Jewish Rabbi

Job Description: Rabbis serve as heads of congregations in one of four branches of Judaism (in order of traditional orthodoxy): Orthodox, Conservative, Reform, and Reconstructionist. The denominations differ in how literally they follow the teachings of the Torah. Because of this, the rabbis' duties regarding worship services vary among branches, and they can vary within a branch. Maimonides, a twelfth-century Jewish philosopher, described the seven requirements for being a rabbi: "Wisdom. Humility. Fear of God. Aversion to materialism. Love of truth. Pleasant and likeable. An unimpeachable reputation."

Judaism lacks the formal hierarchy of most other religions, giving rabbis more independence in how they choose to lead their congregations. Rabbis are hired by and responsible to a board of trustees of the congregation. Large congregations may also have associate or assistant rabbis. The rabbi is responsible for leading worship services, which take place on Friday nights and Saturday mornings. He also is responsible for maintaining the synagogue and supervising educational and community programs. Rabbis may also teach in theological seminaries, colleges, or universities or serve as chaplains in hospitals, colleges, or the military.

Education: To become a rabbi, a student must complete work in a Jewish seminary, most of which require a college degree to enroll. Courses depend upon the branch of Judaism but generally include the study of the Bible, the Torah, rabbinic literature, Jewish history, Hebrew, theology, education, pastoral psychology, and public speaking. Recently, training for leadership in community service and religious education have been stressed. In general, it takes five years to complete the program at a Jewish seminary. Graduates receive Master of Arts in Hebrew Letters degrees; with additional studies, they can earn a Doctor of Hebrew Letters degree.

Major seminaries include the Jewish Theological Seminary of America (Conservative), the Hebrew Union College-Jewish Institute of Religion (Reform), and the Reconstructionist Rabbinical College (Reconstructionist). About thirty-five seminaries, including the Rabbi Isaac Eichanan Theological Seminary, train Orthodox rabbis. Even though the number of seminaries is high, the number of attendees at each is relatively low. Only about 10 percent of the Jewish population practice Orthodox Judaism.

Clothes: Most of the time, rabbis and cantors wear suits or casual clothes, depending upon the occasion. During worship services they may wear, depending upon the denomination, certain traditional garments, including a *yarmulke* and a prayer shawl (*tallith*).

Number of Rabbis: The approximate number of rabbis in 1999 was, in order of size of membership, Reform, 1,800; Conservative, 1,175; Orthodox, 1,800; and Reconstructionist, 250.

Earnings: Salaries vary widely depending upon congregation size and geographical location. As of 1998, the salary range for rabbis was about $50,000 to $100,000, including benefits such as housing, health insurance, and retirement plans. Some rabbis earn additional fees for performing weddings, Bar Mitzvahs (for boys), and Bat Mitzvahs (for girls).

Further Info:
- General: Jewish. Community at www.Jewish.com/askarabbi/. Answers frequently asked questions about Judaism, including how to become a rabbi or a cantor.
- Orthodox: Rabbinical Council of America
  305 Seventh Ave.
  New York, NY 10001
  www.rabbis.org

- Conservative: Jewish Theological Seminary of America
  3080 Broadway
  New York, NY 10027
  www.jtsa.edu
- Reform: Hebrew Union College-Jewish Institute of Religion
  One W. Fourth St.
  New York, NY 10012
  www.huc.edu
- Reconstructionist: Reconstructionist Rabbinical College
  1299 Church Rd.
  Wyncote, PA 19095
  www.rrc.edu

Jewish Cantor

Job Description: Cantors and rabbis share many of the same general duties, but the cantor is usually responsible for leading hymns and chants. This requires in-depth knowledge of not just Judaism but also music. In addition, they visit the sick and the homebound; teach adult education and religious classes; tutor Bar Mitzvah and Bat Mitzvah candidates; attend monthly synagogue board meetings; create musical programs; work with children; counsel the troubled; officiate at ceremonies commemorating births, weddings, and deaths; and represent the congregation in the community in interfaith events.

Cantors are often admired for their powerful singing voices with which they lead and inspire the congregation. Several cantors have recorded collections of Jewish hymns and prayers.

Not all congregations can afford to pay for a full-time rabbi and a cantor, so most cantors work in urban areas or for affluent congregations. Some congregations have volunteer cantors.

Education: To become a cantor, a student must complete many of the same courses as a rabbi (see "Jewish Rabbi"). However, a cantor must also be proficient in music. It is recommended that the aspiring candidate formally study piano to learn sight-reading, ear training, rhythm, meter, and key. Knowledge of both piano and guitar is helpful.

The cantorial degree is a graduate program. Both the Jewish Theological Seminary of America (Conservative) and the Hebrew Union College-Jewish Institute of Religion (Reform) offer comprehensive programs that combine a Masters in Sacred Music with full investiture as a cantor in Israel. It is recommended that undergraduates preparing to attend a seminary major in both music and Judaic studies or major in music with a minor in Judaic studies. Seminaries may require proficiency in reading and writing Hebrew, so this, too, should be included in undergraduate studies.

Clothes: See "Jewish Rabbi."

Earnings: Cantors earn about the same range as rabbis. Rabbis responsible for more administrative duties may earn slightly more.

Further Info: See "Jewish Rabbi."

Further Reading:
- *From Chantre to Djak: Cantorial Traditions in Canada*, compiled and edited by Robert B. Klymasz. Although this book focuses on cantors of various faiths in Canada, the experiences presented are applicable to many congregations. One chapter presents interviews with six Jewish cantors and details their duties and experiences.

Correctional Chaplain

Job Description: Correctional chaplains minister to prisoners and institution staff in many of the same ways they would with any other congregation: They provide spiritual guidance, develop educational programs, oversee a large number of worship and teaching volunteers, and conduct worship services. The American Correctional Chaplains Association sees the chaplain as one who provides for the prisoners religious study and spiritual development, which are "the most valuable tools for rehabilitation and to prevent recidivism." In addition, they argue that "religion plays a crucial role in managing a prison, and the positive effect that religion can have on an inmate is immeasurable."

Unique dangers and challenges come out of teaching spirituality to those who have broken the law and may seem to have abandoned spirituality. Many stories involving prison chaplains focus on a chaplain's risk of being held hostage, his attempts to reform a particularly heinous criminal, and using prison as a metaphor for the world of material desire that "imprisons" people.

Education: To become a correctional chaplain one must already be ordained. Personal, theological, and professional competency are necessary, and they are represented by required certification. A correctional chaplain must be able to work under stress and cope with crises; be aware of hope, trust, and forgiveness; and have a firm grasp on theological issues relating to the correctional setting. The chaplain must demonstrate sensitivity, communication skills, and organization.

Earnings: One of the biggest problems facing prison chaplains comes not from the prisoners but from the administration. As budgets have been tightened, many prisons have eliminated this position altogether. Others have fired chaplains then re-hired them on a contract basis so the chaplains no longer receive benefits for full-time employees.

Professional Associations: The American Correctional Chaplains Association (ACCA) is an affiliate of the American Correctional Association (ACA).

Further Info:
- American Correctional Chaplains Association (www.correctio nalchaplains.com). This site provides specifics about duties, ethics, and certification programs.
- For further information about standards for certification, write to Chaplain Margaret Graziano, Chair of ACCA Certification 3540 Pearl St.
  Eugene, OR 97405.

Further Reading:
- *Dead Man Walking*, Helen Prejean. A nun's account of her experiences ministering to death row inmates. This story was made into a movie of the same name.
- "Wiccan Chaplain Brews Storm," Stephanie Simon (*Los*

Angeles Times, 7 January 2002, p. A14). News account of the first Wiccan prison chaplain in the U.S. and of the surrounding controversy.

- "The Role of Jail Chaplains," Margaret Graziano (www.correc tionalchaplains.com). Informative article about the duties of a prison chaplain and the emotional toll of working as one.

Military Chaplain

Job Description: Military chaplains minister to military members at home and abroad. Their duties are very similar to those of the prison chaplain (see above). Like prisoners, military personnel are often isolated from friends and family who are outside the military. This brings spiritual challenges that military chaplains are trained to deal with.

Education: To become a military chaplain one must already be ordained.

Clothes: A military chaplain wears the uniform appropriate to her rank and military branch.

Earnings: The average annual salary is $57,330.

Further Info:
- See individual branches of the armed forces. Individual branches of the armed forces offer more specific information about chaplains specific to their branch.

Instant Minister

Job Description: Becoming a nondenominational minister is very simple. One need only visit a Web site, fill out a form, and pay a small fee to become legally able to perform weddings and officiate at other ceremonies—provided someone wants such a minister. A person may register his own church as well, even if he's the only member of that church. No specific religious beliefs are involved, though these ministers are cautioned to uphold some form of moral standards.

Education: No education is required.

Further Info:
- Universal Life Church (www.ulc.org) is the most famous and

popular of the instant ministries. To find more information, call CompuChurch directly at (504) 927-4509 (the FidoNet address is 1:3800/6.0).

Additional Occupations

Not all clergy members lead congregations. Some serve in the military or work in hospitals as chaplains, some are involved in overseas or community missions, and some work as administrators and teachers in schools supported by their denominations. Training for the clergy prepares one for many positions, including the following:

- campus minister
- chaplain
- director of religious education
- ecumenical worker
- provider of hospice spiritual care
- liturgist
- minister to separated or divorced spouses
- minister to the grieving
- parish administrator
- parish pastoral minister
- pastoral care minister
- pastoral counselor
- retreat center director
- youth minister

Potential employers for workers in the above positions include

- churches
- colleges and universities
- hospices
- hospitals
- nursing homes
- correctional facilities
- parishes
- retreat centers
- social service agencies

Clergy Members in Fiction

Books

- *A Canticle for Leibowitz*, Walter M. Miller Jr. A cult sci-fi classic set in a Catholic monastery in postapocalyptic Utah.
- *The Mackerel Plaza*, Peter De Vries. One of the funniest writers ever tells the story of a widower minister in search of a wife.
- *The Power and the Glory*, Graham Greene. A "whiskey priest" seeks salvation in Mexico. Greene, a convert to Catholicism, wrote extensively on religious themes.
- *True Confessions*, John Gregory Dunne. Explores the complex relationship and similarities between two brothers, one a police detective and the other a monsignor in the Catholic church. Also made into a movie in 1981.
- Books by Andrew Greeley. Greeley, himself a priest, has written many novels using the Catholic church as a setting. Several novels feature Bishop Blackie Ryan solving mysteries.
- Books by Harry Kemelman. Rabbi Kemelman presents Rabbi David Small as the sleuth who solves mysteries for his congregation.
- Books by William X. Kienzle. Using his experiences as a priest, the author has written novels about sleuth Father Robert Koesler.
- Books by Ralph McInerny. Father Roger Dowling solves mysteries, both in McInerny's novels and the TV series based on the novels.

Movies

- *The Exorcist* (1973). Frightening tale of demonic possession; two priests sacrifice themselves to save the soul of a young girl. Based on the novel by William Peter Blatty. Spawned many inferior imitations, such as *Stigmata* and *End of Days*.
- *Lanigan's Rabbi* (1976). In this TV movie, an Irish Catholic cop and Rabbi David Small team up to seek a murderer.
- *The Mission* (1986). Eighteenth-century Jesuit mission in Brazil is threatened by greedy merchants and political factions within the church.
- *Black Robe* (1991). Gritty tale of a seventeenth-century Jesuit

priest who travels to Quebec to colonize the natives.

- *Priest* (1994). A priest struggles with his faith as well as his homosexual feelings.
- *Diary of a City Priest* (2000). The life of a priest working in a rundown neighborhood.

Television
- *Father Dowling Mysteries* (1989–1991). Series featuring priest and nun as sleuths. Still available in syndication.
- *Touched by an Angel* (1994–). Angels teach moral values to humans.
- *7th Heaven* (1996–). Features a minister and his family. Focuses on his duties as a minister and the struggles of raising children with moral values.
- *Oz* (1997–). This HBO series about life in prison features a prison chaplain and a nun working as a counselor who interact with the prisoners.
- *Six Feet Under* (2001–). HBO series that deals with a family that lives in a funeral home. One son is a mortician who is gay and an elder in the Catholic church, causing him to experience moral conflict.

Web Sites

- **Adherents.com (www.adherents.com)**. A directory with over fifteen thousand religious adherent statistics for over twelve hundred different faith groups. Also includes a section on religions in literature.

- **Institute for the Study of American Religion (www.america nreligion.org)**. Focuses upon smaller religions in the U.S., such as minority religions, alternative religions, nonconventional religions, spiritual movements, and new religious movements.

- **Venerable Thubten Chodron's Home Page (www.thubtenc hodron.org/buddhist_nuns)**. An American Buddhist nun offers various articles explaining her beliefs and duties.

Book Excerpts

There had been a continuous stream of pen-
itents from eight to ten—two hours of the
worst evil a small place like this could
produce after three years. It hadn't
amounted to very much—a city would have made
a better show—or would it? There isn't much
a man can do. Drunkenness, adultery, un-
cleanness: he sat there tasting the brandy
all the while, sitting on a rocking-chair
in a horse-box, not looking at the face of
the one who knelt at his side. The others
had waited, kneeling in the empty stall—Mr.
Lehr's stable had been depopulated these
last few years. He had only one horse left,
which blew windily in the dark as the sins
came whimpering out.

   —The Power and the Glory, Graham Greene

''Lavabo inter innocentes . . . '' Bishop
O'Dea intoned.
   Appearances. They were very much on Desmond Spellacy's mind today. Augustine
O'Dea, for example. Tall, in his late fifties, with massive shoulders and the mane
of snow-white hair. The very picture of a
bishop. He had only one drawback: he was a
boob. A view, Desmond Spellacy knew, that
was shared by the Cardinal. That big, boom-
ing voice always ready to discourse on Saint
Patrick and the snakes or the day Babe Ruth

said hello to him at Comiskey Park. Two favorite topics. (Desmond Spellacy had once pressed him on the Babe and what the Babe had actually said was, ''Hiya, keed.'') But . . . Always the *but*. There was something about Augustine O'Dea that seemed to amuse the Cardinal. With rapt attention, Hugh Danaher listened to the endless monologues about the day little Bernadette met Our Lady at Lourdes or the absence of snakes on the Emerald Isle. Is that right, Augustine. I didn't know that, Augustine. It was as if the vicar general provided the cardinal with his only relief from the Byzantine tedium of running the archdiocese.

—True Confessions, John Gregory Dunne

''I'd like to answer that question by asking another. Just what does that statement mean—'Jesus Saves'?''
''What do you mean, 'mean'?''
''What does Jesus save us from?''
''From our sins. What else?''
''I see.''
I struck a match on the side of a box and extended the flame to him. He took a few puffs and emitted a cloud of smoke, which he dispensed with a wave, as though from some points of view he deplored the habit.
''And what will happen to us if we aren't saved from them?'' I inquired. ''What then?''

''Why, we'll go to hell,'' he answered, and lapped at a tatter in the side of his cigar.

''And where will we go if we are?''

''To heaven.''

I sank into my chair and dropped my arms over the sides. ''Another backslider,'' I thought wearily. It was this damned religious revival. They were everywhere, these converts, defecting to pie-in-the-sky from hard-won positions to which they have been urged and hauled by rational and honest men. Looking at the codger, I thought, Can this man be educated? Or is he beyond salvation?

—The Mackerel Plaza, Peter De Vries

CHAPTER 4

Courtroom Professionals: Lawyers

Criminal Attorney, Public Defender, Civil Attorney, District Attorney, Judge, Bailiff

The Lowdown

The legal profession embodies society's highest aspirations: to create a safe but fair community that protects our freedoms and ideals. The fact that we live in such a diverse society is a strength, but it creates conflicts. One group's morals may conflict with another group's, and sometimes those conflicts can be settled only in court. Even then, the law is fluid, ever changing as society changes its mind about issues. Laws governing women, gays, and racial minorities have continually changed.

A writer gains many advantages when choosing a courtroom professional as a character:

1. The courtroom setting is familiar to most readers, so they bring enough legal knowledge to get involved in the case without having to read explanations of mundane procedures.

2. The stakes can be high or low, depending upon the nature of the case. If the stakes are low, the writer

can play scenes more for comic effect, as in the courtroom comedies where two lovers profess under oath their love for each other. Remember when Santa Claus takes the stand in *Miracle on 34th Street*? If the stakes are high, more suspense can be generated.

3. High stakes can take several forms. A person may go to prison or be executed. A case can affect a lawyer's emotional state, and this generates suspense. A ruling can affect society at large and create enormous stakes, especially where issues such as abortion, women's rights, and affirmative action are concerned.

Because the law involves so many details, a courtroom professional who uses all those intricacies can be portrayed as a highly intelligent, clever, and earnest character. Since most people know the law only superficially, an intricate case that educates the reader about aspects of the law can be compelling. The fact that hot topics—euthanasia, sexual harassment, etc.—are always before the courts means the writer of legal fiction will never run out of material.

Job Description

Lawyers practice either civil or criminal law. Criminal lawyers support their clients by acting as either a prosecuting or defense attorney, most often in court. While all lawyers are licensed to practice in courts of law, not all attorneys are trial lawyers. In the practice of civil law, attorneys counsel their clients on business matters and act as litigation attorneys or transactional attorneys. Litigation attorneys represent their clients in court, whereas transactional attorneys draft legal documents—anything from simple wills to complex documents that affect global corporations.

Whether a case is criminal or civil, lawyers are vital to the exercise and defense of their clients' rights. Sooner or later, everyone will end up needing one of the more than 680,000 lawyers who practiced in the U.S. as of 1998.

Seventy percent of lawyers work in the private sector, either in independent law practice or in a law firm. A small number work as house counsel, advising and working for institutions such as banks, insurance companies, nonprofit organizations, and public utilities. The remaining lawyers are employed by the government. While lawyers are on staff for the Department of Justice, the Department of the Treasury, and the Department of Defense, the majority of government lawyers work at the local level in such positions as district attorneys and public defenders. Most salaried lawyers work in some kind of urban setting.

What makes a lawyer successful? Success for house counsel may be measured by how well they're able to protect their employers from litigation and lawsuits. A successful district attorney has a high number of convictions, which demonstrates her ability to argue the guilt of criminal elements and put them away. A public defender may measure success not by his number of legal victories but by his ability to efficiently move large numbers of defendants through the legal system and provide the counsel to which his clients are entitled. For a civil lawyer, success may come in her knowledge of the finest intricacies of the law, allowing her to defend clients from huge lawsuits—or to file them on her clients' behalf. But in the end, the hallmarks of a successful lawyer are the ability to conduct exhaustive research, convey arguments effectively in writing and speech, survive burnout, and retain a fierce sense of competition and justice.

Salary

The competition to enter prestigious law schools is fierce, and landing a top job in a law firm can be downright Darwinian. After seven or more years of studying the intricacies of law, new lawyers want high compensation from the start. Those who are successful and work in private practice often get it, earning an average salary of $60,000 just six months out of law school. Lawyers who pursue public employment, such as a public criminal lawyer, face a leaner beginning, averaging a salary of just $31,000 six months out of law school.

As of 1998, the average income for all lawyers was a little over $78,000, with the lowest-paid attorneys averaging $37,000 and the middle half pulling in between $51,000 and $114,000 a year. Litigation and transactional attorneys and house counsel can expect to earn an average of $78,700 annually, while lawyers working for the federal, state, and local governments can expect an average income of $78,200, $59,400, and $49,200, respectively. Contingency lawyers, who eat all costs unless their clients win, have the most varied salaries. At the high end, a victorious prosecuting attorney is richly compensated—possibly millions of dollars—if his client is awarded exceptionally high damages.

Some lawyers move into positions as judges. State judges can make between $68,000 and $133,000 a year, while federal judges average $133,000 a year.

Benefits

Most law firms and government offices offer generous benefits packages. Typically, the larger the firm, the greater the benefits package. Lawyers may enjoy 401(k) plans in which employers match employee contributions, programs to pay off student loans, health and life insurance, child care benefits, and low home mortgage rates through financial institutions.

Expenses

Depending on its size, a law firm may reimburse lawyers for bar association dues, continuing education courses, and business mileage. Smaller firms or government institutions may reimburse the cost of continuing education courses, but not travel or meal costs.

Rewards and Perks

Lawyers' job satisfaction is based on their law specialty. Public defenders feel gratified as defenders of the constitution and citizens' rights. Criminal and civil prosecutors can feel proud on having carried out justice for those who have been wronged. With an enviable track record, a lawyer can aspire to higher posts such as a law partner, a judge, or an elected official.

Daily Life

Work Schedule

Lawyers who work for the government, a law firm, or a corporation generally have a structured day, though about 50 percent work fifty or more hours per week, especially during court proceedings. Lawyers in private practice have more flexible hours, though they may have to work odd hours to keep abreast of the law and to meet with clients.

During an economic slowdown, lawyers who handle real estate, wills, and estates usually experience less demand for their services, while other lawyers, particularly those who deal in foreclosures and bankruptcies, may experience a greater daily workload.

The schedule for a prosecutor or defender on the opening day of a trial might look like this:

- Assemble jury instructions, visual aids, and notebook for trial.
- Attend conference in the judge's chambers. Only the judge and lawyers are present.
- Discuss options with client.
- Fifty potential jurors are brought into the courtroom. The judge asks them hardship questions, then he gives the lawyers two to three hours to pick a jury. Once selected, the twelve jurors assemble in the jury box and answer the judge's questions about their names, places of work, jury experience, and knowledge of any parties to the case.
- The lawyers make opening statements. Witnesses are called to testify and be cross-examined.
- The lawyer may spend the remainder of the workday working on that case or on other pending cases or doing research—all of which may continue at home in the evening, depending on a lawyer's caseload.

Dressing the Part
Civil and criminal lawyers are expected to wear suits in court and often out of court as well. Attorneys in private practices may dress more casually especially on days when they will have no face-to-face client contact.

Keys to the Kingdom
Both civil and criminal lawyers can access court files, such as legal documents and motions. If they show their bar association card to the court clerk to check out materials, the court

clerk first records the lawyer's name. Laypersons can look at court records, too, and just a photo ID is required. These instances are not recorded by the court clerk, so some lawyers present a photo ID instead of a bar card in order to research cases without tipping off the opposing counsel. Theoretically, an unscrupulous lawyer could remove files from the court records and not be blamed for the records' absence.

Lawyers also have physical access to courthouses, even on weekends when the courts are closed and manned by only a few security persons. During a criminal trial, a district attorney has access to evidence held in police stations.

Tools of the Trade

To prepare and try cases, lawyers use a wide range of research options, including traditional law library holdings, microfiche, and online legal databases. Trial lawyers enhance their courtroom presentations with audiovisual equipment, charts, and blowups of photographs of crime scenes and other evidence.

The Courtroom

Bailiff: A bailiff controls each courtroom. Bailiffs serve in rotation from their primary jobs as sheriffs. Bailiffs can also be other law enforcement employees or individuals who have undergone training to be a bailiff. As bailiffs are in charge of the jury, it's wise for a lawyer to maintain a good rapport with bailiffs.

Clerk: The clerk, or judicial assistant, marks and keeps items brought into evidence.

Judge: Among the judges in a courtroom, a master calendar judge may assign a judge to each case, ensuring that judges are more or less impartially assigned. The presiding judge controls the courtroom proceedings, double-checks the impartiality of the jury, rules on motions and objections from lawyers, and issues sentences or verdicts depending on the case type.

Jury: A jury is selected from a pool of fifty potential jurors; the pool is known as the "veneer." Lawyers for the prosecution and defense accept and reject candidates until a complete jury is impaneled.

Tricks: Tricks can be part of a lawyer's strategic arsenal. While a lawyer is required to reveal evidence to opposing counsel, sandbagging may occur in this process. For instance, a district attorney's aide might need a dolly when picking up a requested document at the public defender's office; the document may be stuffed in one of a few unorganized boxes containing hundreds of legal documents.

Subpoena: A subpoena is used to compel a witness to appear in court, and serving a subpoena can be time consuming. The recipient must acknowledge receipt of the subpoena, and a "proof of service" attesting that the person was served is required. In addition, no subpoena power exists beyond a hundred-mile radius of the courthouse where a trial is to be held. A witness outside that area or in another state must be served with a subpoena by someone from that area. To aid her client, a lawyer could "bury a witness" by encouraging a witness she does not plan to call to leave the state.

Elbow Rubbing

Lawyers, particularly trial lawyers, deal with a wide range of professionals: jurors; other lawyers; judges; bailiffs; library staff; expert witnesses; subject experts, who specialize in fields such as confessions, alcohol, and forensics; toxicologists; investigators; law enforcement officials; and paralegals.

Slang Titles
- Brief: Prison/underworld slang for *lawyer.*
- D.A.: District attorney.
- P.D.: Public defender.
- Ambulance chaser: Any opportunistic lawyer, especially one who specializes in cases involving car accidents.

Buzzwords

187, et al.: Lawyers sometimes refer to crimes by their legal code numbers; for example, 187 might be a murder. However, each state has its own legal code, so the references differ from state to state. A list of criminal codes by state is on the Web at www.law.cornell.edu/topics/state_statutes2.html.

ace: A felony DUI.

DA in a robe: A judge—especially one who was once a DA—who might be seen by the defense as favoring the prosecution.

deuce: A misdemeanor DUI.

dog: A case where a guilty client won't plead guilty. A bad case, especially one with no plausible defense, may be considered a "barking dog." A dialogue between two lawyers might go something like this:
"I'm trying a dog."
"Is it a barking dog?"
"Yeah. It's a howler."

dumptruck: A case where the lawyer can get a client to plead guilty and the case doesn't go to trial.

mailers: Lawyers, especially those handling cases of driving under the influence (DUI), who provide printed flyers to people in jail.

MSJ: Motion for summary judgment.

NG or *I got an NG.:* Not guilty verdict.

no contest: To plead neither innocent nor guilty; to not dispute an accusation.

rack 'em up: Select a jury

summary judgment: Decision made in cases where no facts are in question and no trial is needed.

take it to the box: Go to trial.

Education

Law School

Becoming a lawyer is no easy task. In addition to earning a bachelor's degree and passing the Law School Admission Test (LSAT), a lawyer must attend three years of law school at an institution certified by the American Bar Association (ABA).

Law students spend the first half of law school studying civil procedure, constitutional law, property law, torts, legal writing, and contracts. Then they can take courses in their field of interest, such as corporate, environmental, labor, or international law.

The Bar

To graduate with the professional degree of juris doctor (J.D.), law students must pass the bar examination. While no nationwide examination exists, prospective lawyers in forty-seven states are required to take the six-hour Multistate Bar Examination (MBE) in addition to a state bar examination. Some states also incorporate a three-hour Multistate Essay Examination (MEE) as part of the bar exam. Most jurisdictions also require students to pass a written ethics examination.

Additional Study

Some lawyers elect to pursue another professional degree in the field of law, specializing in such subjects as dispute resolution or taxes. Thirty-nine states require continuing legal education (CLE) for lawyers, which consists of classes and seminars to keep lawyers up-to-date on changes and developments in law and procedure. In addition, lawyers may have to take another bar exam if they decide to practice in another state.

Getting Around the System

While law school is by far the most common route taken by prospective lawyers, it is not the only means to that end. Apprenticing for a lawyer can prepare one to sit for the bar exam. In addition, the state of California allows a candidate to sit for the bar exam if he's studied law by correspondence.

Job Conflicts

The professional life of a lawyer, especially a trial lawyer, is rife with conflict that extends beyond the innate clash between prosecutor and defense counsel.

Law vs. Personal Beliefs

A lawyer may have internal conflicts when she must put the law before her personal beliefs. For example, this can happen in cases involving the death penalty. In addition, without fully embracing one's role as a provider of a person's civil rights, a beginning lawyer may feel uneasy defending a guilty client.

Lawyer vs. Client

Whether clients are delinquent, demanding, or uncooperative, they can be a source of stress and difficulty. When a client is unlikable a lawyer can find it challenging to fully defend or support the client. In addition, some clients sabotage their own cases by committing perjury, withholding information from their lawyers, etc., making a working relationship tense at best.

Lawyer vs. Judge

A judge's perceived bias can quickly put a lawyer at odds over evidentiary and admissibility rulings. Personality conflicts aside, the fairness and impartiality of the court can be severely tested depending on how a judge fulfills his role. Given that most judges have been lawyers and many served as prosecutors, relationships between judges and defense attorneys can be most interesting, especially given the right circumstances. For example, if a judge doesn't want to waste time and the taxpayers' money on a case she sees as having no merit, she may inform the defense attorney up front that if the prosecution wins, the defendant will be sentenced to so many years; this can scare the defendant into changing his plea to guilty.

Stress

The law profession is a breeding ground for stress. Those incapable of handling the demands inevitably face alcoholism, drug use, or burnout. Law firms may require attorneys to submit time sheets showing hours that can be billed to the client; this adds the stress of appearing financially productive besides being skilled in law. To combat burnout, some firms and public offices rotate the law staff and ensure that no lawyer remains too long on one particular type of case or has too many trial dates in a row.

Myths About the Job

All Lawyers Are the Same

For some reason, lawyers have wound up being viewed as a clump—especially as the collective butt of jokes. But lawyers are often at odds with other lawyers, sometimes for the sake of a client and sometimes out of deep-rooted convictions on how justice should be carried out.

The stereotypical big-money, high-stakes, gala-events lawyer is usually a civil lawyer, at least in the eyes of a criminal attorney. There's almost a white-collar vs. blue-collar division between civil and criminal lawyers. Criminal attorneys see civil lawyers as being concerned primarily with money, which is most often the award in arbitrations and mediations, settlements, and lawsuits that end up in court. Civil lawyers can bury themselves in paperwork as they nitpick the details of a settlement offer or prepare legal documents designed to avoid lawsuits.

Criminal lawyers, both district attorneys and defense counsel, deal with a more earthy crowd as they try or defend cases of murder, sexual assault, molestation, robbery, carjacking, drug trafficking, and other crimes against individuals and society. The hierarchy of respect among criminal lawyers starts with successful lawyers who try capital cases and works down through those who defend lesser crimes. In short, if you put a civil lawyer and a criminal lawyer together at a party, they might be cordial although they don't see eye to eye or have much in common. Put two opposing criminal lawyers together—a district attorney and a defense attorney—and an argument may erupt.

The World Would Be Better Without Lawyers

Chances are good that you or someone you know has been sued, convicted of a crime, drowned in legalese, or otherwise adversely affected by a lawyer. Yet for every victim of a lawyer's success in mediation or in court there's a party who benefited from his advocacy or defense. As advocates of society's laws, lawyers can be the last defense for victims—both those accused and those harmed by others.

Being a Lawyer Is Always Exciting

Thanks to TV dramas, a day in the life of a lawyer seems to be full of brutal crimes, courtroom intrigue, impassioned speeches, and emotional turmoil. While this can happen, the daily routine of a lawyer is usually just routine. Consisting of paperwork and routine procedure, 80 to 90 percent of the job can be drab. From filing motions to serving subpoenas, from scanning law databases on a monitor to writing novel-length documents in legalese, a lawyer does plenty dull work before the excitement of a trial can begin.

Jobs Within the Profession

Criminal Attorney, Public Defender

Job Description: Attorneys practicing criminal law sometimes represent or defend clients accused of a wide range of crimes: white-collar crime (credit card fraud, embezzlement, and insider trading), violent crime (murder, kidnapping, and burglary), drug offenses (possession, sale, and trafficking), motor vehicle offenses (drunk driving, speeding, and vehicular homicide), and sex crimes (sexual misconduct, molestation, and rape). Attorneys interview clients and witnesses, research related cases to find precedents, and prepare defenses for their clients. Criminal lawyers appear in court, question witnesses, and present defenses. When a defendant cannot afford an attorney's services, the court appoints a public defender to the case. Public defenders tend to work more cases for less pay than successful private criminal attorneys. Employed by the government, public defenders are the defense equivalent of a district attorney.

Education: Lawyers must hold a college degree and a law school degree and pass the bar examination. (See "Education" on page 81 for more details.)

Earnings: Please see "Salary" on page 76.

Further Info:
- American Bar Association
  740 Fifteenth Street, N.W.

Washington, DC 20005-1019
www.abanet.org
- Association of American Law Schools
1201 Connecticut Ave., Suite 800
Washington, DC 20036
- National Lawyer's Guild
55 Sixth Ave.
New York, NY 10013
- ABA Journal
750 N. Lake Shore Dr.
Chicago, IL 60611

Further Reading:
- Chicago-Kent Law Review
College of Law
565 W. Adams St.
Chicago, IL 60661
- Duke Law Journal
Duke University School of Law
Science Drive and Towerview Road
P.O. Box 90371
Durham, NC 27708
- Harvard Journal of Law & Technology
28 Pound Hall
Harvard Law School
Cambridge, MA 02138
- Stanford Law & Policy Review
Stanford Law School
Stanford, CA 94305-8610

Civil Attorney

Job Description: Clients retain civil attorneys for a variety of civil suits, including damage claims and breach of contract. Civil attorneys draw up a variety of contracts, including mortgages, wills, leases, and deeds. Civil lawyers also may serve as executors of estates, as specified in wills. If the situation warrants, a civil attorney may prepare a case and appear in court to try it for the client. Many civil attorneys are employed by large corporations and specialize in such areas as patent law, tort law, and intellectual property rights. They typically earn more than criminal attorneys.

Education: See "Education" on page 81. A civil attorney also needs a specialization in an area of civil law.

Earnings: Annually, a civil attorney can earn $50,000 and up, depending on the size of the law practice.

District Attorney

Job Description: A district attorney prosecutes cases on behalf of the city, state, or federal government. A D.A. carries out interviews, develops the case, and presents it to a grand jury, which, in turn, determines whether enough evidence exists to warrant a trial. A district attorney may try jury cases for crimes ranging from drunk driving to capital murder. Like public defenders, D.A.s often deal with gritty crimes rather than the white-collar crimes addressed by civil attorneys.

Education: Please see "Education" on page 81.

Earnings: Please see "Salary" on page 76.

Further Info:
• National District Attorneys Association
  99 Canal Center Plaza, Suite 510
  Alexandria, VA 22314
  www.ndaa.org

Judge

Job Description: Judges are responsible for overseeing the legal process in the courtroom. A judge decides whether a case deserves to be heard in court, dismisses a case if circumstances warrant it, and sentences parties who are found guilty. Half of all state judges are appointed; the remainder are elected. Terms vary from four to six years. Federal administrative judges are appointed by federal agencies, while federal judges are appointed by the president to lifelong terms. The executive branch of the government employs federal administrative judges. These judges conduct hearings for people or companies affected by government actions. Instead of holding trials, administrative judges hold hearings and make judgments without a jury.

Education: Most judges were once lawyers. Federal and state judges are required to be lawyers. Some states require judges to take continuing education courses.

Number of Judges: There are over seventy-eight thousand judges in the U.S.

Earnings: See "Salary" at page 76.

Further Info:
- The National Center for State Courts
  300 Newport Ave.
  Williamsburg, VA 23185
  www.ncsconline.org
- Federal Judicial Center
  Thurgood Marshall Federal Judiciary Building
  One Columbus Cir NE
  Washington, DC 20002

Bailiff

Job Description: A bailiff serves a courtroom and judge by keeping court proceedings running smoothly. Bailiffs are responsible for seating witness and jurors, and they escort jurors to keep them out of contact with the public, especially during deliberations. Bailiffs maintain safety and enforce rules of courtroom conduct, and they may arrest or remove individuals who attempt to cause harm or disrupt the proceedings.

Education: A bailiff has a background in law enforcement and is usually a sheriff.

Earnings: Bailiffs' earnings vary by state.

Further Reading:
- *Bailiff*, Jack Rudman.

Additional Occupations

It takes more than lawyers, judges and juries, to run our legal system. Critical professionals who contribute to the legal process include

- appeals reviewer
- claims adjudicator
- court stenographer
- hearing officer
- judicial reviewer
- legal investigator
- magistrate
- paralegal

Potential employers of those in the above positions include the following:

- state and federal courts
- law firms

Lawyers in Nonfiction

Books

- *Criminal Investigation*, Charles R. Swanson Jr., Neil C. Chamelin, and Leonard Territo. Presents the procedures used to collect evidence for a variety of crimes.
- *Double Billing: A Young Lawyer's Tale of Greed, Sex, Lies, and the Pursuit of a Swivel Chair*, Cameron Stracher. An insider's view of three tough years as an associate at a New York City law firm.
- *Fundamentals of Legal Research*, 7th ed., J. Myron Jacobstein. Covers everything from court procedures to the methods lawyers use to research their cases.
- *Ladies and Gentlemen of the Jury: Greatest Closing Arguments in Modern Law*, Michael S. Lief, Mitchell Caldwell, and Benjamin Bycel. Actual transcripts promote understanding and appreciation of the techniques of court arguments.
- *Law Dictionary for Nonlawyers*, Daniel Oran and Mark Tosti. An easy method for getting a grasp on legal terms and concepts.
- *One L: The Turbulent True Story of a First Year at Harvard Law School*, Scott Turow. Valuable insight into the law school experience.

- *Teach Me to Solo: The Nuts and Bolts of Law Practice*, Hal Davis. A how-to on setting up a solo law practice.

Lawyers in Fiction

Books
- *The Burden of Proof*, Scott Turow. Defense attorney juggles professional challenge with mystery of wife's suicide. Turow has authored many legal novels.
- *Hostile Witness*, William Lashner. Examines the dark side of a corrupt attorney.
- *The Mercy Rule*, John Lescroart. An attorney defends a fellow defense attorney accused of murder.
- *Powers of Attorney*, Mimi Lavenda Latt. Follows the lives of three female attorneys.
- *The Rainmaker*, John Grisham. An inexperienced young lawyer fights an insurance case. Grisham has authored many legal novels (e.g., *The Firm* and *The Client*), most of which have been made into movies.
- *Silent Witness*, Richard North Patterson. An attorney defends a close high school friend in a homicide case.
- *To Kill a Mockingbird*, Harper Lee. Attorney defends an innocent man in a racially charged town during the Depression.
- *Trial*, Clifford Irving. A young Texas attorney tries to resurrect his career.

Movies
- *Adam's Rib* (1949). Husband and wife square off as prosecutor and defense attorney on the same case.
- *Witness for the Prosecution* (1957). The trial after the murder of a wealthy widow.
- *Inherit the Wind* (1960). A Tennessee teacher defends his teaching of Darwinism in drama of the Scopes monkey trial.
- *. . . And Justice for All* (1979). A beginning lawyer's idealism tests the legal system. One of the first films to indict the faults of the legal system.
- *The Verdict* (1982). An alcoholic lawyer is given one more shot to make good.

- *The Accused* (1988). A rape victim uses the legal system to go after her attackers and the onlookers.
- *Reversal of Fortune* (1990). The story of Claus von Bülow's attempts to refute accusations of attempted murder.
- *Class Action* (1991). A crusading lawyer fights an auto company represented by his own daughter.
- *My Cousin Vinny* (1992). A legal comedy about a bad New York lawyer who defends his cousin in a small Southern town.
- *The Firm* (1993). A lawyer must choose between the perks and prestige of a job in a law firm and the cost of knowing the truth. Based on the novel by John Grisham.
- *Just Cause* (1995). A Harvard law professor reexamines a murder case after allegations of a false confession.
- *Ghosts of Mississippi* (1996). Wife of a slain civil rights leader fights for thirty years to convict a white supremacist.
- *Primal Fear* (1996). A lawyer is less interested in guilt and innocence than in his ability to win a murder case.
- *A Time to Kill* (1996). Amid racial tensions, an idealistic young lawyer attempts to bring justice in a murder trial. Based on the novel by John Grisham.
- *Erin Brockovich* (2000). Working for a law firm, a down-on-her-luck woman learns the legal and investigative ropes while uncovering a water pollution cover-up.
- *Legally Blonde* (2001). A comedy about a Valley girl who goes to Harvard and finds her true calling.

Television
- *The Defenders* (1961–1965). An established lawyer takes on challenging cases with his son, a recent law school graduate.
- *L.A. Law* (1986–1994). Life in a large L.A. law firm. Currently in syndication.
- *Law & Order* (1990–). After detectives investigate and make an arrest, the second half of the show focuses on prosecution, but not always with predictable results.
- *Ally McBeal* (1997–). Practicing law, love, and life in a Boston law firm.
- *The Practice* (1997–). Criminal defense attorneys struggle with their clients and their own feelings about the law.

- *Family Law* (1999–). A law practice focusing on family law.
- *Judging Amy* (1999–). A woman returns to her hometown after her divorce and becomes a judge in family court.
- *Philly* (2001–). The gritty side of practicing law.
- *First Monday* (2002–). The inside workings of the U.S. Supreme Court.

Firsthand Research

Almost all trials are open to the public. Ask a security guard at your local courthouse about sitting in on a trial. To research the feel of a specific type of case, contact the D.A.'s office or a public defender's office about the cases currently being tried and where. In addition, you can interview a court bailiff. Bailiffs have seen countless trials and can provide valuable insight into lawyers' differing techniques.

Web Sites

- FindLaw (www.findlaw.com). In addition to being used by lawyers to pull up cases, this Yahoo! of law sites offers federal and state law code sections.

- Westlaw (www.westlaw.com). An essential tool lawyers use to research their cases.

- LexisNexis (www.lexis.com). A valuable Web site for research and for "shepherdizing" cases, i.e., making sure that laws referenced in a case are current and have not been reversed by an appellate court or taken up by the Supreme Court.

Book Excerpts

The District Attorney's office was in a narrow, dirty building sandwiched between two glass skyscrapers. Lawyers with offices in skyscrapers bustled in and out of the revolving doors, the tassels on their loafers swishing, their Rolexes flashing as they hailed the cabs lined up on the street, the drivers all hoping for that apocryphal fare to the airport. Lawyers from the DA's office passed out of their filthy lobby in weary navy blue waves, pushing shopping carts full of their day's files, girded for battle in . . . undermanned courtrooms. There was about this throng of city attorneys the air of a soon-to-be-defeated army pushing forward only because any avenue of retreat had been cut off.

—Hostile Witness, William Lashner

The pretrial conference is held in the middle of January in Judge Kipler's courtroom. He arranges us around the defense table, and stations his bailiff at the door to keep wandering lawyers out. He sits at one end, without his robe, his secretary on one side, his court reporter on the other. I'm to his right, with my back to the courtroom, and across the table is the entire defense team. It's the first time I've seen Drummond since [the] deposition on December 12, and it's a struggle to be civil.

—The Rainmaker, John Grisham

❧

One great advantage in being a rookie is that I'm expected to be scared and jittery. The jury knows I'm just a kid with no experience. So expectations are low. I've developed neither the skill nor the talent to deliver great summations.

—The Rainmaker, John Grisham

❧

This was his least favorite part, but Hardy had to explain his position. ''As it stands now, you're into me for maybe four hundred dollars, two hours.''
''It's been more than that.''
Hardy waved off the objection. ''We're talking round figures. Four hundred gets us to here, but if I continue and we go to trial, then you get most of my time for most of the year.''
''Or else I take the public defender?''
''That's right. There's some good lawyers in that office. I could recommend—''
But Graham stopped him. ''So could I. I know those guys. They got fifty cases going all the time. I'd be one of them.''
Hardy didn't want to waste breath arguing it. Many public defenders were decent

enough trial attorneys, but Graham was right. In general, workload remained a factor in quality of defense.

—<u>The Mercy Rule</u>, John Lescroart

✐

Having told her client to dress conservatively, Kate was appalled when Sandra walked toward her at five minutes to one in a white knit minidress. She should have picked Sandra up. Then she could have made her change. Now it was too late. . . . Kate saw that Donaldson was unable to keep his eyes off Sandra. Kate wasn't pleased. Sandra was purposely flaunting herself as a sex object—not something that was likely to help her case.

—<u>Powers of Attorney</u>, Mimi Lavenda Latt

✐

Now, trapped with Sam in the witness room, Tony felt tense and claustrophobic. ''Whoever's case it is,'' Tony answered, ''I believe I can win it. I think we've got reasonable doubt.''

Sam stared at him, ''*They* think I did it. I've been watching their faces, and they think I'm guilty.''

Tony drew a breath. ''They may suspect that, but they don't *know* it. My job was never to make you look innocent, or even sympathetic. It's only to make you 'not guilty.' ''

—Silent Witness, Richard North Patterson

✍

''I'm no idealist to believe firmly in the integrity of our courts and in the jury system—that is no ideal to me, it is a living, working reality. Gentlemen, a court is no better than each man of you sitting before me on this jury. A court is only as sound as its jury, and a jury is only as sound as the men who make it up.''

—To Kill a Mockingbird, Harper Lee

✍

''I'll repeat the question,'' said Atticus. ''Can you read and write?''
  ''I most positively can.''
  ''Will you write your name and show us?''
  ''I most positively will. How do you think I sign my relief checks?''
  Mr. Ewell was endearing himself to his fellow citizens. The whispers and chuckles below us probably had to do with what a card he was.
  I was becoming nervous. Atticus seemed to know what he was doing—but it seemed to me that he'd gone frog-sticking without a light. Never, never, never, on cross-examination ask a witness a question you don't

already know the answer to was a tenet I absorbed with my baby food. Do it, and you'll often get an answer you don't want, an answer that might wreck your case.

—To Kill a Mockingbird, Harper Lee

The dispositions of a lifetime made it impossible for him to treat legal problems with indifference; the law would ever amaze him, the way some children were always fascinated by a certain toy. Even now, his abilities struck him as unimpaired; yet his commitments were lagging. Clients with their problems, their urgencies—it all seemed beyond his present reserves. There was a limited number of matters to which Stern was inalterably committed. The rest were shifted to the younger lawyers. Each day here he would receive reports from his associates, meet with those clients he was required to see, examine pleadings, make the necessary phone calls or court appearances, and spend the remainder of the day in aimless desultory reflection.

—The Burden of Proof, Scott Turow

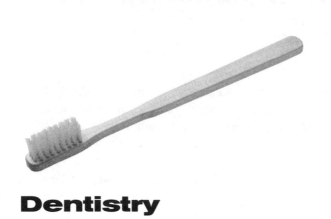

CHAPTER 5

Dentistry

Dentist, Dental Hygienist, Dental Assistant, Orthodontist, Forensic Dentist, Odontologist

The Lowdown

Not surprisingly, dentists in fiction are often characterized by sadism. Writers seem to take gleeful revenge in portraying them as homicidal maniacs who enjoy torturing innocent people strapped helplessly in chairs. Dentist characters do not appear as often as physician characters (see chapter eleven) because the stakes of dentistry are lower: Patients rarely see a dentist for a life-or-death problem. Therefore, with characters in the dental profession, the focus is less on the drama of the daily work and more on the characters' own drama. This is an opportunity to show characters as helpful, caring individuals concerned about their patients' welfare.

The technical aspect of dental work can be used in great detail to reveal a character's intelligence and skill. For certain genres, such as mystery and suspense, the details of dentistry can provide fascinating texture to make the story more interesting. In some stories, dental information can help solve a crime.

Two things make dentistry particularly ripe for comedy: (1) The stakes are generally low, and (2) patients are put in helpless situations. Their pain can be comedic because we know that it's temporary. Patients who are clenching the arms of a chair while they have a mouthful of instruments offer many opportunities for funny situations. The use of anesthetics can also provide amusing results: Novocaine produces muddled speech, laughing gas can cause inappropriate responses to what people say.

Job Description

Dentists work to maintain their patients' oral health. Dentists are both feared and respected by their patients. Although everyone should go to the dentist every six months, many people do not; a successful dentist is one whose patients come back at regular intervals. A successful dentist performs her work well while allaying her patients' fears. Some dentists engage their patients in conversation about such benign topics as favorite radio or television station. (This can also be a source of comedy: A patient with a mouthful of hands and dental equipment can have trouble conversing.)

In addition to the people skills a dentist needs to deal with his patients and staff, attention to aesthetic detail is key. Dental procedures are often costly, painful, and long lasting, and a dentist who seems indifferent to the importance of making his patients look good is as doomed as the dentist who actually does subpar work.

Dentistry is a stable, financially rewarding, respected profession. A dentist's salary varies depending on whether she is in private practice and whether she has a specialty. The average annual net income for all dentists exceeds $125,000, placing them toward the top of the income ladder.

Daily Life

Work Schedule
The average dentist spends thirty to thirty-five hours a week at work; this may include weekend or evening hours. His daily

schedule, however, is filled with direct interaction with patients. Over the course of a day, a dentist might conduct initial exams on new patients and perform filling, crown, or root canal procedures on patients. Most dentists do not stay at the office when they do not have appointments.

Dressing the Part

Under their white coats, gloves, and safety glasses, most dentists dress like businesspeople. Some dentists don scrubs during the workday.

Buzzwords

abutment: The tooth or teeth supporting a bridge.

adhesive dentistry: Dental restoration that involves bonding porcelaine fillings or composite resin to teeth.

air abrasion: A newer method of tooth removal that involves blasting the tooth with air and an abrasive.

anterior: The front; for example, the *anterior* teeth are the six front upper and six front lower teeth.

bitewings: Decay-detection X-rays that show both the upper and lower teeth.

cosmetic or *aesthetic dentistry:* Dental treatments with the primary purpose of enhancing appearance.

cross-contamination: Transmitting bacteria from one patient to the next, usually because the instruments were not properly cleansed.

curettage: The removal of diseased tissue.

freeway space: The distance between the lower and upper jaws when at rest.

tooth preparation: Removing part of a tooth in preparation for a crown.

UCR: "Usual, customary, reasonable": This term applies to fees.

Education

To become a dentist one must complete four years of college and an additional four years of dental school. Dental schools grant either the doctor of dental surgery (D.D.S.) or the doctor of dental medicine (D.M.D.) degrees; these different degrees do not indicate a difference in curriculum. Both degrees indicate completion of a program at a dental school accredited by the American Dental Association (ADA), and both are treated exactly the same by state licensing boards. While a dentist may choose to work as an associate in an established practice before venturing out on his own, he may (and most dentists do) open a private practice right after dental school graduation. Additional training after dental school is required for those who want to specialize as orthodontists, periodontists, or oral surgeons.

Licensing
All dentists must be licensed in order to practice in the U.S. Each state has a licensing board comprised of dental professionals and members of the public. More-experienced dentists who move to another state may obtain a "license by credential" without taking any licensing exams.

Job Conflicts

Dealing With the Public
Interacting with a wide variety of patients can be difficult. Imagine people who are picky when they go to a hairdresser; now imagine those same people with a hairdresser who performs painful procedures. Dentists are sometimes greeted with a little shiver when people find out what they do; many people can't understand why anyone would want to be a dentist. Being in private practice causes the dentist to shoulder considerable expense, and dentists risk losing patients if they do not take appointments on evenings or weekends. In addition to losing patience with patients, dentists can get tired of their relatively unchanging day-to-day work.

Resisting the Temptation to Abuse Drugs

Since most dentists have a solo practice, they have free reign over their office and the inventory therein. Dentists also have easy access to a variety of drugs; they can become addicted to nitrous oxide or prescription drugs without raising suspicion when obtaining them.

Myths About the Job

Dentists Transmit the AIDS Virus

Despite a large scare caused by a singular case in the early 1990s, the risk of HIV being transmitted from dentist to patient is extremely low.

Dentists Have a High Suicide Rate

According to the June 2001 issue of the *Journal of the American Dental Association* there is no evidence that dentists are more prone to suicide than the rest of the population. However, the study also stated that no reliable statistics were available about just how many suicides are committed by dentists each year.

Dentists Are Sadists

This is, of course, mostly a fabrication by filmmakers (think *Marathon Man*) and writers who aimed to titillate audiences and readers. Even so, some dentists have been less than gentle at the chair: In 2000, a New Jersey dentist was accused of restraining children so severely that he hurt them, even breaking the leg of a five-year-old boy. In a more extreme case, Dr. Glennon Engleman is serving three consecutive life sentences for killing seven patients who failed to pay their dental bills.

Jobs Within the Profession

Dental Hygienist

Job Description: Dental hygienists perform cleanings, removing calculus and plaque from teeth. They also take X rays and counsel patients about oral health. Some dental hygienists may work outside dental offices in settings such as schools or hospitals. The overwhelming majority of hygienists—about 98 percent—are women. As of 1999, about 13 percent of enrollees in dental hygiene programs were minorities.

Education: To become a dental hygienist one must have a high school education plus an associate's degree, earned after approximately two years of training. In addition, hygienists must be licensed; upon licensure, a hygienist becomes a registered dental hygienist (R.D.H.).

Clothes: Dental hygienists usually wear scrubs.

Number of Dental Hygienists: More than 100,000 dental hygienists currently work in the U.S.

Earnings: Dental hygienists average about $25 per hour. Many work part-time or split their time between two or more dental offices.

Further Info:
- The American Dental Hygienists' Association
  444 N. Michigan Ave., Suite 3400
  Chicago, IL 60611
  www.adha.org

Further Reading:
- *Clinical Practice of the Dental Hygienist,* Esther M. Wilkins. A comprehensive look at the dental hygienist profession.

Dental Assistant

Job Description: Often the first line of interaction with patients, dental assistants show patients to the exam room and perform office and administrative tasks, including dealing with insurers. Dental assistants also prepare and sterilize equipment. Dental assisting is a popular career choice for women (97 percent of dental assistants are women), with one-fourth of all dental assistants working part-time. About 25 percent of those enrolling in dental assisting programs as of 1999 were minorities.

Education: Training programs are available, but dental assistants can learn on the job.

Number of Dental Assistants: About 200,000 dental assistants are employed in the U.S.

Earnings: The pay for a dental assistant averages about $14 per hour.

Further Info:
- American Dental Assistants Association
203 N. LaSalle St.
Chicago, IL 60601-1225
www.dentalassistant.org

Further Reading:
- *The Dental Assistant*, Pauline C. Anderson and Alice E. Pendleton. Provides the basics for entry-level dental assistants.
- *Journal of the American Dental Assistants Association.* Professional journal of the field.

Orthodontist

Job Description: An orthodontist works to correct a patient's malocclusion, or bad bite. The most common treatment orthodontists perform is fitting braces. Because of the nature of their work, orthodontists interact primarily with adolescents—80 percent of orthodontic patients are under eighteen. All orthodontists are dentists, although most dentists are not orthodontists.

Education: Becoming an orthodontist requires an additional two- to three-year residency in orthodontics upon completion of dental school.

Number of Orthodontists: About 8,500 orthodontists practice in the U.S. and Canada.

Earnings: The median net income for orthodontists is around $175,000 per year.

Further Info:
- American Association of Orthodontists
401 N. Lindbergh Blvd.
St. Louis, MO 63141-7816
www.aaortho.org

Further Reading:
- *Textbook of Orthodontics*, edited by Samir E. Bishara. The foundations of the practice of orthodontics.

Forensic Dentist, Odontologist

Job Description: A forensic dentist identifies deceased persons by consulting their dental records. They also analyze dental evidence (bite marks, etc.) in criminal investigations and help determine abuse or neglect by evaluating dental injuries. Most forensic dentists work for or with coroners, medical examiners, government agencies, or the military, although some work for insurance agencies as consultants in investigating fraudulent claims.

Education: A forensic dentist must be a certified dentist and must pass the American Association of Forensic Odontology (AAFO) examination.

Further Info:
- American Board of Forensic Odontology
  c/o The Forensic Sciences Foundation, Inc.
  P.O. Box 669
  Colorado Springs, CO 80901-0669
  www.abfo.org

Additional Occupations

Dental assistants, dental hygienists, and office staff comprise the people with whom a dentist interacts most. Dentists might also maintain professional relationships with physicians and/or orthodontists.

Dentists in Nonfiction

Books

- *Appointment for Murder: The Story of the Killing Dentist*, Susan Crain Bakos. The account of dentist-turned-murderer Glennon Engleman, who is serving three consecutive life sentences.

- *Confessions of a Modern Dentist*, Sherwin Shinn. A memoir about the struggle and success of a dentist, it includes a section describing his experiences working for a jail.
- *The Dentist of Auschwitz: A Memoir*, Benjamin Jacobs. The extraordinary true story of a young dental student who was imprisoned by the Nazis and used his knowledge of dentistry to stay alive.
- *Doctor Dealer: The Rise and Fall of an All-American Boy and His Multimillion-Dollar Cocaine Empire*, Mark Bowden. The true story of a dentist who became a drug dealer.
- *The Excruciating History of Dentistry: Toothsome Tales & Oral Oddities From Babylon to Braces*, James Wynbrandt. A thorough history of dentistry.
- *Malpractice: What They Don't Teach You in Dental School*, Jeffrey J. Tonner. A legal guide for dentists.

Documentaries
- "Between the Bullet and the Battlefield" (1996). Techniques used by doctors, dentists, and nurses on the battlefield.

Dentists in Fiction

Books
- *Compromising Positions*, Susan Isaacs. A suburban housewife tries to solve the murder of a Long Island periodontist who was a ladies' man. Made into a movie.
- *Death of a Dentist*, M.C. Beaton. Murder, sex, and toothaches in the Scottish highlands.
- *Local Anaesthetic*, Günter Grass. A middle-aged teacher contemplates his life while sitting in a dentist's chair. From the acclaimed German author of *The Tin Drum* and *My Century*.
- *Marathon Man*, William Goldman. Novelist and screenwriter William Goldman turned his fear of dentists into a memorable character: a Nazi murderer who uses dental skills to torture a young graduate student. Made into a movie.

Movies
- *Cactus Flower* (1969). A romantic comedy with Walter Mat-

thau as a successful dentist with a complicated love life.

- *The Dentist* (1996) and *The Dentist II* (1998). These horror films feature lots of gory dental nightmares.
- *Dentists in the Chair* (1960). A British film about dentists involved in crooked schemes.
- *Eversmile, New Jersey* (1989). A traveling dentist traverses South America on his motorcycle.
- *Little Shop of Horrors* (1986). Steve Martin plays a sadistic dentist in this musical comedy.
- *Novocaine* (2001). Steve Martin portrays a dentist who's seduced by a sexy patient and ends up as a murder suspect.
- *The Whole Nine Yards* (2000). Matthew Perry plays a Montreal dentist involved with his hit man neighbor, played by Bruce Willis.

Television
- *The Bob Newhart Show* (1972–1978). A psychologist portrayed by Newhart interacts with his best friend, a dentist. Currently runs in syndication.

Web Sites

- MedBioWorld: Dentistry & Orthodontics Journals (www.sc iencekomm.at/journals/medicine/dentist.html). Journals, including international publications, relating to dentistry.

- Dental Resources (www.onlinedentists.net/resources .htm). A list of dentist-related links.

- The American Association of Women Dentists (www.wom endentists.org/). This group's official Web site.

- Dental Friends (www.dentalfriends.net/). Interactive Web site for dental professionals.

- Zeno's Forensic Site (http://forensic.to/links/pages/Forens ic_Medicine/Odontology/). The odontology portion of a Web site for forensics professionals.

Book Excerpts

One summer visitor complained bitterly that Gilchrest had performed The Great Australian Trench on her. Australian dentists had gained the unfair reputation for casually letting the drill slide across as many teeth as possible, thereby getting themselves a lucrative and steady customer. And although Mr. Gilchrest was Scottish, he was reputed to have performed this piece of supposedly Australian malpractice.

—<u>Death of a Dentist</u>, M.C. Beaton

⤸

But the dentist is equally well read: He traces every abuse of power back to Hegel, whom he refutes elaborately, largely on the strength of the peaceful evolutionary progress of dental medicine. Too many mutually contradictory doctrines of salvation and too little practical advantage . . . he says, and recommends that all government be replaced by his worldwide Sickcare.

Here the teacher discovers common ground: Basically we are in agreement, especially as we both are conscious of an obligation to humanism, humanitas. . . .

But the dentist wants the patient to withdraw his incitements to violence: At the very most I'll tolerate the radical abolition of chlorophyll toothpastes with their unwarranted claim to provide effective protection against cavities.

—<u>Local Anaesthetic,</u> Günter Grass

⤸

He game me a friendly smile. ''Hi, Judy.''

''Judith,'' I replied automatically.

''Okay, Judith it is.'' By that time, I realized I had lost the opportunity to be brilliantly assertive, to establish my adult credentials. I could have said coolly, Mrs. Singer, or, better still, Ms. Singer, or even Ms. Bernstein-Singer. Instead, I sat passively, mouth agape, a napkin resting under my chin, a bib to soak up my infantile dribble. My eyes darted from the word *Castle* on Fleckstein's adjustable light to his princely, large-featured face. He probed, he scraped with one of those ghastly pointed metal dental picks, stopping at intervals so I could rinse my bloodied mouth with Lavoris and water.

''You haven't been using unwaxed dental floss, have you?'' He asked, although he knew the answer.

''No, but I will.''

''You really should. Do you have a Water Pik?''

''Yes,'' I muttered, the draining tube making crude slurping noises in the bottom of my mouth.

''Well, use it. It doesn't do you any good sitting on the sink, does it, Judith?'' He sounded sad and weary, a prophet unheeded by a decadent, self-indulgent people.

—<u>Compromising Positions</u>, Susan Isaacs

CHAPTER 6

Education

*K-12 Teacher, Teacher's Aide, Principal, College
Professor, College Teaching Assistant*

The Lowdown

Everyone remembers a beloved teacher who helped
her find her way through an awkward adolescence.
And most people remember having one teacher (usually a gym or science teacher) who hounded them and
made life miserable. Because of this, teachers in fiction
tend to take on a symbolic role: (1) cheerleaders who
encourage students to become whatever they want to
be or (2) bullies who either abuse the students' self-
esteem or exploit their naïveté.

Schools make wonderful settings because (1) the
stakes are high (things that happen to kids can have
major effects on their adulthood); (2) students are emotionally vulnerable, which makes for powerful scenes;
and (3) conflict occurs between teachers and students,
students and students, teachers and teachers, and
teachers and administrators.

Teachers make compelling characters because the
power they wield has enormous consequences. Many

teachers endure a lot of internal conflict about that, wondering if they teach as effectively as they might and agonizing about decisions they've made regarding students. Unlike physicians, who often see the results of their decisions within a short period of time, teachers may not know the consequences for students for many years—if ever.

Job Description

Teachers are responsible for passing on the important knowledge and skills that develop minds. Teachers at advanced levels, such as college professors, deepen students' appreciation for subjects and help students prepare themselves for careers. The aim of all teachers is to effectively impart their knowledge to their students.

Successful teachers share core traits that allow them to thrive and cope with all the challenges of the teaching profession. Among these traits are organization, confidence in public speaking, patience, creativity, motivational ability, and love of a subject. The ability to adapt to changing class sizes, student backgrounds, and new demands are also essential qualities of a successful teacher. Flexibility is a plus for beginning teachers, as teacher demand is highest in rural and inner-city districts. Teachers must also be lifelong students as they face the challenges of multilingual student bodies, rapidly changing technology, and new developments in both a subject and how it's taught.

Teachers hold different motivations for pursuing this vocation, but they share the satisfaction of passing knowledge to their students. Their reward is helping those students to develop their skills and focus their energies. In the early grades, when students are willing to learn and excited about it, teachers introduce language, math, science, art, history, and other subjects to students. Teachers in middle school and high school must continue students' development in math, science, language arts, and other subjects in a climate where students may be less motivated to learn. In these later grades, discipline becomes an increasingly large portion of a teacher's duties, which cuts into the time spent educating.

Daily Life

Work Schedule

Kindergarten teachers, who typically have their students for a half day, and grade school teachers, who typically have their students for an entire day, teach and supervise activities in a variety of subjects. Secondary school teachers have five to six classes a day in one or a few subject areas, and they have a five- or ten-minute break between classes and a half hour to an hour for lunch. A typical day for a high school math teacher could look like the schedule on page 113.

Dressing the Part

Many private schools have a strict dress code for staff. Public schools tend to be more relaxed, encouraging, but rarely enforcing, a business casual dress code.

Keys to the Kingdom

Teachers of subjects such as gym, shop, chemistry, and physics may have access to recreational facilities, sports equipment, scientific apparatus, and hazardous chemicals and materials. A biology teacher might have everything from an ant farm to a boa constrictor. A typical teacher has keys or access to his own classroom, the bathroom, and the teachers' lounge, with additional access to other classrooms or facilities depending on the structure and policy of the school.

Tools of the Trade

Most teachers use general office supplies in the course of their work, as well as audiovisual equipment, copy machines, and computer networks and software.

Elbow Rubbing

While teachers spend the majority of their time with their students, teachers do meet and confer with a variety of other professionals both on and off campus. These professionals may include assistants, student teachers, librarians, school administrators, speech pathologists, nurses, counselors, special

Time	Duties
7:30–8:00	Check mailbox and e-mail. Prepare assignments for the day. Write up homework assignments for absent students. Write the day's agenda on the board. Set up overhead. Make copies.
8:00–8:55	Period 1 (Homeroom), Algebra I: Take attendance (this must be done in each period). Go over last night's homework assignment. Quiz. Present a section of the text.
9:00–9:55	Period 2, Geometry I: Practice questions for tomorrow's exam.
10:00–10:55	Period 3, Algebra I: Quiz.
11:00–11:55	Period 4, Algebra II. (Fire drill.)
11:55–12:30	Lunch
12:30–1:25	Period 5, Remedial Math.
1:30–2:25	Period 6, Precalculus AP (an advanced placement course offering college credit).
2:25–3:00	Parking lot duty.
3:00–3:30	Conference with a parent. Teachers often spend additional hours on nonteaching tasks such as school safety and assembly duties, committee service, conferences, and open houses.
7:00–8:30 (at home)	Grade Algebra I quizzes. Prepare lesson plan for next day. Finish writing exam for Geometry I.

education assistants, psychologists, social workers, and police officers.

Buzzwords

Like many professions, teaching has an ever shifting, abundant vocabulary. Meanings of the terms are usually apparent.

at their own pace: Students' own natural inclination to learn sets the rate at which they learn.

attention deficit disorder (ADD): An inability to focus attention while learning.

attention deficit hyperactivity disorder (ADHD): This is like ADD, but with a marked tendency toward hyperactivity. Both ADD and ADHD can be treated with medication.

child-centered schooling: This theory promotes cooperative exercises over individual achievement as motivation for learning.

cooperative learning: Teacher-to-student education is shifted to group and student-to-student exercises.

critical thinking: The application of logic and acquired skills to examine a problem.

discovery learning: This method encourages creativity and imagination to unlock a problem or understand a situation.

drill and kill: Rote memorization and repetition with the implied effect of burning out the student.

factory-model schools: Schools seen to turn out students like products as they travel down the assembly line of subjects.

hands-on learning: Students are given the opportunity to learn by firsthand experience, such as direct involvement in experiments in a biology lab.

higher-order skills: Higher levels of cognitive thought, including knowledge, comprehension, application, analysis, synthesis, and evaluation.

learning to learn: Developing the necessary skills to increase the efficiency and effectiveness of future learning.

lifelong learning: Education is seen as a lifelong process with new subjects to be learned or refined according to changes in the student's age, status, and role, as well as in response to changes in society and technology.

multiage classroom: Students of mixed ages, rather than one age group, in a class.

multiple intelligences: This includes skills in linguistics, math, music, visual and spatial concepts, movement, interpersonal ability, intrapersonal ability, naturalist ability, and existential thought.

performance-based assessment: This measurement recognizes a student's skill according to her ability shown in the classroom and on exams.

promise of technology: The concept that computers and technology provide students with the resources to make them brighter and more successful.

self-fulfilling prophecy: This occurs when a teacher's initial attitude about a student sets that student's performance.

thematic learning: Instruction where multiple subjects are centered around a unifying theme.

Education

All public school teachers hold a minimum of a bachelor's degree, and some have advanced degrees in their fields of instruction or in general education. Many teachers pursue continuing education activities, either during summer vacation or in the evening, to keep up with changing subject matter. Public school teachers have also successfully completed a teacher education program, typically one year in length, which certifies them with teaching credentials. Some new teachers in school districts with teacher shortages may be employed with short-term emergency credentials. Private K-12 institutions may not require teacher certification or an undergraduate degree. Instructors at the college level usually hold a master's degree or doctor's degree.

Job Conflicts

With such a wide range of subject areas, school district policies, and student bodies, both new and seasoned teachers walk through a minefield of potential conflicts. At the most basic level are classroom discipline problems and parents' or administrators' criticism of a teacher's methods of controlling a classroom. The disparity between a teacher's rating of a student's performance and the parents' indefatigable belief in their child's talent can lead to conflicts. Teachers may also find themselves embroiled in debates over censorship and teaching materials, usually stemming from parents' concerns over what their children are being taught. An English teacher may have to deal with the threat of not being able to teach *The Adventures of Huckleberry Finn*, or a biology teacher may find herself having to teach natural selection and creationism on equal footing. In both cases, teachers—especially new and idealistic ones—face everything from discipline to alienation depending on how they react to what they consider outside interference to *their* classroom.

Student Testing
Teachers face increased amounts of student testing. More and more school districts are adopting standardized testing, and the schools' funding levels are affected by their students' performance on these tests. Teachers in core disciplines such as math, English, and science, find themselves preparing their students to take standardized tests; they do not get to teach with the flexibility previously afforded to teachers. In addition, teachers may feel pressured to artificially lift students' grades on the ordinary tests in order to help lift the perceived achievement of the school in which they teach.

Burnout
Due to the relatively low pay for the amount of education they hold, as well as discipline problems and other issues, teachers can burn out quickly. Although some teachers migrate to other educational positions, including librarians, curriculum specialists, or administrators, up to one-third of new teachers leave the profession near the beginning of their careers.

Violence on the Job

While teachers try to safeguard students by creating safe environments, teachers themselves are victims to violent attacks at schools. According to the Bureau of Justice Statistics's *Indicators of School Crime and Safety, 1999*, from 1993 to 1997 over 1.7 million crimes were committed against teachers; of these, over 650,000 were violent crimes, including assault, robbery, and sexual assault. This amounts to 84 crimes per 1,000 teachers, with 4 serious violent crimes committed for every 1,000 teachers. A total of 12 percent of teachers working at the K-12 level received threats of injury. Statistics in the "Youth Risk Behavior Study" conducted by the Centers for Disease Control and Prevention (CDC) in 1997 demonstrate the real threat facing teachers in the classroom. In the period thirty days prior to the student survey, 18.3 percent of high school students admitted they had carried a weapon, and 5.9 percent admitted to having carried a gun. Of those students, 8.5 percent had carried a weapon while at school.

Threats of extreme violence, like the sprees in Columbine, Santee, Jonesboro, and other schools, demonstrate that teachers can no longer afford to attribute even the mildest student intimidation or anger to adolescence. Elementary schools are not immune, either. The recent shooting of a six-year-old girl by a seven-year-old student at a Michigan elementary school illustrates that, despite the law's presumption that someone so young can't possibly form an intent to kill, students of all ages can have easy access to weapons of violence and use them.

Myths About the Job

Those Who Can, Do; Those Who Can't, Teach

The cynic sees teachers as failed or untalented practitioners of the subject they teach. In reality, only because teachers are well versed in their fields can they transmit their knowledge of a subject to their students in an engaging, authoritative way. Furthermore, many teachers use their vacation time to pursue their interest in their subjects through obtaining continued education, writing, or attending conferences.

Teachers Are in This Only for the Vacation Time

Teachers do receive more vacation time than most other professionals, but the time off must be judged in light of the workload during the school year. The average teacher works a ten-month school year with two months off during the summer. In addition, most schools observe federal and state holidays, and the calendars include winter and spring breaks. Teachers working a year-round schedule have one week of vacation every eight weeks and a five-week winter break. However, teachers may spend breaks writing or grading exams, writing progress reports, completing report cards, or preparing for the coming term. During the beginning and end of a summer vacation a teacher may prepare for or wrap up the school year. To supplement the teacher's salary and avoid going two months without a paycheck, many teachers teach summer school or take other jobs during the summer. Unlike some other professionals, teachers work at home in the evenings, which can add pressure to their home lives. They spend an average of more than forty hours a week teaching, grading, planning, conferencing, meeting with school administrators, and keeping abreast of changes in their subjects. A teacher can easily put in ten or more hours per school day and spend weekends grading exams or preparing for the coming week. Teachers view the generous summer vacation as a time to unwind, avoid burnout, and rejuvenate themselves after the stresses of the past school year.

Teachers Aren't Accountable and Have Too Much Job Security

Teachers and the schools in which they teach are regularly reviewed for performance, pedagogy, and students' scores on standardized tests. While some teachers do enjoy the benefits of tenure after a three-year probationary period, they can be and do get fired for failing to perform their duties. Tenure merely affords a teacher the promise of due process.

Jobs Within the Profession

K-12 Teacher

Job Description: Teachers' duties include creating lesson plans; developing exercises; evaluating students' performance through quizzes, exams, and class participation; and meeting with parents. Teachers must also enforce discipline if their teaching efforts are to have any effect. Teachers also have a responsibility to identify physical or mental impairments in their students and make recommendations for diagnosis and aid. Teachers also must report instances or suspicion of child abuse or other violence, making them an essential component of a child's safety. Some teachers may also serve as mentors to new and prospective teachers who observe the experienced teachers' teaching methods and develop and hone their own skills.

The average teacher spends less time lecturing than he spends facilitating discussions, aiding group work, and creating problem-solving exercises for the students.

When it comes to vacation time, benefits, and job security, few professions can compete with teaching. Few teachers complain about eight or more weeks of vacation time each year, in addition to winter and spring breaks. Nor do they complain about getting home from work by the time the evening rush hour begins. Most teachers are quick to defend their generous time off by citing their relatively low salaries, the high-stress environments, and the foot-high stacks of tests they must grade in the evening.

Education: A minimum of a bachelor's degree, along with student teaching experience and pedagogy instruction, are re quired for teachers.

Earnings: The average annual salary for public elementary and secondary teachers is $39,000, and private school teachers typically earn less. The lowest paid 10 percent of public school teachers earn $19,000 to $24,000 a year; the highest paid—typically those who've taught the longest—earn $53,000 to $70,000. In the 1999–2000 school year, New Jersey, at over $52,000, topped the list of average salaries. South Dakota, at $29,000, came in last.

Expenses: Many teachers receive allocated funds—or can apply for reimbursement—for the purchase of books, videos, and educational software. While funding varies from school to school, the amount is typically so low that some teachers pay for some essential classroom supplies, including photocopies, supplies, and instructional materials, out of their own pockets.

Unions: For help in negotiating their pay and benefits pack-ages, more than half of all teachers in public schools belong to unions. The National Education Association and the American Federation of Teachers collectively bargain with districts to set pay increases, benefits packages, and other employment issues. Most public school teachers receive cost-of-living increases as well as automatic pay raises based on their contracts with school districts.

Benefits: A well-negotiated contract includes medical insurance benefits for the teacher, and sometimes the teacher's family, as well as a retirement package. Teachers in some states have their own retirement systems and do not receive social security upon retiring. To cut costs, school districts may offer retiring teachers a "golden handshake"—a financial enticement to retire early— and replace a high-salaried teacher with a low-salaried beginning teacher. Some teachers receive a generous number of sick days which can be accumulated and carried from one year to the next; this prevents a lapse in pay and provides a great deal of job security in the event of illness. In addition, many teachers may open accounts at credit unions that offer higher yields on savings and lower interest rates on loans than banks do.

Number of K-12 Teachers: With 3.4 million teachers in the U.S., chances are you have a friend or family member who's engaged in the profession. As of 1998, there were over 1.9 million kindergarten and elementary school teachers and over 1.4 million junior high and high school teachers. Based on a 1993–94 survey, the majority of teachers in public schools are white (87 percent) and female (73 percent), and these percent-ages are even higher at private schools. In public schools, 52 percent of teachers are over the age of forty, and 47 percent have a master's degree. Private schools generally have younger teachers (56 percent are under forty) and fewer teachers that hold master's degrees (34 percent).

Further Info:

- American Council on Education
  One Dupont Circle NW
  Washington, DC 20036
- American Federation of Teachers
  Paraprofessional and School Related Personnel Division
  555 New Jersey Ave. NW
  Washington, DC 20001
- National Education Association
  1201 Sixteenth St. NW
  Washington, DC 20036
- National Resource Center for Paraprofessionals in Education
  and Related Services
  365 Fifth Ave.
  New York, NY 10016

Further Reading:

- *American Journal of Education*, University of Chicago Press.
- *The American School Board Journal*, National School Boards Association.
- *Education Week*, Editorial Projects in Education.
- *The Elementary School Journal*, University of Chicago Press.
- *Inside Education*, Achieve Communications.
- *NEA Today*, National Education Association.
- *Teacher Magazine*, Editorial Projects in Education.

Teacher's Aide

Job Description: Teacher's aides support teachers in the classroom through instruction or clerical work. They often grade student work, set up a classroom for activities, and supervise the school yard. Some aides deal exclusively with students with disabilities or language deficits.

Education: Teacher's aides must hold at least a high school diploma. Those working in specialized areas, such as language skills, may require additional training.

Number of Teacher's Aides: There are over 1.2 million teacher's aides, most of whom are employed in elementary schools.

Earnings: Half of all aides work part-time. Most aides typically earn less than $10 an hour.

Further Info:
• *Handbook for Teacher Aides*, Howard Brighton.

Principal

Job Description: A school principal oversees the daily operation of a school, including the budget, discipline, and building maintenance. Principals must be able to handle pressure from students, parents, and teachers, as well as from school district administrators. The average principal works between forty and sixty hours per week, often attending evening meetings or functions.

Education: Principals often begin their careers as teachers. The post of principal requires a teaching or education degree and often graduate study in administration.

Number of Principals: Though in the 1920s, 55 percent of principals were women, that number has dropped to roughly 20 percent.

Earnings: Pay varies by district, but principals' salaries are higher than teachers'.

Further Info:
• American Association of School Administrators
  1801 N. Moore St.
  Arlington, VA 22209

Further Reading:
• *A Survival Kit for the Elementary School Principal*, Abby Bergman.

College Professor

Job Description: College professors may hold lectures for hundreds of students or work in small seminar-level courses. They may also conduct research projects or take on administrative duties as a department head. Positions include professor, associate professor, full professor, and professor emeritus. A college professor's position and advancement are determined by education, publication, and teaching experience. Undergraduate faculty teach between twelve and fifteen hours a week. Those teaching graduate courses teach about ten hours per week.

Preparation and meeting times bring the average workload to fifty-five hours a week. While there are many teaching positions, securing one is highly competitive. Perks enjoyed by some professors are free tuition for their dependents and the ability to take sabbaticals.

Education: A college professor needs to have at least a master's degree. Associate professors most often must have a Ph.D. and prior teaching experience.

Number of College Professors: Approximately 700,000 professors teach at the college and university level. Women hold over 30 percent of college professor positions.

Earnings: Pay varies widely according to school, ranging from the low $30,000s to $100,000 for established professors at well-endowed schools. Salary is usually based on a nine- or ten-month work period.

Further Reading:
- *The Art and Politics of College Teaching: A Practical Guide for the Beginning Professor*, R.M. Sawyer.

College Teaching Assistant

Job Description: Teaching assistants aid professors in teaching, grading, and conducting class and lab assignments. They often teach general undergraduate courses in part or in whole. Most of these positions are filled by graduate students.

Earnings: Pay is low and often lacks benefits. However, the position lets graduate students gain teaching experience prior to earning graduate degrees.

Further Reading:
- *Handbook for New College Teachers and Teaching Assistants*, Charles Davis.

Additional Occupations

Some other occupations within education include
- coach

- custodian
- librarian
- physical education instructor
- PTA member (a volunteer)
- research librarian
- school board member (an elected official)
- school nurse
- secretary
- teacher for the developmentally delayed
- teacher for the learning disabled
- teacher for the mentally impaired
- teacher for the physically impaired
- textbook writer
- campus policeman

Potential employers for those in the above positions include the following:

- libraries
- police departments
- private school districts
- textbook publishers

Teachers in Nonfiction

Books
- *The ABC's of Running an Elementary Classroom*, Peggy E. Wicker and Harriet U. Schultz. Demonstrates how to engage students and achieve results through various programs.
- *After the Lesson Plan: Realities of High School Teaching*, Amy Puett Emmers. Provides insight into student discipline, the challenges of engaging students, and other day-to-day realities facing high school educators.
- *Among Schoolchildren*, Tracy Kidder. Describes a fifth-grade teacher's everyday experiences in fostering a learning environment for her students.
- *The Essential Career Guide to Becoming a Middle and High School Teacher*, Robert W. Maloy and Irving Seidman. An invaluable resource for understanding the practical issues of be-

coming a teacher. Includes state salaries, accreditation information, and education associations.

- *The First Days of School: How to Be an Effective Teacher*, Harry K. Wong and Rosemary T. Wong. Introduces classroom management techniques for teachers at all levels. Includes practical strategies and lesson plan how-tos.
- *A Lifetime of Teaching: Portraits of Five Veteran High School Teachers*, Rosetta Marantz Cohen. Recounts the teaching experience from the point of view of five high school teachers.
- *On Being a Teacher: The Human Dimension*, Stanley J. Zehm and Jeffrey A. Kottler. Guidance and suggestions for grappling with the challenges of teaching.
- *The Water Is Wide*, Pat Conroy. Memoir of an educator's experience teaching children on an island off the South Carolina coast.

Documentaries
- "The First Year" (2001). Davis Guggenheim's chronicle of the first year of teaching for five young teachers.

Teachers in Fiction

Books
- *Animal Dreams*, Barbara Kingsolver. Story of a thirty-year-old woman returning to her hometown to teach at the local high school for one year.
- *Goodbye, Mr. Chips*, James Hilton. English schoolmaster shapes boys' lives in the late 1800s.
- *Lessons in Survival*, Laramie Dunaway. A high school biology teacher has her life turned upside down when her hippie, bank-robbing parents are released from prison after twenty years.
- *Plainsong*, Kent Haruf. Teachers and students intersect in small-town America.
- *The Prime of Miss Jean Brodie*, Muriel Spark. Set at a girls' school in Edinburgh during the 1930s, this book explores the responsibility of teachers to their pupils. Made into a powerful movie.

* *Up the Down Staircase*, Bel Kaufman. An idealistic first-year high school English teacher faces the realities of inner-city public education.

Movies
* *Blackboard Jungle* (1955). An idealistic English teacher faces the challenges of an inner-city school.
* *To Sir, With Love* (1967). An engineer without teaching experience becomes an instructor at a rough London school where students are in need of real-world lessons.
* *Getting Straight* (1970). Based on an excellent Ken Kolb novel about a grad student trying to become a teacher without losing his moral bearings. The film also explores the protest movement on campuses in the 1960s.
* *Fame* (1980). Follows students through four years at the New York City High School for the Performing Arts.
* *Teachers* (1984). A high school teacher battles both flunking students and school board officials.
* *The Principal* (1987). A high school teacher finds himself promoted to principal of a crime- and gang-filled school.
* *Stand and Deliver* (1987). A high school math teacher in East Los Angeles motivates his students to take and pass an advanced placement exam.
* *Dead Poets Society* (1989). An unorthodox prep school English teacher fosters in his students the idea of carpe diem.
* *Lean on Me* (1989). A high school principal confronts school violence and student underachievement with both encouragement and heavy-handed tactics.
* *Kindergarten Cop* (1990). An urban cop, finding himself in an unexpected role as a kindergarten teacher, juggles new responsibilities.
* *Dangerous Minds* (1995). A high school English teacher battles the school administration and tough students in northern California.
* *Mr. Holland's Opus* (1995). A high school music teacher and aspiring composer faces everyday realities as he inspires his students.
* *Election* (1999). A high school teacher gives an overachieving

student some competition for student council president by fronting his own candidate.

- *Music of the Heart* (1999). A music teacher raises students' esteem by establishing a music program in East Harlem.
- *October Sky* (1999). A high school student, with help from a special teacher, tries to avoid a future in coal mining by winning a science scholarship.

Television

- *Fame* (1982–1987). Based on the movie, kids attend a high school for the performing arts. Currently in syndication.
- *Popular* (1999–2001). Satiric show about high school kids and their teachers. Currently in syndication.
- *Boston Public* (2000–). Series that depicts the interaction of teachers and students at a Boston high school.
- *The Education of Max Bickford* (2001–2002). Richard Dreyfuss plays a college professor overcoming a midlife crisis while raising a family and caring about his students.

Firsthand Research

Get a firsthand impression of the duties, stresses, and rewards of a teacher by visiting a classroom. Most schools and teachers welcome visitors. Contact a school's principal or vice principal directly with your research request.

Web Sites

- **LessonPlansPage.com (www.lessonplanspage.com)**. Sample lesson plans that can be used or supplemented by teachers in a variety of subject areas.

- **AskERIC (http://ericir.syr.edu)**. AskERIC provides a comprehensive index of education links covering subjects such as learning theories, school safety, teacher assessment, and more.

- **Sites for Teachers (www.sitesforteachers.com)**. An index of hundreds of links to resources such as lesson plans and activity ideas.

- Inner-City School Teacher Blues (www.rjgeib.com/biogra phy/inner-city-blues/innerblu.html). Observations on the experience of teaching in the inner city.

- Middle School Diaries (www.middleweb.com/mw/aaDiari es.html). Diary entries chronicling the efforts and experiences of teachers and principals as they face the challenges of the teaching profession.

Book Excerpts

I found the room where I would be teaching General Biology I and II, and made it through the homeroom period by taking attendance and appearing preoccupied. I'd finally paid my preparatory visit to the school a few days earlier, so I knew what to expect in the way of equipment: desks and chairs; some stone-topped lab benches with sinks and arched chrome faucets; an emergency shower; a long glass case containing butterflies and many other insects in ill repair; and a closet full of dissecting pans and arcane audiovisual aids. . . .

The girls seemed to feel a little sorry for me as I stood up there brushing chalk dust off my blazer and explaining what I intended for us to do in the coming year. But the boys [looked] at me like exactly what I was—one of the last annoying things standing between them and certified adulthood.

—<u>Animal Dreams</u>, Barbara Kingsolver

The principal raised the sheet of paper.
Here it is. Russell Beckman. According to
what I see here you're failing him this
first quarter.

That's right.

How come?

Gabriel looked at the principal. Because,
he said. He hasn't done the work he's sup-
posed to.

That's not what I mean. I mean how come
you're failing him.

Guthrie looked at him.

Because hell, Lloyd Crowder said. Everybody knows Mr. Beckman isn't any kind of
student. Unless he gets struck by lightning
he never will be. But he's got to have American history to graduate. It's what the state
mandates.

Yes.

Plus he's a senior. [. . .] Do you want
him back next year?

I don't want him this year.

Nobody wants him this year. None of the
teachers want him. But he's here. You see
my point. Oh hell, give him a downslip if
you want. Scare the son. But you don't want
to fail him.

—Plainsong, Kent Haruf

〰️

As I walked around my new fiefdom, the kids
earnestly applying themselves to the task
at hand, I had my first moment of panic. Some

of them could barely write. Half of them were incapable of expressing even the simplest thought on paper. Three quarters of them could barely spell even the most elementary words. Three of them could not write their own names. Sweet little Jesus, I thought, as I weaved between the desks, these kids don't know crap. Most of them hid their papers as I came by, shamed for me to see they had written nothing. By not being able to tell me anything about themselves, they were telling me everything.

—<u>The Water Is Wide</u>, Pat Conroy

At the end of eight weeks of class, the following entries were the sum of Harry's notes for Education 266B, the required course for all candidates for the secondary teaching credential:

ED. 266B—Prin. Sec. Educ. Subtitle Educ. As Soc. Integ.—Dr. Grumbacher. G moves like a toy with a broken spring. Voice old record Henry Burr, dearly beloved we are gathered here to teach teaching to teachers. 'response—building dynamics' etc. etc.
pretty girl in 4th row sits with legs apart. G sneaks peeks. got it figured. G. warming up to deliver same old

GOLDEN PLATITUDES
1. We teach children, not subjects. (Cause

we don't know the subjects.)
  2. Learning is Socio-Environmental Integration. (I learns to be Them.)
  3. We all Learn by Doing. (or as Einstein said, $E=mc^2$)
Learning must be made Enjoyable. (No biz like the teach biz.)

—<u>Getting Straight</u>, Ken Kolb

CHAPTER 7

Firefighting

Arson Investigator (aka Fire Investigator), Smoke Jumper, Fire Dispatcher, Fire Chief

The Lowdown

It's easy to see why firefighters are so popular in fiction. They risk their lives in dramatic fashion, rushing into infernos that most sane readers fear. A primary difference between firefighters and cops (see chapter nine) as characters is that firefighters do not necessarily deal with crime on a daily basis, therefore their lives are not as impacted by the inhumanity that cops see. However, firefighters can be affected by the tragic loss of life and property that fires cause. In addition, a dark cloud of worry hangs over every firefighter's family because he may be killed on the job. This adds a dramatic intensity to firefighters' lives and relationships.

Many readers are fascinated with the details of firefighting, and this gives writers an opportunity to exploit settings, whether the fire station or the scene of a fire. The specifics of who does what and when offer compelling insight into this dangerous profession.

For mystery and suspense writers, arson is an exciting crime because (1) the stakes are high, (2) evidence is hard to come by, and (3) new technology for investigating fires is constantly being developed, which allows writers to present fresh information to the readers.

Job Description

In addition to putting out fires, firefighters work on most forms of fire prevention, including building inspection. They also lend help at the scenes of catastrophic events such as earthquakes, floods, and other disasters. Firefighters enjoy the benefits of being seen as benevolent protectors (think of the classic image of the fireman rescuing a kitten stuck in a tree) without having to endure the negative sentiment associated with law enforcement public servants (e.g., police officers). Firefighting can be physically and emotionally taxing; firefighters spend much time lying in wait, then they leap to action, frantically hauling eighty- to one hundred-pound equipment into burning buildings. It is also a dangerous occupation, with 112 line-of-duty deaths reported throughout the U.S. in 1999. The attack on the World Trade Center on September 11, 2001, alone resulted in the deaths of more than three hundred firefighters, pushing the total line-of-duty deaths up to 442 for that year. Injuries—everything from minor abrasions to smoke inhalation to disabling damage—are also par for the course for those who fight fires.

A much sought profession (most departments have a long wait to get in), firefighters often come from a long line of firefighters; in fact, family members often work in the same department. Fire departments are organized in a pseudomilitaristic fashion, with a strict hierarchical structure. Like in war, firefighters depend on one another to live, creating a close-knit bond between them. Firefighters work long shifts, requiring them to sleep and eat on the premises) and this also helps them forge close relationships.

The overwhelming majority (more than 90 percent) of firefighters work for city and county fire departments. Some are employed by the federal government, and a small number work for private firefighting companies. A firefighter's salary is modest—between $22,000 and $40,000 per year. One way firefighters can increase their salaries is to pass promotional exams, instrumental in moving them up through the ranks. More-experienced firefighters might hold titles including lieutenant, captain, battalion chief, or chief.

Daily Life

Work Schedule
Firehouse schedules differ by department, but in general firefighters work shifts that are at least twenty-four hours long. Often, firefighters work for one to three days then are off for two to four days. While on duty, firefighters might carry out routine maintenance on their equipment or engage in public service activities. However, they spend much of their time waiting to be called to duty. Most firehouses have recreational amenities such as gyms to help ease boredom. Firefighters fall into a domestic pattern while on duty, sharing chores such as cooking and passing the time by playing games, watching TV, or bickering with one another. When an alarm sounds, they must respond immediately, and each firefighter performs her respective task necessary to mobilize the fire truck(s) and deal with the situation at hand. Working on weekends and holidays is inevitable.

Dressing the Part
A firefighter's uniform is not unlike a police officer's uniform: slacks and a dark blue or tan shirt adorned with identifying badges. However, a firefighter is most recognizable in the uniform worn while battling fires—the trademark yellow jacket, pants, and hard hat. While on duty at the firehouse, firefighters often dress casually. As a show of pride in what they do, many firefighters sport T-shirts, hats, and patches indicating that they belong to the profession. In the wake of the September 11 tragedy, hundreds of New York City firefighters have gotten tattoos of a design available exclusively to them as a show of solidarity with their fellow firefighters.

Buzzwords

apparatus: A fire truck. Also called an *engine*, but never called a truck.

defensive mode: Fighting a fire from the exterior (see also *offensive mode*).

drafting: Extracting water from a source other than a hydrant (e.g., a lake or stream).

master streams: Large-diameter, fixed-location water vessels, including the deck gun and ladder pipe.

M.P.O.: Motor pump operator.

nozzle man: The firefighter who handles the hose line.

offensive mode: Fighting a fire from the interior.

opening up: Extinguishing small hidden pockets of fire.

P.P.E.: Personal protection equipment.

proby: A rookie.

snags: Burned-out trees.

turnouts: Uniforms.

Education

The level of education required to become a firefighter varies depending on the department. Most departments require at least a high school diploma; college-level study in fire science or another field is helpful. Emergency medical technician (EMT) certification is also required for all firefighters.

More important than the number of years spent in school is the satisfactory completion of the many tests would-be firefighters must take. In addition to taking written exams, prospective firefighters are rigorously tested for agility, strength, and overall physical health. Subsequent exams are usually requirements for a firefighter to move up through the ranks.

Job Conflicts

Toll on Personal Life

Because of the unusual demands of the job—especially the firefighter's schedule—home life can be tough. Male firefighters are among the fantasized-about men in uniform, and this, coupled with the long hours spent away from home, can cause tension within marriages.

The inherent danger of the job, however, does not seem to create conflict. While family and friends may worry, firefighters are proud of their chosen career and accept the risks that come with fighting fires.

Tension between firefighters presents a potential job conflict. Firefighters form familial relationships with their co-workers, and while this is often represented positively, the "brotherhood" of firefighters can be as negative as it is positive. Even if bad feelings develop between two firefighters on the same squad, they have to deal with one another day in and day out. This is also true of firefighters and their chiefs. Some chiefs have reputations as easygoing or otherwise pleasant to work for, whereas others are considered hard-assed, lazy, or unwilling to stand up for his firefighters. All of this is compounded by firefighters' direct responsibility for one another's lives; if one is deemed incompetent, the damage to his reputation can be enormous. Add to all this the egotism that can erupt from professional pride and the machismo that some firefighters affect. While firefighters can request to be transferred, a firefighter who has difficulty getting along with others will find it difficult to excel at his job.

Sexism and Racism

The face of firefighting is changing. The adoption of the term *firefighter* in place of *fireman* illustrates one of the biggest potential conflicts within firefighting: women in the department. In what is traditionally a very male-oriented community, many firemen struggle to accept women as their firefighting equals. The most common argument is that the physical testing standards have been lowered for female firefighters. Other concerns include the safety of pregnant firefighters, the need for privacy in undivided quarters, and the family-unfriendly work schedule. The number of female professional firefighters is still quite low; for example, New York City currently has twenty-nine female firefighters in a department of more than eleven thousand.

A different set of conflicts surrounds minority firefighters. As with gender issues, the popular argument regards lowering testing standards to increase diversity. Firefighting is seen by many to have a strong Anglo tradition (despite a legacy of African-American and other minority firefighters), and some of those Anglo firefighters bristle at the idea of nonwhites with lower test scores "stealing" available jobs and appeasing liberals. Much of the conflict is more subtle, falling into grayer areas. For example, a recent attempt to erect a statue depicting the famous flag raising at "Ground Zero" on September 11 ruffled many feathers when it was announced that two of the three firefighters would be represented as minorities even though all three firefighters who raised the flag were white.

Myths About the Job

Firefighters Sit Around Playing Cards Until There Is a Fire

This is, in part, true. Firefighters must be available in case of an emergency; therefore, they cannot get too involved in an activity or be too far from the firehouse at any given time during a shift. This mythical element is that the firefighters enjoy all that waiting. Being in close quarters with a large group—mostly men—and an extremely limited number of things to do can be very frustrating.

Keep in mind that firefighters do not just fight fires and wait around. Firefighters often handle administrative tasks and public service projects. They must also perform routine maintenance on their equipment.

Jobs Within the Profession

Arson Investigator (aka Fire Investigator)

Job Description: An arson investigator looks into the origins of a fire to determine its cause. Arson investigators also enforce arson laws. They sometimes must disarm or remove explosive or incendiary devices and apprehend arson suspects. Like other types of detectives, arson investigators have some administrative tasks: They compile reports based on incidents that involve arson or explosive devices, and they arrange for the safe transport, disposal, and storage of explosives.

Many arson investigators are employed by insurance companies to investigate fraudulent claims. Others go into business for themselves as private investigators.

Education: Experienced police officers and firefighters both can transition to the field of arson investigation. They must pass a battery of physical and psychological exams, including hearing and color vision tests. A bachelor's degree is usually required, preferably in fire science, criminal justice, or one of the social sciences.

Clothes: Arson investigators wear civilian clothes, protective gear, or a firefighter's uniform, depending on the stage of an investigation.

Number of Arson Investigators: No data on the exact number of arson investigators currently working in the U.S. is available, but the International Association of Arson Investigators has over 7,200 members.

Earnings: An investigator just starting out in public service might earn as little as $15,000 a year, and experienced federal investigators earn almost-six-figure annual salaries.

Further Info:
- International Association of Arson Investigators
  12770 Boenker Road
  Bridgeton, MO 63044
  www.firearson.com

Further Reading:
- *Arson Investigation: The Step-by-Step Procedure*, Thomas J. Bouquard.
- *Blaze: The Forensics of Fire*, Nicholas Faith. Reconstructs investigations of famous fires.

- *Fire Cops*, Michael W. Sasser and Charles W. Sasser. Stories from real arson investigators.

Smoke Jumper

Job Description: Smoke jumpers fight forest fires by parachuting into areas that cannot be reached on foot, an extremely demanding job. A smoke jumper must orient himself in the forest using a compass and map; find the supplies and equipment, which also get parachuted in; and determine the best plan of attack. This may include felling trees or digging trenches in addition to suppressing the fire in more conventional ways. Smoke jumpers must maintain contact with their base and/or plane. During periods of fire inactivity, smoke jumpers can be responsible for everything from clearing brush in fire-susceptible areas to consulting other government agencies about environmental and safety issues.

Education: Emphasis is placed on physical fitness rather than formal education. This extremely competitive field requires top physical condition as well as experience in wildland firefighting. Classes to help educate prospective smoke jumpers are available, though these classes are not requirements.

Number of Smoke Jumpers: According to the United States Department of Agriculture (USDA) Forest Service's *2000 National Smokejumper Operations Report*, there were 291 Forest Service smoke jumpers. Two Bureau of Land Management smoke jumper bases employ seasonal and full-time jumpers.

Earnings: This is not a career that someone pursues for the money. Smoke jumpers earn incredibly modest salaries, with jumpers starting at as little as $11 per hour. Additionally, the nature of the business requires that most employees work only seasonally or as needed, making their income as unstable as it is low.

Further Info:
- Bureau of Land Management
  Office of Public Affairs
  1849 C St., Room 406-LS

Washington, DC 20240
Phone: (202) 452-5125
Fax: (202) 452-5124
www.blm.gov
- National Smokejumper Association
www.smokejumpers.com
- USDA Forest Service
Fire & Aviation Management
3833 S. Development Ave.
Boise, ID 83705
Phone: (208) 387-5100
www.fs.fed.us/fire/fire_new/

Further Reading:

- *Firefighter's Handbook on Wildland Firefighting*, William C. Teie. Written by a firefighter for firefighters.
- *Jumping Fire: A Smokejumper's Memoir of Fighting Wildfire in the West*, Murray A. Taylor and Kati Steele. A popular memoir written by a smoke jumper with over thirty-five years of experience.
- *The Smoke Jumper*, Nicholas Evans. A romantic novel by the author of *The Horse Whisperer*.

Fire Dispatcher

Job Description: Fire dispatchers take emergency and non-emergency calls and send fire personnel, paramedics, and equipment to the scenes. If necessary, a dispatcher provides medical and other instructions to the caller before the firefighters or paramedics arrive.

Education: A high school diploma or its equivalent is necessary for one to gain employment as a dispatcher. As with many other civil service jobs, one must take an exam that tests basic reading, writing, and math skills. Medical training and other emergency training are provided on the job.

Number of Fire Dispatchers: There are countless dispatchers throughout the country, as every fire department must have them on hand twenty-four hours a day, seven days a week.

Earnings: Compensation for fire dispatchers varies widely. For example, a fire dispatcher in a small Midwestern town might earn a starting salary of around $20,000 per year, whereas one in a major West Coast city can earn upwards of $40,000 a year to start.

Fire Chief

Job Description: A fire chief is in charge of the fire department and acts as a liaison between firefighters and city officials. The fire chief is likely required to attend fire commission meetings, provide reports, set budgets, and basically make the department look good. Part of this involves enforcing department policy and procedures, but a good fire chief must also have the respect of his firefighters. The fire chief is responsible for hiring and firing firefighters, as well as coordinating any volunteer fire departments.

Education: A solid background as a firefighter (usually ten or more years) is essential for one to become a fire chief. A college education also becomes important at this stage: Most departments require an Associate's Degree in Fire Science, and many require a bachelor's degree. Computer and organizational skills are necessary, but EMT certification and firefighting proficiency are still essential. Fire chiefs, like firefighters, must undergo physical testing, though a much lower level of physical fitness is required.

Number of Fire Chiefs: Each fire department has one fire chief.

Earnings: Fire chiefs earn modest salaries compared to other types of management positions. A new hire could start as low as $50,000 a year, and annual salaries usually cap off before they hit six figures.

Further Info:
- International Association of Fire Chiefs (IAFC)
  4025 Fair Ridge Dr., Suite 300
  Fairfax, VA 22033-2868
  Phone: (703) 273-0911
  Fax: (703) 273-9363
  www.ichiefs.org.

- Most states also have their own fire chiefs associations.

Additional Occupations

Other jobs related to firefighting include EMTs, paramedics, and police officers.

Firefighters in Nonfiction

Books
- *The Fire Inside: Firefighters Talk About Their Lives*, Steve Delsohn. A journalist interviews firefighters.
- *Report From Engine Co. 82*, Dennis Smith. A memoir of a South Bronx firefighter circa 1972.

Firefighters in Fiction

Books
- *California Fire and Life*, Don Winslow. A mystery novel involving arson.
- *The Rescue*, Nicholas Sparks. Story of a volunteer firefighter. By the author of *Message in a Bottle*.
- *The Smoke Jumper*, Nicholas Evans. A romantic novel by the author of *The Horse Whisperer*.

Movies
- *Always* (1989). A Steven Spielberg film about pilots who douse forest fires.
- *Backdraft* (1991). The definitive movie about brothers—one a firefighter, the other an investigator.

Television
- *Emergency!* (1972–1977). A series about emergency workers, including firefighters. Available on video.
- *Third Watch* (1999–). A drama about a group of firefighters and paramedics in New York City.

Web Sites

- Firehouse.com (www.firehouse.com). A useful Web site designed for firefighters. It includes many helpful links.

- Fire Department, City of New York (www.fdny.org). The official FDNY Web site.

- Women in the Fire Service, Inc. (www.wfsi.org). An international nonprofit organization that considers issues relating to female firefighters.

Book Excerpts

''We don't even know if it's arson.''
''Yeah, we do. I do.'' The statement stopped Georgia cold. Carter never made definite judgments this early in a case. He must have read the shock on her face, because he beckoned her over to a swirling bluish-green depression on the basement floor, about fifty feet from the stains they'd noted earlier. It was shiny and sleek, almost like glass. And it was etched deep into the concrete, as permanently as a tattoo.
''You see this pretty burn?'' He ran his fingers across the mark. ''Something very bad and very deliberate caused it.''
''Nothing burns concrete,'' Georgia insisted. ''That's why they call concrete buildings fireproof.''
''Fireproof,'' Carter mumbled. ''Well, maybe y'all gonna have to change the term.''

—The Fourth Angel, Suzanne Chazin

Fire has a language.

It's small wonder, Jack thinks, that they refer to tongues of flame, because fire will talk to you. It will talk to you with its burning color of flame, color of smoke, rate of spread, the sounds it makes while it burns different substances, and it will leave a written account of itself after it's burned out.

Fire is its own historian.

It's so damned proud of itself, Jack thinks, that it just can't help telling you about what it did and how it did it.

Which is why first thing the next morning Jack is in the Vales' bedroom.

He stands there in that dark fatal room and he can hear the fire whispering to him. Challenging him, taunting him. Like, Read me, you're so smart. I've left it all here for you but you have to know the language. You have to speak my tongue.

It's okay with me, Jack thinks.

I speak fluent fire.

—California Fire and Life, Don Winslow

Friends and neighbors mill around, rubber-
necking. Terrifying, they say. The flames
were taller than the trees. They're fright-
ened because as far as they're concerned it
was an accident, an act of God, something
that could happen to anyone at any time, no
warning. And simultaneously they're re-
lieved because it's not their house, it's
not their stuff spread out on the grass. It
didn't happen to them.

—Music for Torching, A.M. Homes

CHAPTER 8

Journalism

Editor, Reporter, Publisher, Photo Editor, Copyeditor

The Lowdown

Who can resist the fast-paced, high-stakes world of news reporting? The deadlines at a daily newspaper can create a natural ticking bomb in a plot. If information is not gathered within a certain time period the story may not run, which can affect millions of lives. After all, if something is newsworthy, then high stakes may be involved. Add to that the fact that many other journalists are after the same story, so you get plenty of plot suspense.

Characters who work for newspapers are appealing because the public tends to see them as modern crusaders: seekers of truth who are willing to risk their lives and jobs in order to share information that the entire community will benefit from. Because of that perception, presenting characters who will do anything to get a story just to further their own careers offers conflict. News reporting also provides an obvious plot structure: The reporter must interview a series of characters. Each scene introduces another character, so the writer can slowly provide clues in an active way.

Newspapers deal with big issues, so a fiction writer who wishes to tackle such an issue can use a news setting to do so without being preachy. A reporter has access to a lot of information that would provide background to any issue. A reporter character also can show readers the many effects of an issue merely by interacting with characters who have been affected.

Job Description

Newspaper and magazine editors are instrumental in creating the look and feel of publications. Editors must be up-to-date on all the news pertaining to their section or sections and assign (or accept from freelancers) stories that are relevant to the publication. In addition to editing the submitted articles, editors often write stories of their own.

Daily Life

Work Schedule

The typical work schedule for an editor varies immensely depending on the publication and the editor's personality. Regardless, editors—especially newspaper editors—are known for working long hours. In a big city, editors must cover a lot of ground and produce a large newspaper every day. In a small town, the editor might be one of only a handful of people producing the newspaper for the whole community. The same principle is true of magazines: The editor at a large magazine might work late into the evening and on weekends to sort through his many queries and press releases, determined to keep his magazine on top; the editor of a smaller magazine is less deluged with material but likely wears many hats (proofreading, booking photographers, or even layout).

In any case, most editors divide their time between attending editorial meetings to determine what to include in the next issue, dealing with phone and e-mail correspondence with news sources and reporters, editing articles, and keeping up with the news relevant to their sections. In fact, newspaper and magazine editors are usually saturated with information: They subscribe to dozens of periodicals and also may have to keep televisions in their offices so they can keep CNN (or HGTV, or E!, depending on their focus) playing in the background.

Dressing the Part
The culture of the publication determines appropriate dress. At a fashion magazine, being stylish is part of an editor's job. At a business publication, business attire is required. At most newspapers and general-interest magazines, editors use their own judgment and usually settle on business casual.

Buzzwords
ABC: Audit Bureau of Circulation—the organization that compiles circulation statistics for publications.

above the fold: Stories appearing on the top half of page one of a newspaper.

backgrounder: An informal meeting with the press that gives information not meant for publication.

beat: A beat is the section to which a reporter is assigned, and the reporter is expected to alert the editor to issues that might be newsworthy. A city newspaper might have a school district beat, for example, and the reporter on that beat must keep up with any news involving that district and its schools.

byline: The reporter's name carried atop a story.

clips: Newspaper or magazine clippings of a writer's own story. A writer uses clips to help her land other jobs.

dope: Advance information, usually based on gossip or rumor.

evergreen: An article that is not directly linked with that day's news and could run anytime.

news hole: The space for news amidst advertisements.

press cycle: One press cycle is the schedule for producing one issue, and it varies by publication frequency.

Education

Most editors have college educations, and many have graduate degrees in journalism or a field relevant to the subject they edit. However, some editors become involved in journalism by first distinguishing themselves in another field; for example, an artist without a college education might successfully write about art and become the arts editor for a publication.

Job Conflicts

Editorial Goals vs. Advertising Goals

To a publisher, a newspaper or magazine is a business with revenues generated from circulation and ad sales. The content is important because it draws people to read the publication. Effective content therefore drives up circulation, which then drives up the amount charged for advertising. Editors take an inverse view: Ad sales bring in enough money to keep the periodical afloat so that content can be published. Most publications, particularly newspapers, keep advertising and editorial functions as separate as possible, and they even run negative stories on major advertisers when the situation calls for it. However, publications sometimes hold certain topics— so-called sacred cows—above rebuke due to the politics of the publication or to its advertising dollars.

Editorial Duty vs. Ownership

This conflict also deals with a reality of corporate America: Can newspapers owned by corporations that also own many other businesses be trusted to give the reader impartial truth? For example, if Disney owns a TV network (which it does), can that channel's news programs be trusted to impartially report on Disney's legal hassles? Can the channel be trusted to air objective reviews of movies made by Disney or to question consumer products made by a Disney subsidiary? An editor can be conflicted if her journalistic responsibilities put her meal ticket at risk.

Editorial vs. Editorial

Editors can clash with publishers and reporters over vision for the publication. Editors constantly work to keep their sections fresh and innovative while maintaining the spirit of the publication. People are fiercely protective of their ideas and reputations as journalists, and many egos get stepped on when the editing process begins.

Editorial Output vs. Society at Large

An editor's job is centered around conflict: The news business means, after all, capturing and distilling issues for readers. When an editor chooses to run a story, he faces potential criticism from readers. For example: "Running a story about this issue is just sensationalism"; "The facts are twisted, and people are quoted out of context." Because the news media has a reputation of being cutthroat, many people are wary of being interviewed for a newspaper or magazine story. The old news adage "If it bleeds, it leads" sums up the popular opinion of how newsrooms are run.

Print vs. Television

The rise of television viewing has brought about a decline in newspaper circulation. Newspaper editors admit that television can publish breaking news fast and provide dramatic visual coverage. However, editors contend that TV tends to prioritize news according to its video footage rather than its importance. For example, a story about a car chase, a fire, or a celebrity in court will lead the TV news. Newspaper journalists claim that they give more in-depth information than TV can.

Myths About the Job

The News Media Has a Liberal Bias

This is one of the most hotly debated topics about the media. In the late 1990s, David Croteau of Virginia Commonwealth

University set out to settle this debate scientifically. The result was his 1998 publication of the results of a landmark study. Surveying hundreds of journalists from print, radio, and TV media, the study concluded that journalists' political views were overwhelmingly centrist. In fact, Croteau's study found that the media leans to the right on economic issues including Social Security, taxes, and trade. They were more liberal than the average citizen on social issues including environmental law. Still, certain publications such as *The New York Times* are considered to be left of center overall; while others, including the *New York Post*, can be quite conservative. Of course, a fundamental sticking point in this debate is how one defines *liberal* and *conservative*.

Reporters—Hard-boiled and Willing to Do Anything to Get a Story—Are Always Hitting the Street to Get the Scoop

Bob Woodward and Carl Bernstein (or Fox Undercover News) notwithstanding, newspaper and magazine editors and reporters rarely practice the covert aspects of journalism. For starters, few reporters have exciting beats. In introductory journalism classes, professors often remark that the obit section is the starting point for young reporters. This is usually not far from the truth. While not all reporters start off with obits, most begin their careers reporting on school board or city council meetings and writing about new parking restrictions or other mundane civic business. Even reporters assigned to city hall or Capitol Hill are overwhelmingly businesslike, conducting work on the phone and developing friendly relationships with their colleagues and news sources. (This puts to rest the myth that all interviews are antagonistic.)

Jobs Within the Profession

Reporter

Job Description: A reporter writes up to several articles per day for the newspaper or magazine for which he works. Reporters must track down and interview sources for stories and write articles in a clear voice and a timely manner.

A reporter pursues her journalism career by working on staff at a particular publication or as a freelance writer. Reporters who are employees, especially at newspapers, write exclusively or almost exclusively for that publication. Freelancers roam about independently, pitching ideas to publications and selling each story individually. A freelancer can be contracted to produce a certain amount of content for a publication over a specified period of time; this does not, however, make him a part-time employee of that organization.

Education: Most reporters have a bachelor's degree or an advanced degree, but experience is often valued as much as education.

Clothes: Reporters must dress to fit the occasion—a war correspondent in the Middle East obviously dresses differently from someone who is covering a charity ball.

Number of Reporters: Tens of thousands of reporters, employees and freelancers, work in the U.S. Thousands of writers work or freelance for *The New York Times* alone each year.

Earnings: The pay for reporters varies widely. Someone just starting out might work without pay or for perks only at small magazines or newspapers. A major newspaper might pay a reporter more than $1,000 for one piece.

Further Info:
- Reporter.org (www.reporter.org). A great resource for professional organizations relating to reporters.

Further Reading:
- *The Art and Craft of Feature Writing*, William E. Blundell.
- *Creative Interviewing: The Writer's Guide to Gathering Information by Asking Questions*, Ken Metzler.

Publisher
Job Description: The publisher is the top person on the business side of a publication. A publisher's concerns focus on increasing circulation and advertising while lowering expenses. The publisher is usually the owner of the publication and,

therefore, is the boss. She may change everything from the target demographic to the editor in chief in an attempt to keep circulation and advertising rates up.

Education: To own a publication a publisher needs money, not an education. Most publishers have college degrees, but that is more of a matter of culture than necessity.

Number of Publishers: The number of publishers is shrinking. Few major magazines or newspapers are independently owned. For example, Condé Nast owns the *New Yorker, Gourmet, Lucky, GQ, Wired,* and many others; the *Los Angeles Times* is owned by Tribune Company, publisher of the *Chicago Tribune* and countless other newspapers. Large publishing companies such as these may have several associate publishers—each is often an MBA the owner of the company hires to oversee one particular publication. For many small publications, the person who conceived the idea for the publication is also the publisher and editor in chief, and a tiny staff runs the production.

Earnings: Publishers are usually paid a salary along with bonuses depending on how well the publication does. It is safe to say, however, that the publisher of a major newspaper or magazine is likely to be quite wealthy.

Further Info:
- Newspaper Association of America (NAA)
  1921 Gallows Rd., Suite 600
  Vienna, VA 22182-3900
  Phone: (703) 902-1600
  Fax: (703) 917-0636
  www.naa.org

Further Reading:
- *The Newspaper Publishing Industry,* Robert G. Picard and Jeffrey H. Brody.
- *Personal History,* Katharine Graham. Pulitzer prize–winning memoir by the publisher of the *Washington Post.*

Photo Editor
Job Description: A photo editor works with editorial and design staff to develop ideas and content. He also commissions

and produces original photography for the publication while working within the confines of its budget.

Education: Photo editors usually have a bachelor's degree from an art school or college, but experience may be substituted for education.

Number of Photo Editors: This varies depending on the size and budget of the publication. A large daily newspaper may have several photo editors, whereas a smaller circulation magazine may combine the duties of the photo editor with other design duties.

Earnings: Photo editors earn anywhere from about $20,000 to six figures each year.

Further Info:
- National Press Photographer's Association
  3200 Croasdaile Dr., Suite 306
  Durham, NC 27705
  Phone: (919) 383-7246
  Fax: (919) 383-7261
  www.nppa.org

Further Reading:
- *Body Horror: Photojournalism, Catastrophe, and War,* John Taylor. A critical study of photography, ethics, and culture.
- *The Digital Journalist* (http://digitaljournalist.org). An online magazine for photojournalists.
- *ei8ht.* A new print magazine of photojournalism that features photos, news, and links. From the creators of *foto8* (http://foto8.com), a Web-based magazine of photojournalism.

Copyeditor

Job Description: The copyeditor makes sure every *i* is dotted and every *t* is crossed. The copyeditor is responsible for correcting typographical, spelling, and grammatical errors, and she is also expected to ensure conformity with the style guide set by the publication. Further, copyeditors write headlines and captions and are sometimes responsible for page layout.

Education: Copyeditors almost always have bachelor's degrees. Some copyeditors hold advanced degrees in English or related fields.

Number of Copyeditors: Like other newspaper and magazine positions, it's difficult to estimate the number of copyeditors working in the U.S. One copyeditor handles four to six stories per shift at a major newspaper; work volume may be higher at a newspaper with a smaller budget.

Earnings: Copyeditors can earn anywhere from $20,000 to $60,000 annually, depending on their experience and the rigors of the job.

Further Info:
- American Copy Editors Society (ACES)
  Phone: (800) 393-7681
  www.copydesk.org

Further Reading:
- *Copy Editor.* A newsletter published by McMurry Publishing.
- *The New York Times Manual of Style and Usage*, Allan M. Siegal and William G. Connolly.

Additional Occupations

Other jobs related to journalism include paperboys, newsstand operators, cartoonists, and columnists.

Journalists in Nonfiction

Books
- *All the President's Men*, Carl Bernstein and Bob Woodward. Fascinating account of the reporters that broke the Watergate scandal. Made into an equally compelling movie.
- *The Associated Press Stylebook and Briefing on Media Law*, Norm Goldstein, ed.
- *Bias: A CBS Insider Exposes How the Media Distorts the News*, Bernard Goldberg. An insider tries to make a case that the news media is liberal.

- *Jack the Ripper and the London Press*, L. Perry Curtis Jr. A book comparing the ways different London publications dealt with stories about the notorious killer.
- *Personal History*, Katharine Graham. The Pulitzer prize–winning memoir by the publisher of the *Washington Post*.
- *The Times of My Life and My Life With the Times*, Max Frankel. The memoir by retired *New York Times* executive editor Frankel, who had a total of forty-five years with the newspaper.
- *Within the Veil: Black Journalists, White Media*, Pamela Newkirk. An NYU journalism professor's study of African-American reporters in the media.

Journalists in Fiction

Books
- *Basket Case*, Carl Hiaasen. Recent novel about an investigative reporter demoted to the obits desk.
- The Cat Who . . . series, Lilian Jackson Braun. This best-selling mystery series features journalist Jim Qwilleran and his sleuthing kitty sidekicks.
- *Flinch*, Robert Ferrigno. A tough Los Angeles tabloid reporter unwillingly becomes a serial killer's confidant.
- *The Fourth Hand*, John Irving. A broadcast journalist undergoes an experimental medical procedure. By the author of *The Cider House Rules* and *The World According to Garp*.
- *Panic on Page One*, Linda Stewart. Fast-paced, highly readable novel about a newspaper following a grisly story.

Movies
- *His Girl Friday* (1940). A fast-talking and morally ambivalent reporter, played by Cary Grant, works a death penalty story and his girlfriend at the same time. Based on the play *The Front Page*, which has also been made into several movies.
- *Citizen Kane* (1941). This mother of all newspaper movies is based on the life of news mogul William Randolph Hearst.
- *Gentlemen's Agreement* (1947). Based on the Laura Z. Hobson novel, this film features a journalist who poses as a Jew

in order to write about anti-Semitism. It has some surprising twists.

- *Absence of Malice* (1981). A reporter, played by Sally Field, uses her journalistic skills to wrongly implicate Paul Newman's character in a crime. Does a good job of debating journalism ethics.
- *Broadcast News* (1987). This movie addresses love and journalistic integrity in television news. Excellent characterization and dialogue.
- *The Paper* (1994). Michael Keaton's character runs a newspaper and tries to have a personal life.
- *I Love Trouble* (1994). This film tries to be an edgy *His Girl Friday* and stars Nick Nolte and Julia Roberts as competing reporters.

Television

- *Lou Grant* (1977–1982). An excellent series about a Los Angeles newspaper staff struggling with the moral implications of their news stories.
- *Everybody Loves Raymond* (1996–). A sitcom about a sports writer and his family, including his omnipresent parents.
- *Just Shoot Me* (1997–). A sitcom about the eccentric staff at a New York fashion magazine.

Web Sites

- **American Society of Newspaper Editors (www.asne.org).** This site covers legal and other issues for editors of daily newspapers.

- **Mediabistro.com (www.mediabistro.com).** A site of collected job information and news related to journalists. This site focuses heavily on magazines.

Book Excerpts

Caroline's old office in the Tribune building had been kept exactly as it was when she had finally sold out of her remaining shares in the newspaper to Blaise, with the understanding that even as a minor stockholder she would be considered, when she chose, what indeed she was: the creator of the modern Tribune, and its copublisher. Blaise seemed more pleased than not to have her back, if only as a pipeline to the White House.

On one wall there had been placed a map of Europe; each day, Harold Griffiths would move about different-colored pins to show the advance of the German armies across the Rhine and the retreat of the French and British armies toward the sea. Above the map there was a modernistic clock, first revealed at the World's Fair in New York the previous summer. It told the hour in every one of Earth's zones as well as the dates. Thus far, it was May 10, 1940, in Washington, D.C.

—The Golden Age, Gore Vidal

⊜

''You're taking that out?'' Betsy had said as the editor drew a blue line through a sentence.

In rough copy, a *Time* story could sometimes look like modern art after an editor's blue pencil was finished with it.

''Yes, I am,'' Still Norris had said. ''I hardly think it's in the interest of our subscribers to make them sick at their stomachs.''

''It's true,'' Betsy had said. ''You can see it in a newsreel.''

''Oh, I have no doubt.'' The editor had smiled agreeably, resuming his zigzag marks with the blue pencil.

—Fast Copy, Dan Jenkins

However much homework you did before an interview, you never felt easy until it was over. Peter had told her where the general-turned-politician would be most vulnerable, and this morning Zoe began by playing up to his achievements. Then when he thought everything was going his way and relaxed, she asked why he had shouldered none of the responsibility for American troops being pulled out of Irkuk without toppling the dictator first. He blew his top. That's when she got the meat she wanted.

On her way to the paper afterward, she felt the relief of a journalist who knows the tape and notebook in her bag contain what she needs to produce a good piece. Minutes later, of course, came the annoyance of realizing that if she'd put a further question to him, the piece would be better still.

—The Magnates, Susan Crosland

CHAPTER 9

Law Enforcement

Police Officer; Prison Warden; Federal Bureau of Investigation (FBI) Agent; Secret Service Agent; Central Intelligence Agency (CIA) Agent; Alcohol, Tobacco and Firearms (ATF) Agent; Drug Enforcement Administration (DEA) Agent; Immigration and Naturalization Service (INS) Agent

The Lowdown

This is many writers' favorite fictional profession. From literary mainstream darlings to genre hacks, writers know that crime and those who wallow in it are natural subjects. Some crime writers—such as Elmore Leonard, Ross Thomas, Raymond Chandler, Dashiell Hammett, and Ross Macdonald—elevate the subject matter through their literary style and keen insight into characters. Others merely exploit the exciting circumstances of law enforcement in order to thrill the readers. Some manage to do both.

Law enforcement characters provide high stakes. On the surface, the stakes are simply life and death, but the stakes can be subtler, yet equally high, in the hands of a good writer. The stakes for law enforcement characters are similar to those for priest characters: living with the role of being symbols that people can do the right thing for the sake of their community despite physical dangers, the toll on their personal lives, and temptations of the evil they fight. These conflicts are enough to fuel thousands of books, TV shows, and movies—and they have. The stakes for the criminal—the risk of getting caught—can provide many shades of characterization. The criminal can be a deadly mastermind who cares for no one and for nothing but his own ambition. Conversely, she can be a decent person in terrible circumstances. The spectrum is so vast that the writer can introduce familiar character types but give them a unique essence.

Crime symbolizes an assault on our values as a community. Besides the personal safety of citizens, the ideals we hold dear and teach our children are at stake when criminals threaten. If law enforcement can't uphold the ideals of truth and justice, how can we expect our children to embrace those ideals? The futures of our children and, therefore, the future of society itself are ultimately at stake.

(Wonder why we haven't included the private detective in this section—or anywhere in this book? The reason is simple: Many terrific books that cover this area thoroughly are already out there.)

Job Description

Law enforcement is made up of a range of agencies, each one filled with employees serving different roles. Occupations include police officers, detectives, and various federal agents—ATF, INS, DEA, FBI, and even the Secret Service. For many, the attraction of law enforcement is the real sense of purpose the job provides. With a clear mandate to uphold the law and protect society, police officers and federal agents alike can enjoy seeing how their work affects the community and the nation. In addition to satisfaction from preventing crime, apprehending criminals, and protecting society, law enforcement professionals enjoy the camaraderie of a tightly knit profession. A career in law enforcement can come with a price, though. The job often can be dangerous, and the fight against criminal elements can seem daunting and overpowering.

Daily Life

Work Schedule

The most visible law enforcement presence is the patrol officer. Unlike many operations, police work continues twenty-four hours a day. A police officer's hours depend on how his department schedules shifts. Some departments have a day shift and a night shift, while others break a workday into three watches. A police officer's beat and seniority come into play in scheduling. Some officers may work four consecutive day or night shifts then receive three days off. A rookie officer is more likely to be assigned less-desirable late-night or early-morning shifts. Emergencies can extend an officer's workday and interfere with scheduled time off.

In the course of a day, a patrol officer may tackle everything from tedious, uneventful periods to chasing armed suspects. An officer may assist stranded motorists or take measurements and conduct interviews to ascertain the cause of a car accident. Officers are called to investigate complaints of excessive noise, child abuse, vandalism, domestic violence, robbery, or car theft. At the scene of a crime, an officer collects and catalogs evidence. A law enforcement officer makes arrests, interviews victims, questions suspects, and testifies in court. When involved with community policing, a patrol officer may spend several hours meeting with local community representatives. During large public occurrences, such as special events or protests and riots, law enforcement officers engage in crowd control and traffic management.

Dressing the Part

A police officer's uniform includes most, if not all, of the following articles: shirt, pants, shoes or boots, hat, holster, and badge. Special items such as a motorcycle or bicycle helmets are issued to specific officers. To fit a variety of climates, police officers have special uniforms and footwear including shorts, heavy jackets, and rain gear.

Keys to the Kingdom

Most patrol officers use an assigned patrol car that holds or is outfitted with special equipment. The officer uses the police radio to communicate with other officers and the department. She can use the computer to run driver's license and vehicle license checks, and onboard video cameras record citations, chases, and arrests. An officer operates sobriety-testing equipment during traffic stops and at sobriety checkpoints. Traffic and highway patrol officers use radar guns to detect speeding motorists.

Police officers have access to multitudes of equipment that allows them to deal with a variety of circumstances. Some officers routinely use body armor. Specialized equipment is available to officers who engage in underwater recovery, search and rescue, or bomb disposal. Specially trained officers operate bicycles, motorcycles, or even helicopters in the course of duty. Special weapons and tactics (SWAT) divisions have access to a much larger arsenal of nonlethal and lethal weapons, from flash grenades used in raids to high-caliber rifles.

Tools of the Trade
A patrol officer is commonly equipped with a collapsible baton; a semiautomatic sidearm, either 9mm or .40 caliber; handcuffs or other restraints; and nonlethal weapons such as pepper spray.

Elbow Rubbing
During the course of the workday law enforcement officers encounter a variety of people: community residents; business owners; officers from other police departments; fire, rescue, and emergency personnel; lawyers; judges; jail personnel; and prison inmates. Police officers work with animals if they patrol in a K-9 unit or on horseback.

Slang Titles
- Cop (Constable on patrol)
- Dick
- Fuzz
- Heat
- The Law
- Pig

Buzzwords

Law enforcement personnel employ a rich vocabulary of jargon and radio codes.

10-9: Repeat last message.

11-8: Person down.

11-45: Attempted suicide.

11-46: Death report.

11-47: Injured person.

11-85: Send tow truck.

AC: Aircraft crash.

ADW: Assault with a deadly weapon.

BOLO: Be on the lookout.

BT: Bomb threat.

bus: Ambulance.

check-by: Provide low priority aid to an officer.

code 3: Proceed with siren and red lights.

code 6: Out of car to investigate.

code 6A: Out of car to investigate, assistance may be needed.

code 6C: Suspect is wanted and may be dangerous.

code 9: Jailbreak.

code 10: Request clear frequency.

code 100: In position to intercept.

DB: Dead body.

dog call: Uninteresting response call, or a situation that shouldn't require police involvement.

DT: Detective.

GTA: Grand theft auto.

gun run: Weapons search.

HBD: Has been drinking.

hit: An active warrant.

hook: Tow truck.

jaws or Jaws of Life: A device for opening badly damaged vehicles.

OC: Organized crime.

OD: Off duty.

perp: Perpetrator.

pop: To make an arrest.

rabbit: A subject who runs from the police.

rat squad: Internal Affairs Bureau.

rip: Disciplinary loss of pay.

white shirts: Lieutenants and higher. Office types.

Education

Some state police departments require candidates to hold a two-year college degree. All departments encourage candidates to have some college experience. Officer candidates need between 448 and 823 hours of police academy classroom training in subjects such as constitutional, family, criminal, and traffic law. Students also receive instruction in sobriety testing, arrest control methods, radar certification, courtroom protocol, and cultural diversity. State law enforcement candidates require the most classroom hours, while sheriff's department candidates require the least. New officers must also complete between 360 and 480 hours of field training. In addition, new police officers must have passed a personal interview; a medical exam; and criminal record, background, and driving record checks. Ninety percent of agencies require some form of psychological testing and a written aptitude test. Eighty percent of agencies require a drug test, and 66 percent require a polygraph test.

Job Conflicts

Danger
The law enforcement profession is fraught with the potential for harm. Despite vigorous training, safety measures, and safety equipment, officers can be injured or killed in the line of duty. This potential danger can be a major source of stress for a police officer's spouse and loved ones and for the officer himself.

Immersion in the Job
An inability to distance work from family life can impact a police officer's relationships. Nationwide, divorce rates among police officers, estimated at between 60 and 75 percent, are significantly higher than the national average.

Burnout
The high level of stress experienced and the unending tide of crime and suffering that some officers witness—while having to show extreme restraint—can easily lead to a sense of hopelessness and depression in those who work in law enforcement. It's no surprise that police officers suffer from high rates of alcoholism. Of police officers who drink, 23 percent become alcoholics; the rate is 10 percent for the general population.

Desperation
While it's true that police officers face potential harm on the job, the most serious injuries may be self-inflicted. The effect of seeing so much violence and working in the toughest areas of the country can take its toll. The suicide rate among police officers is more than twice the national average. In 1994, 300 officers committed suicide; 137 officers were killed in the line of duty.

Myths About the Job

Police Officers Are Corrupt

With recent arrests and indictments within the ranks of law enforcement, there's no denying that law enforcement has an image problem. According to a 1998 FBI report, 508 people in law enforcement were convicted from 1994 to 1997 as a result of FBI investigations, and even more were convicted in cases involving organized crime. Drugs and drug money were involved in almost 45 percent of the convictions, and officers were arrested in departments of every size in every area of the U.S. While damaging to the reputation of law enforcement, these numbers are relatively low given the thousands of police officers who serve without succumbing to bribes or kickbacks, even in the face of modest salaries.

Police Officers Spend Most of Their Time Writing Tickets

Some people assume that an officer wastes time writing tickets when she could be arresting criminals. However, routine traffic stops often result in arrests for outstanding warrants, drug or weapons possession, or smuggling. A high-profile example is that Timothy McVeigh was arrested after being stopped for a traffic violation only hours after the Oklahoma City bombing.

Jobs Within the Profession

Police Officer

Job Description: Police officers have a highly stressful job that utilizes a wide variety of skills. From courage to quick thinking to effective communication, police officers must have a basic skill set in order to protect and serve their communities and to survive potentially dangerous situations. Officers need to be proficient in handling firearms, driving in pursuit at fast speeds, using computers and police radios, and maintaining accurate and succinct records. While a sharp memory and accurate judgment benefit any police officer, a successful officer also commits to an unwavering code of ethics, one that strengthens his commitment to the community and serves to bridge difficult periods that might otherwise lead to burnout.

Most law enforcement officers are entitled to health and life insurance and paid vacation and sick leave, as well as paid overtime, which can amount to a considerable amount of added income. Expenses for uniforms, weapons, and protection are paid by the police department. Police officers have the option to retire after only twenty to twenty-five years, so they can retire or switch careers in their forties if they so choose. Early retirees receive half of their previous employed salary.

Number of Police Officers: As of 1998, over 760,000 police and detectives were working in the U.S. Sixty-five percent of the officers at the state and local levels worked on patrols. The majority of police officers are white men. The percentage of females employed ranges from 15 percent in sheriff's departments to 5 percent at the state level. Police officers who are ethnic minorities make up a high of 23 percent of the force at the county level to a low of 12 percent at the state level.

Earnings: Recent salaries for police patrol officers have ranged from $28,000 to $63,000 a year, with an average of $37,700. Police and detective supervisors take home an average of $48,000 a year, detectives earn an average of $46,000 annually, and sheriffs and deputy sheriffs make an average of $28,270 a year.

Further Info:
- Federal Law Enforcement Officers Foundation
  P.O. Box 1306
  Grand Central Station
  New York, NY 10163
- National Sheriffs' Association
  1450 Duke St.
  Alexandria, VA 22314

Prison Warden

Job Description: Prison wardens are responsible for prison operations, including security of, budgeting for, and maintenance of prison facilities. In addition, wardens handle custody, rehabilitation, and medical care for inmates. Prison wardens also work with the local community and remain on call for prison emergencies. A successful prison warden excels in administration, communication, and dealing well with crisis situations.

Education: No formal education requirement exists for the position, though many prison wardens previously worked in law enforcement or as correctional officers.

Earnings: Prison wardens can gain increased salaries by earning promotions to positions at larger prisons or by taking on more complex administrative duties.

Further Info:
- The American Jail Association
  2053 Day Rd., Suite 100
  Hagerstown, MD 21740
- Association of State Correctional Administrators
  National Institute of Correction
  Spring Hill West
  South Salem, NY 10590
- North American Association of Wardens and Superintendents
  Kentucky State Penitentiary
  Route 2, Old Eddyville Road
  Eddyville, KY 42038

FBI Agent

Job Description: As part of the Department of Justice, FBI agents investigate a wide variety of crimes, including espionage, sabotage, organized crime, bank robbery, and embezzlement. They conduct interviews, participate in surveillance and raids, and give court testimony. They work out of field offices and are on call at all times. FBI agents must be U.S. citizens, college graduates, and between twenty-three and thirty-five years old when joining the FBI, and they must retire at age fifty-five if they've worked for the FBI for over twenty years. Requirements for FBI agents include maintaining excellent physical condition and passing physical, oral, and written exams.

Education: Agents are trained for sixteen weeks at the FBI Academy at the U.S. Marine Corps Base in Quantico, Virginia.

Earnings: Agents start at $36,000 a year. An agent can climb to a senior administrative role with a salary approaching $100,000 a year.

Further Info:
- The Federal Bureau of Investigation
  U.S. Department of Justice
  Washington, DC 20535

Secret Service Agent

Job Description: As part of the Department of the Treasury, Secret Service agents protect the highest-ranking political leaders and their families. These agents also carry out investigations in the realm of counterfeiting and forging. They are sworn to protect the current president and vice president and their families, the president- and vice president-elect and their families, former presidents and their families, presidential candidates, and visiting foreign leaders. Leaders elected after 1997 receive protection for ten years after leaving office. Agents protect and patrol the White House grounds, the vice president's residence, and the Treasury building. Those agents engaged in protection work in shifts, conducting patrols from cars, on foot, and sometimes with dogs. Secret Service agents must be in top physical shape; possess acute, uncorrected vision; and be under thirty-five years old when joining the Secret Service. Agents are employed in Washington, DC, or at one of the more than one hundred locations throughout the U.S. Agents can retire at age fifty if they've served for twenty years.

Education: To become an agent, one must possess a bachelor's degree or its equivalent and pass the Treasury Enforcement Agent Examination. Agents are trained in protection, investigation, and criminal law at the Federal Law Enforcement Training Center in Brunswick, Georgia, and in Washington, DC.

Further Info:
- United States Secret Service

950 H St. NW, Suite 8400
Washington, DC 20223
www.treas.gov/usss
- United States Secret Service Personnel Division
1800 G Street NW
Washington, DC 20223

CIA Agent

Job Description: Since 1947, CIA agents have contributed to national and international security through administrative work, fieldwork, analysis, and policy recommendations. To become an agent, one must be at least eighteen years old and a U.S. citizen. The application process involves an extensive background investigation and may take over a year. Agents analyze and report on foreign developments with implications on national security. They develop and utilize high-tech methods for gathering and processing information. In addition, they engage in counterintelligence and counterterrorism. The CIA is made up of professional, analytical, technical, and clandestine personnel, and CIA agents often specialize in one field. They usually are fluent in a foreign language. As an agency, the CIA employs sixteen thousand to twenty thousand people, including a wide variety of professionals, from attorneys to graphic artists to economists. Agents receive federal health and life insurance benefits as well as a retirement package.

Education: CIA agents commonly hold at least a college degree.

Earnings: The starting annual salary is $34,000 to $52,000, depending on experience and skills.

Further Info:
- Central Intelligence Agency (www.cia.gov). The organization's official Web site.

ATF Agent

Job Description: ATF agents, made independent of the Internal Revenue Service in 1972, work for the Treasury Department. They gained prominence in their attempts to enforce the ban on the manufacture, sale, and transportation of alcohol during Prohibition. Their chief responsibilities are to enforce laws regarding tax collection on alcohol and tobacco and to oversee laws regarding firearms and explosives. In addition, ATF agents investigate arson and violent crimes, particularly those involving firearms. Agents may lend their expertise in ballistics, arson, and explosives to other agencies. In recent years, ATF agents have developed computer systems for matching ammunition with weapons, and they have refined the use of canine units to detect explosives and weapons. The ATF is the most efficient federal agency, collecting thirteen billion dollars annually—thirty-five times as much as the agency spends.

Education: ATF agents must hold a bachelor's degree or have equivalent work experience. Training includes ten weeks in Glynco, Georgia, at the Federal Law Enforcement Training Center followed by an additional seventeen weeks of training with the ATF.

Earnings: The starting salary is $25,000 to $40,000 a year.

Further Info:
• Bureau of Alcohol, Tobacco and Firearms
  650 Massachusetts Ave. NW
  Washington, DC 20226
  www.atf.treas.gov

DEA Agent

Job Description: The Drug Enforcement Administration enforces U.S. drug laws by reducing the availability of drugs and arresting individuals and groups who produce, distribute, or sell illegal drugs. Agents investigate drug dealers for potential prosecution and seize assets associated with drug trafficking, including cars, boats, and planes. In addition, DEA agents engage in crop eradication to reduce the availability of raw materials. They also train foreign law enforcement agents and work with international law enforcement agencies.

Education: Training takes place at the Justice Training Center in Quantico, Virginia, and includes courses in law enforcement and laboratory operations.

Number of Employees: The DEA has over nine thousand employees, of which over half are special agents. The remainder work as diversion investigators, intelligence specialists, chemists, administrators, and technical staff.

Further Info:
- Drug Enforcement Administration
  Information Services Section (CPI)
  2401 Jefferson Davis Highway
  Alexandria, VA 22301
  www.usdoj.gov/dea
- National Drug Enforcement Officers Association
  Drug Enforcement Administration
  Office of Training/TRDS
  FBI Academy
  P.O. Box 1475
  Quantico, VA 22134

INS Agent

Job Description: Part of the Department of Justice, the INS processes millions of immigration applications a year. Agents enforce immigration laws and work with refugees and asylum seekers. They also administer naturalization to qualified legal immigrants. INS agents make workplace inspections that uncover undocumented workers, they handle deportation of tens of thousands of criminal aliens, and they inspect more than three hundred ports and other means of entry into the country. Border patrol agents cover the six thousand–mile border between the U.S. and Mexico, and they apprehended over 1.5 million illegal aliens in 1999. New border patrol agents must be under thirty-seven years old and possess U.S. citizenship. Border patrol agents are part of the INS; however, not all INS agents patrol the border.

Education: A bachelor's degree or applicable experience is required.

Number of Employees: The INS employs more than twenty-eight thousand people who carry out duties in thirty-three districts and twenty-one border patrol areas.

Further Info:
- U.S. Border Patrol
  Chester A. Arthur Building
  425 I St. NW
  Washington, DC 20536
  www.ins.usdoj.gov
- U.S. Department of Justice
  Immigration and Naturalization Service
  Washington, DC 20536

Additional Occupations

Enforcing the law and protecting the public keeps a range of law enforcement professionals busy. Some of these are

- airport police officer
- bailiff (see chapter four)
- correctional officer
- customs inspector
- deportation officer
- harbor police
- immigration inspector
- parking enforcement officer
- radio dispatcher
- state trooper
- traffic sergeant
- U.S. Capitol police officer
- vice squad detective

Employers for the above positions include the following:

- Department of Immigration and Naturalization
- highway patrol
- police department
- prison

Firsthand Research

Nothing can bring you closer to the day-to-day workings of a police patrol unit than going along for the ride. To accompany an officer in a squad car (without having committed a crime first), see if your local police department offers ride-along programs. You'll need to sign up well in advance: This gives them time to review your request and process any release and indemnity agreement you have to sign. Some departments also offer a citizens' police academy. By attending a series of classes over several months, you can gain valuable insight into the methodologies and tactics police officers employ.

Law Enforcers in Nonfiction

Books

- *Basic Patrol Procedures: A Foundation for the Law Enforcement Student, a Review for the Veteran Officer*, Tim Perry. This book details practical street tactics in use by law enforcement.
- *Cops: Their Lives in Their Own Words*, Mark Baker. Learn what it's really like in law enforcement from these interviews with officers.
- *Fatal Fascination: Where Fact Meets Fiction in Police Work*, Phil and Karen McArdle. The subtitle says it all.
- *Force Under Pressure: Why Cops Live and Why They Die*, Lawrence Blum. A psychologist delves into the effects of high-stress tactical encounters on police officers.
- The Howdunit series, Writer's Digest Books. This is the best series available for learning about the nitty-gritty of everything from police work to private detectives to poisons. Includes titles such as *Police Procedural*, *The Writer's Complete Crime Reference Book*, and *Howdunit: How Crimes Are Committed and Solved*.
- *Inside the CIA: Revealing the Secrets of the World's Most Powerful Spy Agency*, Ronald Kessler. A history and an analysis of the CIA.
- *Guide to Careers in the FBI*, John E. Douglas. Explores various opportunities within this organization.
- *Lady Cop: True Stories of Policewomen in America's Toughest City*, Bryna Taubman. The beat as seen from the eyes of policewomen.

- *Law Enforcement and the INS*, George Weissinger. A study of and interviews with INS agents.
- *Police Procedural: A Writer's Guide to the Police and How They Work*, Russell Bintliff. The ins and outs of police procedure, including crime scene investigation.

Law Enforcers in Fiction

Books

- *Forty Words for Sorrow*, Giles Blunt. The search for a serial killer.
- *The Glitter Dome*, *The Choirboys*, and others, Joseph Wambaugh. Ex-cop Wambaugh breaks fresh ground with his energetic and gritty portrayal of cops.
- *Middle of Nowhere*, Ridley Pearson. A Seattle police lieutenant tries to uncover an attacker.
- *Over Tumbled Graves*, Jess Walter. A detective investigates murders in the Pacific Northwest.
- *The Tin Collectors*, Stephen J. Cannell. Internal affairs in the LAPD.

Movies

- *The Naked City* (1948). A documentary-style look at a Manhattan homicide squad.
- *Dirty Harry* (1971). A San Francisco cop bends the rules.
- *The French Connection* (1971). New York City narcotics cops attempt to seize a heroin shipment.
- *Serpico* (1973). Based on the nonfiction book about police corruption, this film is equally compelling and frightening—and still topical after thirty years.
- *The Big Easy* (1987). A detective and a D.A. tussle in New Orleans.
- *The Untouchables* (1987). A Chicago police officer aids the Feds in fighting the Mob.
- *The Hard Way* (1991). An actor researches a role by riding with a New York City cop.

Television

- *Police Story* (1973–1977). Ex-cop-turned-writer Joseph Wambaugh's series. Rather than a set cast, different characters are presented in each episode. Most of Wambaugh's novels have been made into movies. His nonfiction book, *The Onion Field*, about a true-life crime, is also noteworthy.
- *Hill Street Blues* (1981–1987). Still the best cop series ever. See Dennis Franz as one of the most original villains in TV fiction. Famed writer-director David Mamet wrote at least one episode. Currently in syndication.
- *Law & Order* (1990–). This series and two spin-offs currently are being aired, and the original also is aired in syndication. The series does a good job showing how detectives often have to go beyond the obvious clues to find the truth. It's similar to a ninety-minute TV drama, *Arrest and Trial* (2001–), which spent the first half of the show pursuing the criminal and the second half prosecuting.
- *NYPD Blue* (1993–). By the creator of *Hill Street Blues*. This series uses the same shaky camera technique as *Hill Street Blues* and features Dennis Franz as a protagonist.

Web Sites

- **Law Enforcement Online** (www.pima.edu/dps/police.htm). A listing of five thousand sites.
- **USACOPS** (www.usacops.com). Listings of law enforcement departments.
- **The Police Marksman** (www.policemarksman.com). A law enforcement magazine.
- **Central Intelligence Agency** (www.cia.gov). The official CIA site.
- **Federal Bureau of Investigation** (www.fbi.gov). The official FBI site.
- **Bureau of Alcohol, Tobacco and Firearms** (www.atf.treas.gov). The official ATF site.

- Drug Enforcement Administration (www.usdoj.gov/dea). The official DEA site.

Book Excerpts

She smiled at the department's euphemism for its psychiatrist—professional services. She knew who went to see the dour woman in professional services: drunks just before they were fired, wife beaters, attitude problems, and burnouts, the guys who beat the shit out of people at routine traffic stops. ''Sarge, I don't need this.'' Caroline lifted a hand to rub her jaw, but became self-conscious and dropped it back in her lap.

''You work sixty-hour weeks,'' he was saying. ''I get my ass chewed for carrying your comp time and sick days over from the year before . . . at this rate, you'll be able to retire at forty.''

He was thinking of another theory, how if you paired a young man and a young woman on patrol duty, they would end up sleeping together. Other cops attributed that to adrenaline or the huge amount of trust required for the job, but Dupree had a better explanation: The attraction between two people was directly proportional to their proximity to death.

—<u>Over Tumbled Graves</u>, Jess Walter

Malcolm Musgrave and his team were encamped at the Pinegrove Motel. The room was a standard-issue box, with faux colonial furniture and violent orange curtains. Maid service had apparently been suspended. Between tape recorders, video monitors, and radios, a heap of pizza boxes and Chinese food containers had grown into a precarious pyramid.

The place stank of sweat and old hamburgers.

—Forty Words for Sorrow, Giles Blunt

❧

''You're still intent on leaving Special Investigations, I suppose . . .''

''Well, Chief, you're not losing me. I'm just moving over into CID.''

''I know, I know. But Special Investigations—one could make the case that it's the most important part of the department. Take away Special Investigations, you've got a brain, certainly—all the motor functions are intact—but without Special Investigations, you've got a brain without a conscience. And that, my young friend, is a dangerous thing.''

—Forty Words for Sorrow, Giles Blunt

❧

''Take off your gun and hand me your badge. You're suspended from duty without pay pending your Internal Affairs Board of Rights.''

''Don't you have to write up a 1.61 before you can suspend me?''

''Consider it written.''

''The Police Bill of Rights really seems to have its limits where I'm concerned, doesn't it?''

''The 1.61 will be in your hands before nine o'clock. Take off your gun and give me your badge and ID card.''

—The Tin Collectors, Stephen J. Cannell

The Arrowhead Sheriff's Department was in turmoil. Earlier that day they had found a dead body in the lake. From what Shane could pick up, it was so decomposed that they hadn't been able to make an ID. In L.A., a dead body was no big deal, but up here an unexplained death was the unusual tragedy it should be everywhere. . . .

''If you're a cop, why did you run?'' the sheriff said, looking at him critically.

''I'm out of my jurisdiction and I didn't take the time to check with you guys like I should have, so I just decided to get small,'' he said. ''Bad choice. You guys were magnificent.''

''Put away the jar of Vaseline,'' Conklyn said. ''You got a CO we can call?''

—The Tin Collectors, Stephen J. Cannell

Life Sciences

*Zoologist, Biologist, Microbiologist, Animal Behaviorist,
Animal Caretaker, Biochemist, Botanist*

The Lowdown

Professionals in the life sciences (zoology, botany, biology, biochemistry, etc.) are favored as characters among science fiction writers because these are the men and women who deal with the various strange life forms from this planet and beyond. A typical line from such a character might be: "For the love of God, I've never seen anything like this!" In such stories, the scientist is there to provide information to the reader. She provides plausibility by providing some pseudoscientific explanation for the origins of a creature and how to defeat that creature.

Writing about a life science professional also offers several thematic opportunities. One such theme is humanity's mixed emotions about our relationship with animals; zoologists and animal behaviorists embody this theme. How we study and treat animals reflects community values. On one hand, we like to think we love and cherish animals and treat them humanely; on the other hand, we enslave, imprison, experiment on, torture, and eat them. Characters with careers in life sciences allow the writer to explore this conflict between our animal selves (which exploit others for personal gain) and our spiritual selves (which place the welfare of others above ourselves). Another theme arises from the schism between philosophy and religion: those who emphasize human reason and learning over instinct and feeling vs. those who emphasize emotional response and spiritual influences over logic. This is a gross simplification, but those who champion reason are often represented in fiction by scientists, while those who champion instinct and emotion are represented by artists and members of the clergy.

The professions discussed in this chapter are often used in mainstream stories to symbolize humanity's efforts to understand the universe and our place in it. Generally, these efforts are portrayed as falling short because (1) humans use their senses to know the universe, and senses are faulty information gatherers, so we can never be confident about what we know; and (2) the universe is too vast and our methods are too inadequate for us to ever know enough to reach absolute conclusions. We are like one of the six blind men who feels only the trunk of an elephant and, therefore, believes the elephant looks like a snake. Often this theme is embodied by a scientist who tries to do something unnatural, such as Dr. Frankenstein's work to re-create life. Such stories are meant to warn us to acknowledge our limitations and to not act too godlike. Of course, other writers counter this by demonstrating that every scientific inquiry was at some point in history thought to be blasphemous.

Whether used by sci-fi or literary mainstream writers, life sciences provide fascinating settings and texture for stories. The details of what goes on in laboratories can be compelling to the reader. Obscure details about animal behavior, for example, provide lively backdrops for scenes.

Job Description

Biology is a branch of science centered on the study of animal life. Biologists examine and explore the life processes and history of birds, fish, reptiles, insects, mammals, invertebrates, and microscopic organisms. They identify, classify, and record the behavior of animals and gauge the impact of animals on the environment, as well as the environment's influence on life. For example, zoologists may monitor the effect of the introduction of wolves to an area where the original wolves had been hunted to extinction, such as those introduced into Yellowstone National Park. Marine biologists may monitor and count migrating whales to assess population and health, while biologists may track down hibernating bears who have been fitted with radio collars.

Life scientists may further the understanding of animal life for the sake of pure knowledge or to help affect the course of animal life. Areas of applied biology include environmental preservation, wildlife management, fisheries, and educational arenas such as zoos. In wildlife management, zoologists may recommend the reduction in the numbers of a species that lacks predators. They may recommend the number of fish to be stocked in lakes based on sustainability and recreational use. In zoos, they help design habitats based on their knowledge of an animal's natural home and may develop educational programs about the animals in the exhibits.

Other life scientists focus on animal interaction and study the behavior of animals. Animal behaviorists can train, handle, and sometimes communicate with animals—from basic commands to responses to the sign language employed by some primates. Microbiologists uncover the workings of biology at the molecular level, including the mechanics and influence of genetics. Even paleontology draws from the life sciences by using current knowledge of plant and animal life to help illustrate how extinct animals may have walked, fed, and reproduced.

In many respects, biologists are the counterparts of botanists, who concentrate their study on plant life. A broad science, zoology encompasses marine and land animal life at every level from the molecule to an entire ecosystem.

Daily Life

Work Schedule
The type of work carried out by life scientists varies greatly. Some spend much of their time in the field, conducting studies

that may include counting species, notating behavior, and postulating the impact of environmental changes on a species. Life scientists may be found cramped in blinds or tents, dangling from cliff walls to observe nesting sites, or hiking through rain forests to search for an endangered species and formulate the reasons for its shrinking numbers. Other zoologists and biologists may spend much of their time doing laboratory work, examining species collected in the field, and enjoying the luxury of a full set of lab instruments. Still others perform administrative duties such as writing extensive reports on animal populations and documenting impact studies on development's effect on a species. Those working for the federal government to carry out lab or administrative duties have a fairly regimented workday that may include set hours which get recorded on time sheets. Scientists in the field, especially in remote locations or between seasons, may work longer days because their schedules are at the mercy of the weather, the animals, and project budgets.

Dressing the Part

Life scientists wear lab coats when performing dissection and experiments, business casual clothing when completing administrative tasks, and casual outdoor wear—even camouflage—when in the field. Those employed by a government agency, such as the National Park Service, wear uniforms designed for different seasons and weather. Some life scientists, such as marine biologists, may wear clothing adapted to their environment, such as a wet suit, snorkeling gear, or scuba gear.

Buzzwords

biotechnology: A fairly new industry that uses living organisms, usually genetically modified, for human benefit.

cloning: Creating an identical copy of an existing animal; for example, Dolly is a cloned sheep.

gene therapy: Treating disease by altering genetic structure.

genome map: A blueprint of the genetic structure of a living thing.

Education

Life scientists hold at least a bachelor's degree in science in their particular field. Many also hold a master's or doctor's degree in biology, especially if they conduct research. Unlike many other sciences, biology was once a fairly stable field involving the study of life in the field or laboratory. Today, with the advent of genetic alteration, cloning, and other manipulation of life, zoologists and biologists must continually educate themselves on the latest scientific advances and wrestle with new discoveries and ethical dilemmas.

Job Conflicts

Cloning

One of the hottest topics in the science community is cloning, the ability to create an exact genetic copy of an individual. While it's been practiced for a while without controversy in areas such as orchid farming, the cloning of a sheep brought the capability to clone complex mammals into the modern scientist's toolbox. The conflict for zoologists, biologists, and all life scientists lies in deciding what to do with this ability. The logical next step of cloning humans forces scientists into a hot ethical arena. While the idea of cloning a human is condemned by many scientists, others are open to the idea. At issue is not so much the ethical responsibility of life scientists in disrupting natural reproduction processes but rather their responsibility in potentially creating deformed, disease-prone, or otherwise flawed humans. In the event that human cloning proves successful, biologists will have opened a Pandora's box of controversies ranging from the use of cloning to enhance traits such as strength or intelligence—a disturbing Aryanlike idea—to the potential psychological suffering of clones—who might feel and be treated as less than human.

The Biotech Industry

The life sciences used to focus on observing and learning about the processes that govern life, from the simplest organisms to huge mammals. Today's biotechnology industry has changed the relatively passive role of the biologist and botanist into an active one involving the creation of modified plants and animals. Beginning biologists and botanists must make an ethical choice if they consider going to work for companies who create genetically modified food products. Are the sciences of biology, botany, and genetics so significantly advanced that genetically altered crops are safe? Is it ethical to market seeds modified to produce sterile crops—forcing farmers to buy new seed each season? Are genetically modified crops dangerous to preexistent crops? What will happen if those two types of crops crossbreed? For some, the heart of the conflict is the hubris of the scientist vs. the path of nature in determining which crops grow and survive. The biotechnology explosion has raised other questions: How can a life scientist be sure the release of a genetically altered crop will not adversely affect the environment and those who consume the crop? Is it safe to take genes from animals and insert them into plants or vice versa—alterations that would never take place in the wild? How does the influence of a profit-driven employer affect scientific judgment?

Evolutionism vs. Creationism

In the 1925 Scopes trial the issue of teaching evolution in the classroom drew national attention. Since that time, much in science has been built upon the fundamentals of Darwin's theory of evolution, specifically natural selection. While these theories, the basis for modern biology, are taught in all universities as one of the basic principles governing the development of life, some public school systems, particularly in the South, continue to be in the center of the conflict between science and religion. In Kansas, the use of the word *evolution* has been omitted from textbooks, and no mention is made as to the age of the universe—the scientific estimate might conflict with a biblical timeline. While it's rare for the teaching of evolution in a public school to be off limits or even frowned upon, pressure is increasing for teachers to include instruction on creationism, the theory that all life was created by God. For creationists, the theory of evolution discounts the existence of God. Many modern biologists believe that creationism is pseudoscience. For biology and life science teachers of either persuasion have a simple dilemma: They must teach students the fundamentals of biology without confusing the students or presenting personal bias. Additionally, in states such as Kansas, Tennessee, and Alabama, a biology teacher may have difficulty teaching the principles of evolution when the approved curriculum makes no mention of it.

Myths About the Job

Zoologists Work Only in Zoos

Zoology concerns all animals, not just those in zoos. People who maintain exhibits and care for animals for a zoo are zookeepers. A zoologist who works for a zoo usually is an expert on a certain animal and may contribute to or head the design of an exhibit at an animal park. Overall, zoologists are most interested in the kind of animal research that can't be conducted in a typical zoo. Even educational zoos and aquariums are still public exhibits and present limited research opportunities for the zoologist. Many zoologists are employed by state and federal government agencies. A large number work for private companies, where they conduct biotechnological research that leads to the creation of pharmaceuticals, medical treatments, and agricultural innovations.

Biologists Spend Much of Their Time With Animals

A large number of students pursue biological sciences with the idea that their careers will resemble those of Jane Goodall or Dian Fossey. Only the truly devoted can struggle through a multitude of difficult biology and chemistry courses and accept the reality that they probably won't spend much time with animals. Budding ocean biologists may end up studying invertebrates. Others may spend nearly all their time in front of a computer conducting research or working with huge online catalogs of biological data. Biologists tend to specialize in narrow fields within the life sciences and spend much of their time in the lab. When they do work with animals, they may work only with lab animals rather than animals in the field.

A wildlife photographer may spend more time in the wild than the average zoologist does.

Biologists Care More About Animals Than About People

The typical image of the biologist is that of a lone scientist living in some remote jungle location and noting on a clipboard the observations for week forty-seven of an animal that's just a stone's throw away. Such an image supports the idea that zoologists are more concerned with animals than with people. While some biologists do work tirelessly to preserve the environment and the animals they study, the basic data collected by biologists benefits other scientists, not animals. Many biologists work closely with animals in order to help understand diseases in humans and develop treatments. Others may actively participate in animal testing, subjecting animals to cancers, AIDS, and other ailments. Again, the motivation for watching the effects of pollution and disease on animals is improving the lives of people.

Jobs Within the Profession

Zoologist

Job Description: Zoologists study animal life, including life cycles, distribution in an environment, and classification. They also investigate animal diseases, behavior, and origin. Zoologists usually specialize in a set group of animals. Mammalogists study mammals, herpetologists study reptiles, ornithologists study birds, and ichthyologists study fish. Other areas of specialization include animal husbandry, aquatic biology, ecology, entomology, genetics, invertebrate zoology, marine biology, oceanography, paleontology, parasitology, physiology, and veterinary medicine. Zoologists may specialize in one area of study with regard to animal group, such as insects' pollination activities or whale migratory patterns.

Zoologists who contribute to the basic understanding of animal life tend to work for universities and government agencies or independently through grants. They may conduct research using lab-raised animals or by examining and collecting specimens in the field. Zoologists whose duties are administrative may oversee programs at zoos and aquariums. Zoologists practicing applied science apply their knowledge and the basic findings of other life scientists to the creation or refinement of medicines and other treatments. Applied zoology may entail more laboratory time, including the testing and monitoring of animals. This branch of zoology is influenced by the private sector, including pharmaceutical companies and the biotech industry, which employs many life scientists.

Education: Zoologists hold a minimum of a bachelor's degree. Zoologists who conduct research usually hold a Ph.D.

Clothes and Tools: Zoologists wear appropriate lab apparel when conducting experiments and comfortable outdoor wear when in the field. Depending on the location of an expedition, a zoologist may need extensive outdoor equipment—including a backpack, a tent, and climbing gear—in addition to an array of scientific and computer equipment. Field studies focused on mating or migration, for example, may require short but intensive periods outdoors.

Earnings: The median annual income for biological scientists is $46,000. The beginning salary for one with a bachelor's degree is $29,000.

Further Info.
- The Society for Integrative and Comparative Biology
  1313 Dolley Madison Blvd., Suite 402
  McLean, VA 22101
  www.sicb.org

Further Reading:
- *Opportunities in Zoos and Aquariums*, Blythe Camenson.

Biologist
Job Description: Biologists study all forms of life and the major processes that govern life, including growth, metabolism, reproduction, adaptation, and evolution. Most biologists specialize in one aspect of biology, such as cellular growth, DNA sequencing, the effects of radiation exposure, or pollution. Bi-

ologists play important roles in determining and regulating population sizes, controlling imbalances, and developing pesticides and pest-control solutions. Biologists can teach, work for government departments ranging from agriculture to the National Park Service, or work in the private sector. If they choose the latter, biologists apply their knowledge to activities for financial gain: developing pharmaceutical products or perfecting cloning techniques, to name a few. Marine biologists focus on marine life and may work for government agencies, educational institutions, or private industry.

Education: A biologist has taken college courses in animal biology, chemistry, biochemistry, genetics, and more, but her education continues for the rest of her career. As with all life sciences, a Ph.D. is usually required for one to be a research biologist.

Earnings: See Zoologists.

Further Info:
- The National Science Foundation
  4201 Wilson Blvd.
  Arlington, VA 22230
  www.nsf.gov
- American Institute of Biological Sciences
  1444 I St. NW, Suite 200
  Washington, DC 20005
  www.aibs.org

Further Reading:
- *On Becoming a Biologist,* John Janovy Jr.

Microbiologist

Job Description: Microbiologists study life forms—bacteria and other forms of microscopic life—that can't be seen with the naked eye. Microbiologists identify, study, and research the development, structure, and spread of microscopic life—most often on a slide beneath the lens of a microscope. Samples from the lab or the field are grown, or cultured, until they're sufficient in number to be observed. Culturing involves placing a small amount of the microscopic material into a medium and applying the right balance of temperature, humidity, and nutrients to cause the microscopic sample to grow. Microbiology isn't limited to observations in the lab, however.

Microbiologists also examine how life forms such as bacteria and viruses affect plants and animals. Microbiologists report on characteristics for the bacteria or viruses, and this data can be used in the development of antibiotics and other remedies. Microbiologists also study other biological structures such as enzymes and acids, and this research leads to the creation of polymers and vitamins and in the execution of other applications. Like most life scientists, microbiologists are employed by various federal agencies, the medical community, or private industry.

Earnings: See Zoologists.

Further Info:
• American Society for Microbiology
  152 N St. NW
  Washington, DC 20036
  www.asmusa.org

Further Reading:
• *Clinical Microbiology Made Ridiculously Simple*, Mark Gladwin.

Animal Behaviorist

Job Description: Animal behaviorists participate in a range of practical tasks, from the traditional—e.g., the study of breeding to improve livestock—to the cutting edge—e.g., applying psychological principles to unlock animal thought. Behaviorists observe animal behavior, including feeding, communication, and mating, in the wild or in a laboratory or artificial environment. Animal behaviorists are essential in the creation of exhibits in aquariums and zoos. Applying his knowledge of an animal's habits regarding feeding, sleeping, and mating, an animal behaviorist can help create an exhibit that applies the least amount of stress on the animals.

Animal behaviorists usually fall into three groups. Ethologists study animals in the natural habitat. Applied animal behaviorists train animals such as misbehaving pets. Animal behaviorists such as psychobiologists study the origins of animal behavior—physiological, psychological, and neurological—and may apply their knowledge to help understand human behavior.

Education: An animal behaviorist usually has a degree in zoology or biology and perhaps an additional degree in psychology.

Earnings: See Zoologists.

Further Info:
- American Society of Animal Science: a professional organization for animal scientists.
  1111 N. Dunlap Ave.
  Savoy, IL 61874
  www.asas.org
- The Association for the Study of Animal Behaviour www.soci eties.ncl.ac.uk/asab. This organization promotes the study of animal behavior.

Further Reading:
- *Essentials of Animal Behaviour*, P.J.B. Slater.

Animal Caretaker
Job Description: Animal caretakers work with animals in zoological parks, aquariums, boarding kennels, pounds, laboratories, animal hospitals, and stables. Caretakers who specialize in grooming are called groomers, while those working in stables are grooms. Caretakers engaged in work in animal hospitals and clinics are known as veterinary assistants. Groomers have relatively fixed hours. Grooms may travel with horses used in competition or races. Veterinary assistants working in animal hospitals may be on call twenty-four hours a day.

The focus of an animal caretaker's job is the well-being of animals kept in captivity. Caretakers mix food with food supplements and medication according to instructions by curators or veterinarians. Caretakers provide food, water, and exercise to animals and maintain strict records on the vital statistics of the animals. Caretakers also observe animals for signs of stress, illness, or injury and may give inoculations. Some animals, chiefly in boarding kennels and stables, must be exercised. Animal caretakers also clean animal cages, pens, stables, and exhibits to ensure a safe environment.

Caretakers who work in zoological parks are known as zookeepers and usually specialize in one type of animal, such as mammals or birds, or in one main exhibit area. They may help raise young animals or care for the sick and injured. They may need to enter exhibits to move animals into other quarters for breeding, feeding, or birthing. Zookeepers who work in certain exhibits, such as aviaries, can expect a constant bombardment of noise. Zookeepers can deal with dangerous animals and risk injuries, including scratches and bites when transferring animals. In addition, they may face emotional stress from bonding with animals that need to be euthanized. Though zoos aren't always open, the animals inside always need to be fed, watered, and cared for. Therefore, many zookeepers work holidays and night shifts. Zookeepers may also answer guests' questions and ensure that guests behave appropriately for their safety and that of the animals.

Education: Zookeepers often hold a bachelor's degree in zoology or biology. Veterinary assistants usually have some veterinary experience.

Earnings: Annual earnings can be more than $30,000 for experienced zookeepers. Animal keepers and assistants make significantly less.

Further Info:
- American Zoo and Aquarium Association
  8403 Colesville Rd., Suite 710
  Silver Spring, MD 20910
  www.aza.org

Further Reading:
- *Primer of Wildlife Care & Rehabilitation*, Patti L. Raley.
- *Wildlife Feeding and Nutrition*, Charles T. Robbins.

Biochemist

Job Description: Biochemists study the chemistry behind physical processes such as breathing and growth, as well as the chemical effects of hormones, vitamins, and drugs on living systems. With the advent of biotechnology, which brings together genetics, biology, and chemistry, biochemists have increased study on how to transfer desired traits from one plant or animal to another. Biochemists play a vital role in adding disease-resistant traits to crops and producing beneficial drugs. Biochemists work for universities, government agencies, and companies in the biotechnology industry. Biochemists design laboratory equipment for research projects; create tests and methods for analyzing the effect of modified genetics, drugs, or other elements on test plants and animals; and make recommendations for further research or practical application.

Education: A Ph.D. is usually the minimum degree requirement for conducting any biological research.

Further Info:
- American Society for Biochemistry and Molecular Biology
  9650 Rockville Pike
  Bethesda, MD 20814
  www.faseb.org/asbmb

Further Reading:
- *For the Love of Enzymes: The Odyssey of a Biochemist,* Arthur Kornberg.

Botanist

Job Description: Botany covers the study of all plant life—even plant life that is only found in fossils. Depending on their specialty, botanists may uncover beneficial aspects of plants, study their classification, or define the functions of all parts of a plant. Botanists also study the relationship between plants and the environment, including the effects of pollution, temperature change, and soil conditions on fungal and plant life. Botanists discover causes of disease in plants and aid in creating heartier crops and timber forests. In addition, these scientists isolate plant characteristics that have applications in the pharmaceutical industry.

Botanists may study and observe plants and fungus in the field or under laboratory conditions. In the lab, botanists raise and maintain test plants, exposing them to varying simulated environmental conditions and observing the effects of temperature, humidity, and other conditions. Botanists are employed by governments, universities, zoological parks, pharmaceutical companies, and organizations in the biotechnology industry.

Education: A Ph.D. is required for most life science research careers.

Further Info:
- Botanical Society of America
  1735 Neil Ave.
  Columbus, OH 43210
  www.botany.org

Further Reading:
- *Careers in Horticulture and Botany*, Jerry Garner.

Additional Occupations

The life sciences cover a broad range of related professions, including
- agricultural zoologist
- animal nutritionist
- animal control officer
- biomedical illustrator
- environmental lawyer
- environmental physiologist
- fisheries biologist
- game park manager
- geneticist
- hatchery operator
- museum curator
- molecular biologist
- ornithologist

- paleontologist
- park naturalist
- park ranger
- physiologist
- wildlife biologist

Employers for the above positions include the following:

- Environmental Protection Agency
- National Park Service
- Department of the Interior
- Department of Agriculture
- U.S. Fish and Wildlife Services
- Bureau of Reclamation
- museums
- aquariums
- zoos
- universities

Life Scientists in Nonfiction

Books
- *Ahead of the Curve: David Baltimore's Life in Science*, Shane Crotty. Nobel prize winner Baltimore is major contributor to the study of biology.
- *Beyond Innocence: An Autobiography in Letters: the Later Years*, Jane Goodall. Goodall discusses her forty years of research in Tanzania with her chimpanzees.
- *The Biology of Science Fiction Cinema*, Mark C. Glassy. A discussion of the biology used in sci-fi films.
- *Borderlands of Science: How to Think Like a Scientist and Write Science Fiction*, Charles Sheffield. Physicist and Nebula- and Hugo award–winning novelist shows how scientific facts can become fiction.
- *The Cosmic Serpent: DNA and the Origins of Knowledge*, Jeremy Narby. A first-person narrative that covers biology, anthropology, and the limits of rationalism.
- *The Elixir: An Alchemical Study of the Ergot Mushrooms*, William Scott Shelley. This book shows just how a scientist works.

- *Essays on Life Itself* (from the Complexity in Ecological Systems series), Robert Rosen. A collection of philosopher and biologist Robert Rosen's essays.
- *The Feejee Mermaid and Other Essays in Natural and Unnatural History*, Jan Bondeson. Zoological curiosities, some real and some legendary.
- *The Trouble With Testosterone: And Other Essays on the Biology of the Human Predicament*, Robert M. Sapolsky. The work of a professor of biology and neuroscience at Stanford who is a recipient of a MacArthur Foundation "genius grant."
- *The Way Life Works: The Science Lover's Illustrated Guide to How Life Grows, Develops, Reproduces, and Gets Along*, Mahlon Hoagland and Bert Dodson. A biologist and artist collaborate to explain life processes from those of bacteria to those of humans.

Life Scientists in Fiction

Books

- *A Botanist at Bay*, John Sherwood. The author combines mystery with botany.
- *Frankenstein*, Mary Shelley. A classic novel about scientist re-creating life.
- *Great Science Fiction: Stories by the World's Great Scientists*, Isaac Asimov, et al. Twenty-three stories, all by scientists both known and obscure.
- *The Secret Laboratory Journals of Dr. Victor Frankenstein*, Jeremy Kay. A fictional diary of Victor Frankenstein.
- *Slightly Mad Scientists*, James Smith. A collection of stories featuring the title characters.

Movies

- *The Neanderthal Man* (1953). A zoologist turns a tiger into a sabertoothed tiger.
- *Rhino!* (1964). A zoologist works to save endangered animals.
- *Mr. Forbush and the Penguins* (1971). A young London biologist spends most of his time pursuing girls.

- *Night of the Lepus* (1972). A zoologist is called in to fight giant rabbits.
- *Jaws* (1975). A marine biologist fights sharks.
- *The Gods Must Be Crazy* (1980). A clumsy biologist's experience among an African tribe.
- *The French Lieutenant's Woman* (1981). Based on the acclaimed novel and featuring a Victorian–era amateur naturalist.
- *Cannery Row* (1982). Based on the Steinbeck novel about a marine biologist.
- *The Serpent Warriors* (1985). A zoologist fights snakes.
- *A Zed & Two Noughts* (1985). Brothers who are zoologists become obsessed with decay.
- *Animal Behavior* (1989). A romantic comedy about an animal behaviorist who loses funding.
- *Love Potion No. 9* (1992). A geek biochemist uses magic to get women.
- *The Beast* (1997). A sea biologist fights an ocean creature.
- *Zeus and Roxanne* (1997). A marine biologist's dog forms an attachment to a dolphin.
- *Next Stop Wonderland* (1998). A man dreams of becoming a marine biologist.
- *Deep Blue Sea* (1999). A medical biologist fights sharks.
- *The Insider* (1999). Jeffrey Wigand, a former research biologist for Brown & Williamson, reveals secrets about cigarette dangers.
- *Adventures in Wild California* (2000). Biologists work with otters and a bald eagle.
- *Evolution* (2001). A comedy about two community college professors discovering life from another planet.
- *Mimic 2* (2001). A biologist fights cockroaches.

Television
- *War of the Worlds* (1988–1990). A microbiologist fights alien invaders.
- *Friends* (1994–). The character Ross is a paleontologist.
- *Crossing Jordan* (2001–). "Bug" is an insect expert.

Web Sites

- Biochemist Online (www.biochemist.com/home.htm). Biochemistry-related news and forums.

- Biosis Internet Resource Guide for Zoology (www.biosis.or g.uk/free_resources/resource_guide.html). Exhaustive index of zoology links.

- Careers in Biotechnology (www.accessexcellence.org/AB/ CC/). Biology-related job descriptions.

- NetVet (http://netvet.wustl.edu/e-public.htm). A list of biology-related electronic publications.

Book Excerpts

The commercialization of molecular biology is the most stunning ethical event in the history of science, and it has happened with astonishing speed. For four hundred years since Galileo, science has always proceeded as a free and open inquiry into the workings of nature. Scientists have always ignored national boundaries, holding themselves above the transitory concerns of politics and even wars. Scientists have always rebelled against secrecy in research, and have even frowned on the idea of patenting their discoveries, seeing themselves as working to the benefit of all mankind. And for many generations, the discoveries of scientists did indeed have a peculiarly selfless quality.

—Jurassic Park, Michael Crichton

In the metamorphosis from Cow to New Cow, the Current-Cow sob story is an important phase: ''I know we just met, but did I happen to mention how sad, miserable, misunderstood, and lonely I've been my whole life?'' This is crucial to introducing the myth of male shyness and the poor-guy persona—common disguises for a wolf in sheep's clothing. ''You're so easy to talk to, not like my Current Cow.''

> —Animal Husbandry, Laura Zigman

I was always fascinated by nature as a boy. I would return to my nursery with pockets full of frogs and insects, only to be quietly admonished by my Nanny. My Tutor always complied with my wishes to discuss these fruits of Our Creator's labors, though his focus was more spiritual than secular.

By my seventh birthday (in 1799) I believed I knew all that was necessary to live in the World.

> —The Secret Laboratory Journals of Dr. Victor Frankenstein, Jeremy Kay

I was driving home still thinking about that dead grasshopper. The one I'd just dissected for my class, its thorax as hard to crack as a tin thimble. Watching me struggle over it, my students had become restless and giddy, so I'd made some offhand joke about the grasshopper being a typical male, afraid to open up to a woman. They'd laughed and groaned, as usual. But then when I'd finally dragged the scalpel across the grasshopper, splitting open his tough skin and exposing his tiny organs, one student in the back, an anorexic seventeen-year-old named Lisa Drought, jumped up and screamed, ''That's what they did to Jesus!'' The class turned and stared at her, then turned and stared at me, waiting for a response, a voice of reason. Stunned, I didn't know what to say except that Jesus didn't have an exo-skeleton.

That's what was on my mind when I turned my car onto the street where I lived. I was wondering if tonight, after sticking her finger down her throat and vomiting up her mother's pot roast dinner, Lisa would doze off in a delirious dream of crucified grass-hoppers and Satanic blonde biology teach-ers. I'd sent a note to the school psycholo-gist, but these things were tricky. Lisa's name would be passed along to all the appro-priate people, but no one would actually do anything, including me. Driving home now, I remembered her huge eyes bulging from her pale skeletal face, the only discernible color coming from her bright red lipstick. I couldn't shake that image.

—Lessons in Survival, Laramie Dunaway

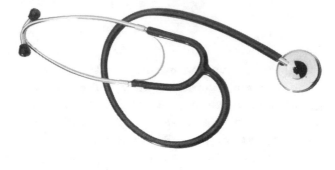

CHAPTER 11

Medical Sciences

Emergency Room Doctor, Obstetrician Gynecologist (OB-GYN), Pediatrician, Surgeon, Plastic Surgeon, Physician Assistant, Licensed Practical Nurse (LPN), Registered Nurse (RN), Emergency Medical Technician (EMT)

The Lowdown

Most of us have had intimate (not the *good* intimate) experiences with doctors, so we know that people feel vulnerable in the presence of a physician. In that cold little room we feel naked without a briefcase or cell phone or any of the trappings that make us feel powerful and in control of our lives outside the exam room—and we are naked but for a thin gown. Fear partly informs our relationships with physicians. Who else in your life has the power to deliver such devastating news as "You have cancer; there's not much we can do." This fear leads to conflicted feelings about doctors: We respect them because they can help us, and we hate them because of what they might tell us.

With so much intense emotion all around them, doctors are natural, popular characters in fiction. Physicians come from every social, economic, and ethnic background, and they provide a writer with several areas of dramatic conflict:

1. Doctors face life-or-death situations, sometimes on a daily basis, so the stakes of a story are high.

2. The weight of the responsibility doctors feel for their patients can take a heavy toll. Doctors have high rates of divorce, suicide, and drug and alcohol abuse. Writers can depict layers of characterization.

3. Doctors can develop a God complex—they feel more important than other mortals and think their own decisions are unquestionable. This establishes internal conflict.

4. For enterprising doctors there's much money to be made, so stories can take place in affluent settings, giving readers a voyeuristic glimpse into lives of the wealthy. The drive for money can provide motivation as well as texture.

5. Some doctors are extremely dedicated to their patients. These characters are modern hero types.

6. Health care is expensive, and many people are uninsured. This allows the grand old theme of "what cost humanity?" to be hauled out again and again, providing a platform for social commentary.

Job Description

There are two major classes of physicians: the Doctor of Osteopathic Medicine (D.O.) and the Doctor of Medicine (M.D.). D.O.s stress holistic health care and preventive medicine, with emphasis on the musculoskeletal system. Some common specialties include family medicine, general pediatrics, obstetrics, gynecology, and psychiatry. M.D.s, also known as allopathic physicians, may concentrate on general or family medicine, internal medicine, treatment of cardiovascular diseases, surgery, or one of many other specialties. Both M.D.s and D.O.s can and may prescribe medication or surgery when needed.

Few occupations can bring the level of satisfaction felt by physicians. From delivering a baby to easing pain and suffering—whether a migraine or a melanoma—doctors know their efforts make a profound difference to their patients. In addition, physicians may be able to expand medical knowledge by means of running clinical trials or developing new surgical techniques, to name just two. Doctors can also gain satisfaction by teaching up-and-coming doctors.

Half of D.O.s and a third of M.D.s practice general, family, and pediatric medicine. These physicians have the most consistent relationship with patients and often refer their patients to specialists when necessary.

As of 1998, there were a little more than half a million physicians in the U.S. Seventy percent practice in an office or a clinic, while another 20 percent work in hospitals. The remaining physicians practice medicine for the government in the Department of Health and Human Services or in Veterans Affairs. The highest concentration of doctors relative to the population exists in New England and the mid-Atlantic states; the lowest concentration is found in the South.

Becoming a doctor is an expensive endeavor. Over 80 percent of medical students borrow money to pay for all or a portion of their educational expenses, which can be as high as $250,000. Scholarships can help offset tuition costs, but the competition is fierce. Figure in the one to seven years of relatively low-paying residency, and you can see why physicians, once out of their residency program, demand high compensation for their services.

While the training is long and expensive and the practice is stressful, most physicians are well compensated. From monetary gain to the prestige of being a successful practitioner, a physician enjoys a wide range of perks. Medical expenses for themselves or family members may be reduced or eliminated: Colleagues may offer services such as surgery free of charge. Physicians who ally themselves in group medical practices are also likely to enjoy more free time.

Perseverance, dedication, and the ability to draw from experience to diagnose illness are basic prerequisites for a physician's success. Traits that can propel the physician through a lifetime of demanding work rest in communication skills, the ability to extract accurate diagnoses through patient examinations, and the ability to remain compassionate despite an endless stream of suffering patients. In addition, a successful physician can concentrate her efforts on serving her patients without letting the long hours or the bureaucracy of the health care system affect her bedside manner.

Salary
In 1998 and 1999, salaries ranged from roughly $34,000 for first-year residents to $42,000 for those in their final year. For physicians out of residency, however, salaries increase dramatically. The average income for physicians in 1997 was nearly $165,000. During this period, the lowest-paid specialty at $120,000 was pediatrics; radiology was the highest, at $260,000. Salaries range widely and depend on specialty and whether a physician is in private practice or a group practice.

Expenses
Physicians in private practice incur expenses for medical assistants, office space, insurance, maintenance, and all other needs that come with running a business.

Daily Life

Work Schedule
While nearly all physicians are bound to have a hectic schedule, the hours and tasks vary widely according to specialty, whether a physician works in a practice or a hospital, and any teaching duties. A typical day for a physician could look like the schedule on page 206.

Dressing the Part
Most physicians with their own practice adopt business casual as the dress code for seeing patients. Hospitals and group medical practices may set dress codes, usually prescribing business dress and even a lab coat for patient care. In settings outside of consultation, such as surgery or emergency rooms, a physician wears the prescribed scrub uniform. At all hospitals, physicians are required to wear visible I.D. tags.

Keys to the Kingdom
While physicians have a vast array of equipment at their disposal, tools such as imaging equipment are usually operated

TIME	DUTIES
7:00–8:15	Make rounds at hospital to check on patients' status, review information from biopsies and X rays, and update patient charts.
8:15–9:00	See three patients at practice.
9:00–11:30	Teach course at medical school.
11:30–12:00	Lunch
12:00–12:30	Answer phone messages from patients, hospitals, and other physicians.
12:30–4:30	See fourteen patients at practice.
4:30–5:30	Visit patient admitted to hospital emergency department. Have remaining appointments pushed back to tomorrow.
5:30–6:00	Attend a staff meeting.
6:00–6:30	Make rounds at another hospital.
6:30 P.M.–7:00 A.M.	On call for emergencies from patients, hospitals, or other physicians.

by trained technicians. These technicians pass the test results on to the physician for interpretation.

Tools of the Trade

Whether they're pediatricians or heart surgeons, physicians use an assortment of tools that runs the gamut from tongue depressors to ultrasound equipment as they diagnose and treat illnesses. The following list shows some of the common tools employed by physicians:

- biopsy needle
- blood pressure cuff
- cardiac monitor
- cast-cutting saw
- defibrillator
- forceps
- operating scissors
- probe
- scalpel
- sponge forceps
- sterilizing aids
- stethoscope
- suction tubes
- surgical blade
- surgical needles

Elbow Rubbing

While physicians deal primarily with patients and patients' families during the course of the day, they also may interact with other medical and nonmedical professionals. A physician specializing in geriatrics may interact with physical therapists and nutritionists. A pediatrician may consult with teachers, counselors, or allergists. Surgeons interact with nurses, anesthesiologists, and imaging technicians.

Buzzwords

bounceback: A patient who returns with the same symptoms after treatment.

champagne tap: A clean lumbar puncture.

D & D: Death and donuts—an M & M with refreshments.

first-degree burn: A burn that takes ten to twenty-one days to heal and leaves little scarring.

GGF: Grandpa's got a fever—a series of tests to discover the cause of a fever in an older male patient.

gork, gorked: Unconscious; e.g., "a gork in room 211."

M & M: Morbidity and mortality—a conference that follows a case that results in a patient's death.

PQRST: Palliative and provoking, quality, radiation, severity, timing—a mnemonic phrase used to assess chest pain.

scoop and run: Describes patients, brought to the hospital by emergency personnel, who could not be aided at the scene of an accident.

second-degree burn: A burn that takes twenty-five to sixty days to heal and leaves a dense scar.

thrill: Cardiac murmurs that can be felt through the chest.

tox screen: Blood analysis that identifies drugs in a person's system.

wheezer: A patient having trouble breathing.

Education

Students in the 144 medical schools in the U.S. must be willing to spend eleven or more years—four years of undergraduate education, four years of medical school, and three to eight years of residency as an intern—studying, training, and honing their medical skills. During the course of undergraduate study, premed students take standard courses such as inorganic and organic chemistry, physics, math, and biology, as well as classes in the humanities. After graduation, students compete for entrance into a medical school based on their academic standing, and Medical College Admission Test (MCAT) scores come into play here.

Medical School

In medical school, students build on courses from their under-graduate studies. The first half of med school involves the study of physiology, anatomy, psychology, biochemistry, phar-macology, pathology, microbiology, and medical ethics and laws. The latter half of med school involves learning, under supervision, to examine patients and diagnose illnesses based on symptoms.

Residency and Certification

After med school, most M.D.s spend up to seven years in a paid residency, most often in a hospital setting where they can gain further experience in a specialty. Residency involves long hours and heavy workloads, thus testing a physician's mettle under extreme conditions. In order for a physician to become licensed, he must pass a licensing exam after the residency period. In addition, a final exam is required to gain board certification by the American Osteopathic Association, the American Board of Medical Specialists, or any other board of a specialty. Receiving further certification in an area of study within a specialty requires one to two years of additional education and experience.

Job Conflicts

Roles, Ethics, and Politics

Physicians deal with a wide array of conflicts during the course of their careers. Their roles and influence are changing due to medical organizations and insurance companies. How a physician acquiesces control or confronts this change impacts her practice. Physicians face ethical challenges, such as receiving money from drug companies for enrolling their patients in clinical drug trials. The barrage of free samples, advertisements, and pharmaceutical sales calls tests physicians' impartiality and their ability to maintain objective judgment on the appropriateness of certain medicines. From abortion to euthanasia, physicians' stances on prolonging or concluding life may place them in conflict with society as well as the medical community. Politics can also present conflicts, as physicians sometimes must choose between supporting (1) legislation that expands patients' rights regarding their insurance companies and medical providers and (2) the medical providers who employ the physicians.

Burnout

Given the high number of patients physicians must attend to each day, the shuttling between home and workplaces, and the potential for being on call all night, it's not surprising that some physicians burn out after only a few years. More than 33 percent of all physicians work sixty or more hours per week. These long stretches of continuous, arduous work can quickly sap even the strongest of physicians. Burnout affects a physician's communication skills and motivation, which in turn affects the quality of patient interviews and patient satisfaction.

Myths About the Job

All Physicians Are Rich
There's no denying that a successful surgeon can earn the kind of income that some people only dream about. However, material rewards such as enormous houses and expensive cars may be little enjoyed because of the long hours physicians work. Physicians who are lower on the financial rung—for example, rural pediatricians or internists who make $35,000 a year and have $150,000 in student loan debt—illustrate that not all physicians live in luxury. Those who do earn handsome sums are quick to point out that their income is commensurate to the lengthy education, intense schedules, and high-stress environments physicians endure in order to improve and extend the lives of others.

Physicians Don't Care About Their Patients
After spending an hour in the waiting room and perhaps a scant fifteen minutes in the examination room, it's easy to conclude that physicians are less interested in their patients than in conducting quick, superficial consultations. However, the time physicians have to examine their patients, and the tests they can prescribe may be constrained by outside factors. Some medical organizations place time limits on patient exams and quotas for the number of patient exams per day. During an office visit, a patient may misconstrue the brevity of a doctor's attention as insensitivity.

Physicians Don't Do Much Beyond Seeing Patients
The practice of medicine is much more than patient examination, treatment, and follow-up. Physicians must keep abreast with changes and advances in medical science, from new pro-

cedures to new drugs to news about common drugs. In addition to lifelong learning, physicians deal with a substantial paperwork burden and must keep up with technological changes that affect their practice.

Jobs Within the Profession

Emergency Room Doctor

Job Description: Emergency room doctors assess the condition of arriving patients and provide treatment. On a hospital's front line, these doctors see a larger variety of ailments than most doctors do. Emergency room doctors encounter, for example, heart attacks; strokes; burns; injuries from car accidents, sports, and assault; asthma attacks; unconsciousness; drug overdoses; suicide attempts; food poisoning; severe allergic reactions; and appendicitis. In triage, doctors and nurses categorize patients' conditions as life threatening to not urgent. The emergency room doctors work with emergency nurses, physician assistants, and emergency room technicians to treat patients.

Number of Emergency Room Doctors: There are over thirty-two thousand emergency physicians in the U.S., representing roughly 2.8 percent of all doctors.

Earnings: Emergency room physicians earn a median income of $184,000 a year.

Further Reading:
- *The Emergency Room Intern Pocket Survival Guide,* Todd Rothenhaus.

Obstetrician Gynecologist (OB-GYN)

Job Description: Obstetricians provide prenatal care, administer ultrasounds, teach, supervise residents, and deliver babies. Gynecologists treat infertility and conditions such as abnormal Pap smears and bleeding. Some have a subspecialty (which requires two to four years of additional study) in infertility, high-risk pregnancy, or gynecological cancer. There are OB-GYNs, though some may only practice gynecology because of their specialty area (e.g., menopause) or because they can't afford the insurance rates necessary to practice obstetrics. Most OB-GYNs work fifty to one hundred hours per week and average sixty hours per week. They are on call twenty-four hours a day.

Number of OB-GYNs: There are approximately thirty thousand practicing OB-GYNs.

Earnings: OB-GYNs earn a median income of $200,000 a year.

Further Info:
- American Medical Association
  515 N. State St.
  Chicago, IL 60610
- American Medical Women's Association
  801 N. Fairfax St., Suite 400
  Alexandria, VA 22314

Further Reading:
- *Night Calls: The Personal Journey of an Ob/Gyn*, Henry Eisenberg.

Pediatrician

Job Description: Where the obstetrician leaves off, the pediatrician takes over, caring for children from birth. Pediatricians diagnose illnesses and abnormalities in child development and prescribe treatment. They administer physicals and prescribe medication and preventive vaccines.

Number of Pediatricians: There are approximately forty-five thousand pediatricians in the U.S.

Earnings: Pediatricians earn a median income of $130,000 a year, which is on the low side compared to other physicians.

Further Info:
- The American Academy of Pediatrics
  141 Northwest Point Blvd.
  Elk Grove Village, IL 60007

Further Reading:
- *The American Journal of Medicine*, University of California

San Francisco.
- *Being a Pediatrician*, Travis Cavens.
- *Medical Practice Management*, Greenbranch Publishing, LLC.
- *The New England Journal of Medicine*, Massachusetts Medical Society.

Surgeon

Job Description: Other physicians usually refer patients to surgeons, who assess a patient's condition and the risk an operation poses to that patient. These physicians perform surgery in their field of specialization—such as heart, brain, or reconstructive surgery—to correct abnormalities and repair injuries. In addition to being skilled in their craft, surgeons must stay current on the latest and most successful procedures being practiced and pioneered by other surgeons.

Earnings: Surgeons have some of the highest salaries among physicians. The median income is about $250,000 a year.

Further Reading:
- *Journal of the American Medical Association (JAMA)*, American Medical Association.
- *The Making of a Surgeon*, William A. Nolen.

Plastic Surgeon

Job Description: The work of a plastic surgeon falls into two categories: cosmetic surgery, which improves a patient's appearance, and reconstructive surgery, which repairs and re builds a patient's appearance and is necessitated by injury, disease, or genetics. In either case, plastic surgeons can improve the physical and emotional well-being of their patients. The most common cosmetic surgeries include abdominoplasty, breast augmentation, collagen injections, ear augmentation, eyelid augmentation, facelifts, liposuction, and nose augmentation.

Number of Plastic Surgeons: Approximately forty-five thousand plastic surgeons practice in the U.S.

Earnings: Annual salary depends on the number of patients

and the complexity of the procedures, but it is comparable to other physicians' salaries.

Further Reading:
- *Skin Deep: The Making of a Plastic Surgeon,* Donald T. Moynihan.

Physician Assistant

Job Description: Physician assistants (PAs) carry out much of the work formerly done by physicians. Working under a physician's supervision, PAs examine, diagnose, and treat patients; order tests; prescribe medication; and check on patients in hospitals. In areas lacking full-time physicians, PAs provide a vital link between patients and physicians.

Number of Physician Assistants: As of 2000, there were 40,000 physician assistants in the U.S.; 32 percent worked in hospitals, and 56 percent worked in offices and clinics. The remainder are employed in public health clinics and by other healthcare providers.

Education: PAs undergo two years of training in an accredited program which offers either an associate's, bachelor's, or master's degree. Courses include human anatomy, microbiology, physiology, clinical medicine, and disease prevention. PAs who want to work in specialized areas such as surgery must take additional courses.

Earnings: PAs earned a median income of $61,000 in 2000.

Further Info:
- American Academy of Physician Assistants
  950 N. Washington St.
  Alexandria, VA 22314
  www.aapa.org

Licensed Practical Nurse (LPN)

Job Description: Licensed practical nurses work primarily in hospitals and nursing homes and give bedside assistance and care. Their duties commonly include taking a patient's temperature and blood pressure, providing medication, and caring for newborns. An LPN may work in a private residence to provide complete services from preparing food to bathing the patient. Nurses working in private homes tend to work more hours—up to twelve hours a day if they have multiple patients—than those in hospitals.

Education: LPNs study nursing for at least one year.

Number of Licensed Practical Nurses: Over 700,000 LPNs work in the U.S.; 29 percent work in nursing homes, 28 percent tend to patients in hospitals, and 14 percent assist in clinics and private medical practices. The remainder are employed by schools and home healthcare agencies.

Earnings: Median income for LPNs is $30,000 a year.

Further Info:
- National Federation of Licensed Practical Nurses
  893 U.S. Highway 70 West, Suite 202
  Garner, NC 27529
- National League for Nursing
  10 Columbus Circle
  New York, NY 10019

Registered Nurse (RN)

Job Description: Registered nurses work primarily in hospitals in one or more special capacities including bedside care, post-surgery care, pediatrics, maternity care, or surgery. Some RNs may be self-employed and care for a single individual.

Education: Compared to an LPN, a registered nurse must have additional training, usually a bachelor's degree in nursing. Some RNs take additional classes in order to become nurse practitioners, who can perform some physician's duties, such as administrating physical exams. All RNs must have a nursing license, which they receive after passing a national licensing examination. Periodic license renewals are also required.

Number of Registered Nurses: Approximately 2.2 million registered nurses worked in 2000.

Earnings: The median income for RNs is $45,000 a year.

Further Info:
- American Nurses Association
  600 Maryland Ave. SW, Suite 100 West
  Washington, DC 20024
  www.nursingworld.org

Emergency Medical Technician (EMT)

Job Description: Emergency medical technicians are employed by private ambulance services, hospitals, and fire departments. When dispatched to the scene of an accident or incident, they provide emergency medical care at the scene and/or en route to the hospital. Common calls include those for automobile accident injuries, gunshot injuries, heart attacks, childbirth, and a need for CPR. Any treatment given to patients in transit is on the advice of hospital doctors. Working either in ambulances or aboard helicopters, emergency medical technicians restrain and stabilize patients to reduce the threat of additional injury during travel. On board EMTs carry a stock of medical equipment and supplies. EMTs range in proficiency and skill level, and they do everything from tending to basic medical needs to administering drugs, performing advanced procedures, and using monitoring equipment on a patient. A key requirement for EMTs is the ability to handle stress in a fast-paced environment. Most EMTs work forty to sixty hours a week.

Education: EMTs are trained at different levels ranging from EMT-1, or basic response, to EMT-4, or full paramedic response. Certification is required by all states, and some states require EMTs to periodically reregister to ensure continued training.

Number of EMTs: Over 170,000 EMTs work in the U.S.

Earnings: The median income for emergency medical technicians is $25,000 a year. Salaries vary by training and geographic location.

Further Info:
- National Association of Emergency Medical Technicians
  408 Monroe St.
  Clinton, MS 39056
  www.naemt.com

Additional Occupations

Physicians value the support and opinions of other doctors, and they rely on nurses, medical equipment operators, and therapists. These professionals include

- anesthesiologist
- dermatologist
- family practitioner
- medical technologist
- nurse-midwife
- oncologist
- pathologist
- physical therapist
- podiatrist
- psychiatrist
- radiologist
- scanning technician
- ultrasound technologist

Employers for those in the above positions include the following:

- hospitals
- clinics
- private medical practices

Medical Professionals in Nonfiction

Books
- *The Clinical I: Scenes From a Doctor's Life and Practice*, Irwin Siegel. First-hand account of a doctor's work and requirements.
- *The Intern Blues: The Timeless Classic About the Making of a Doctor*, Robert Marion. The real-life diaries of three medical interns.
- *On Being a Doctor 2: Voices of Physicians and Patients*, Michael A. LaCombe, ed. Essays, stories, and poems by doctors and patients.
- *Vital Signs: Real-Life Medical Dramas of Doctors and Patients, Pain and Compassion, Hope and Healing*, Dennis L.

Breo. A collection of true medical stories.
- *A Way of Thinking: A Primer on the Art of Being a Doctor*, Eugene Stead Jr. Details the necessary attributes that make for an effective physician.

Medical Professionals in Fiction

Books
- *Bad Medicine*, Ron Querry. A newly arrived physician on a Navaho reservation uncovers a virus.
- *A Case of Need*, Michael Crichton writing as Jeffrey Hudson. A doctor is charged with murder after an abortion goes wrong.
- *Critical Care*, Richard Dooling. The sleepless nights of a second-year resident at an intensive care unit.
- *Critical Judgment*, Michael Palmer. A big-city doctor moves from a hospital to a small-town ER, where her patients have developed an unexplained illness.
- *Harmful Intent*, Robin Cook. A doctor is accused of malpractice.
- *Harvest*, Tess Gerritsen. A new resident joins an organ-harvesting team.
- *The House of God*, Samuel Shem. A tale of six interns struggling to survive.

Movies
- *M*A*S*H* (1970). Humor helps a Korean War field hospital staff battle to save lives.
- *The Hospital* (1971). An overwhelmed doctor is caught up in the inefficiencies of a hospital.
- *Coma* (1978). Having discovered a hospital's sinister practice, a doctor finds his life at risk.
- *The Cider House Rules* (1999). A doctor runs an orphanage and trains a young man to follow in his footsteps.

Television
- *M*A*S*H* (1972–1983). A series based on the 1970 movie.
- *St. Elsewhere* (1982–1988). Life in a run-down hospital. One

of the best-written doctor shows ever.

- *Doogie Howser, M.D.* (1989–1993). Life in a residency program for a precocious teenage doctor.
- *Northern Exposure* (1990–1995). A young doctor sets up a practice in Alaska. Excellent characterization and plots that delve into powerful themes. Currently in syndication.
- *Chicago Hope* (1994–2000). A drama about the lives of those working in a busy Chicago hospital.
- *ER* (1994–). Emergency room staff at a Chicago hospital cope with work and life.
- *Becker* (1998–). A sitcom about a grumpy doctor's life in and outside of his private practice.
- *Scrubs* (2001–). A sitcom about doctors, interns, and staff in a hospital.

Firsthand Research

While there's no substitute for interviewing a physician, medical assistants and hospital staff can give you equally revealing points of view on how a medical practice operates. Familiarize yourself with a local hospital and contact the front desk about the availability of tours. Most hospitals provide free literature on a variety of specific conditions and diseases.

Web Sites

- Internet Resources for Family Physicians (www.medinfo.uf l.edu/cmc/inct/inetres.html). A directory of links for physicians.

- Com-Med.com (www.com-med.com/60559.asp). Links for doctors.

- Yahoo! (http://shopping.yahoo.com/Books/Health___Wel lness/Medicine/Physicians/Titles/). A bibliography of physician-related books.

BOOK EXCERPTS

''Like I said, I think we should open her up
and work on the heart directly. There's not
much to lose at this point.''

Jeffrey watched the flat EKG for another
moment. Then he sighed. ''Okay. Let's try
it,'' he said reluctantly. He had no other
ideas, and he didn't want to give up. . . .

Ted gowned and gloved in less than ten minutes. Once he was prepared, he had the nurse
stop compressing the chest so that he could
rapidly drape and slice into it. Within sec-
onds he was holding Patty's naked heart.

Ted massaged the heart with his gloved
hand and even injected epinephrine directly
into the left ventricle. When that failed
to have an effect, he tried to pace the heart
by attaching internal leads to the cardiac
wall. That resulted in a complex on the EKG,
but the heart itself did not respond.

—<u>Harmful Intent</u>, Robin Cook

The groans startled Werner because he was
not used to sounds coming out of his patients. Most of his patients were on venti-
lators, and the tube that took oxygen from
the breathing machine to the patient went
in the mouth, down the throat, through the
vocal cords, and into the lungs. Once intu-
bated, patients could only mouth silent
words with their lips, gesture, or scrawl

messages on pads. Even gesturing was usually out of the question for these patients,
because their hands were almost always tied
to the bed rails with cotton restraints to
keep them from yanking their tubes.

—Critical Care, Richard Dooling

The sun rose, and the real doctors—tho-
racic surgeons, neurologists, nephrolo-
gists, pulmonologists, oncologists, radi-
ologists, chiefs of this, and heads of that—
began arriving between six and seven. . . .
During the daytime, Werner had to take his
place among the lesser lights in the medical
hierarchy, a mere reflection of the bril-
liance shining down from above. . . .
Refreshed by a solid eight hours of sleep
in houses protected by burglar alarms, the
real doctors arrived, cranked up on caf-
feine and ready for another fast-paced day
of Money and Medicine. They called their
answering services on their new cordless
phones, checked their beepers, grabbed
their stethoscopes out of their glove com-
partments. They parked their luxury sedans
right outside the Emergency Room doors in
privileged parking places. It had been cal-
culated that this simple expedient saved
each doctor almost fifteen minutes a day.

—Critical Care, Richard Dooling

Cardoza was slipping away.

Desperately, Abby tried to remain calm. . . . If he was bleeding that badly into his belly, there was probably nothing she could do. The answer was to start from the beginning—the ABCs. His airway was fine, as was his monitor pattern. But while examining his chest, she hit pay dirt. The tube she had inserted was kinked, and Cardoza's original problem had recurred. She straightened the tube without much difficulty and tacked it down. Once again, Cardoza's pressure came up and his color improved.

—<u>Critical Judgment</u>, Michael Palmer

☙

The scrub nurse handed him the electric saw. Abby took hold of the retractor. As Frobisher cut through the sternum, Abby couldn't help turning away. She felt vaguely nauseated by the whine of the blade, the smell of bone dust, neither of which seemed to bother Frobisher, whose hands worked with swift skill. In moments he was

in the chest cavity, his scalpel poised over
the pericardial sac.

—<u>Harvest</u>, Tess Gerritsen

❧

I have trouble buying life insurance. Most
pathologists do: the companies take one
look at you and shudder—constant exposure
to tuberculosis, malignancies, and lethal
infectious disease makes you a very poor
risk.

—<u>A Case of Need</u>, Michael Crichton writing
as Jeffrey Hudson

❧

As I cut through the corridors and buildings, I remembered my rotation through the
hospital as a resident. Small details came
back. The soap: a strange, cheap, peculiar-
smelling soap that was used everywhere. The
paper bags hung by each sink, one for paper
towels, the other for rectal gloves. As an
economy, the hospital saved used gloves,
cleaned them, and used them again. The little plastic name tags edged in black, blue,
and red depending on your service.

—<u>A Case of Need</u>, Jeffrey Hudson

CHAPTER 12

Modeling

Agent, Talent Scout, Model, Artist's Model, Stylist, Fashion Photographer

The Lowdown

Modeling offers great appeal to many fiction writers because of the apparent glamour of the fashion industry. The models are beautiful, and they hang out with wealthy and powerful celebrities (note how many rock musicians date or marry models). This provides the writer with a vast palette of colors to paint a story.

1. The world of modeling is a setting rich with several arts, including posing, photography, and fashion, giving the writer much opportunity for texture. Screenwriters especially like the modeling setting because it allows them to have attractive women parade around, often skimpily dressed.

2. Character conflicts abound. Models wishing to remain thin in order to be competitive can become self-destructive. The competition itself creates conflict. People who pursue models because of just their appearance leave the models apprehensive or confused about relationships.

3. Because both personal and financial stakes are so

high in modeling, plots involving models can be adapted for many different genres, from literary mainstream to mystery.

4. Modeling provides a powerful theme: Models offer up an image of perfection that is unrealistic for the audience it attracts. Young girls who strive to emulate models get frustrated by their inability to reach their goal—unattainable because the images are manipulated not just with lighting and airbrushing but by reshaping of the models' bodies. Cindy Crawford once said that even she can never look like the Cindy Crawford in the magazines.

Daily Life

Work Schedule
A good agent or talent scout is always working. In a typical day, an agent sorts through countless photographs of prospective models, deals with fashion editors and casting directors to place his models in shows and photo shoots, and takes care of administrative business such as contracts. In this industry, who you know is at least as important as what you know, so agents spend plenty of time schmoozing—everything from lunching with business associates to being seen at the right parties and social events.

Dressing the Part
People in the modeling industry must always be aware of their physical appearance. This involves immaculate grooming and fashionable hair and dress. On the flip side, people in the industry who are not models must exude an air of professionalism, which means treading the line between style and trendiness. A popular refrain is that businesspeople in the industry have sleek, plain hair and tailored, black clothes. There is good reason for this: Plainness keeps them from looking dated and communicates a confidence that they are somehow beyond fashion.

Job Description

The individual jobs within the modeling profession differ greatly. For more detailed information, see "Jobs Within the Profession," starting on page 228.

Buzzwords

catalog: A model who is deemed by the agency to be a catalog model (rather than a model for runway or high-level fashion magazine work).

catwalk: The narrow walkway on which fashions are modeled.

couture: The business of designing and selling fashionable women's clothing. The clothing produced.

haute couture: The most exclusive designers and the fashions they create.

house: A designer's business organization (e.g., the *houses* coming out with the best designs this year include Gucci and Prada).

ready-to-wear: Clothing that is meant to be sold to consumers, as opposed to haute couture, which is intended mostly for runway shows.

supermodel: A model who is also a celebrity, e.g., Claudia Schiffer or Kate Moss.

Education

Many models are most busy during their high school and college-age years, making a formal education nearly impossible. There is specialized education for modeling (e.g., modeling school), but it matters little in actually helping models find work.

Job Conflicts

Job Instability

The fashion industry and the modeling industry, in particular, are notoriously fickle. It takes little or no provocation for to-day's hottest face to become yesterday's news. Women as young as twenty-one often are considered too old to begin a modeling career. For men, the age range is greater, though in both cases this is an industry for the young. Everyone in the business—from photographers to stylists to agents—must stay ahead of the curve in order to have any career longevity.

Media Scrutiny
The modeling industry is under constant scrutiny from political groups and the media. Some criticize models for promoting an unhealthy self-image in young girls and photographers for posing underage models in overly sensual situations. A recent BBC documentary called "MacIntyre Undercover" exposes the seedier side of modeling agencies and has created a major stir in the industry.

Lifestyle
Most models are under great pressure to stay thin. It's not uncommon for a female model to be five-foot-nine or taller and have a twenty-three-inch waist. Models who feel that pressure and mingle with fast crowds at parties can fall into a habit of drug use (particularly cocaine). People at modeling agencies have been complicit in illegal drug use to keep their girls' weight down. In 1999, a Latvian modeling agency was even caught trafficking drugs. In order to maintain their weight, models often adopt unhealthy eating habits and struggle with bulimia or anorexia.

Myths About the Job

Models Lead Glamorous, Jet-Setting Lives
Working models often have fast-paced lifestyles, traveling from city to city all over the world to shoot fashion spreads or work the runway. However, with few exceptions, this is anything but glamorous. Beginning models may live with several other girls in a dormitory-style room. They enjoy little privacy, free time, or money. Only models who have truly made it enjoy a lifestyle with more glamour and less stress.

Models Aren't Smart
Although models make their living based on their looks, many are acknowledged as being smart as well. Supermodel Cindy

Crawford is an industry-savvy businesswoman who has enjoyed longevity with her career and earned the respect of those she works with. In 2000, fashion models Matt Garel and Derry Watkins released a spelling game they had created called Coodju, and it was favorably reviewed by Mensa's newsletter.

Jobs Within the Profession

Agent, Talent Scout

Job Description: Modeling agents and scouts decide who's hot. This is more complicated than it might seem; it's not just a matter of high cheekbones and long legs. It is about finding the person who projects the kind of image that will promote the product or service being advertised. A model used in a successful beer advertisement is very different from one used to promote a hearing aid. Both agents and talent scouts hunt for people with the right kind of look and match them up with the right assignment. Agents also look out for a model's financial interests, negotiating contracts and helping the model select the assignments that are in keeping with her ultimate goal.

Education: The formal education of people in the modeling industry can vary quite a bit. Working in the modeling industry can interfere with getting an education; fashion thrives on youth and trends. Some agents are former models, so many agents do not have a college education. However, some agents enter the industry through the business or editorial side of fashion; these people often have bachelor's degrees.

Earnings: Agents receive a cut (usually between 10 and 20 percent) of a model's earnings. At top agencies, agents make a very good living. Becoming an agent can be grueling, as nobody hands over the most promising models to the low man on the totem pole. An agent gains distinction by discovering a model, which involves time, money, and luck.

Model

Job Description: A model must project a look that makes people notice. If models want to model haute couture, they must also be tall and thin.

Education: Many models work most during what would be their high school and college years, making a complete formal education nearly impossible. There is specialized education for modeling (i.e. modeling school), but it matters little in helping models to actually find work.

Clothes: Though the clothing worn during a shoot is provided, models must also own a wardrobe that is fashionable and flattering for them to wear in public and in meetings with prospective employers.

Number of Models: Thousands of men and women vie for modeling jobs, but only a handful work regularly. Truly famous models number only a few dozen, at best.

Earnings: The top models can make several thousand dollars a day, or even an hour, but most models work for a modest wage. After the agency deducts its expenses, including money they've spent to promote the model, a new model often is left without much money at all.

Artist's Model

Job Description: An artist's model poses for sculptors, illustrators, and painters. This job requires a great deal of agility and the physical fitness necessary to sustain a pose for several hours. Age and physique are much less of an issue for the artist's model than for the fashion model.

Clothes: The model's work clothing is provided by the artist— or not, for art featuring a nude model.

Earnings: An artist's model's pay can be about $15 per hour or more. Some models forego payment, sitting as a favor for an artist they admire.

Further Info:
- How to Become an Artist's Model (www.borsheimarts.com/modeling.htm). This informative personal home page of artist Kelly Borsheim tells about becoming a model.

Stylist

Job Description: A stylist, also called an image consultant, creates a model's look. The stylist works with hair, skin, and clothing. Like a consultant who gives makeovers, a stylist tries to imagine the best overall look for a model.

Education: Stylists are usually certified beauticians who have professional experience cutting hair, applying makeup, etc. However, since stylists are consultants (the actual styling is usually left to a staff hairdresser or makeup artist), it is possible for someone with a good eye to get into the field without any formal training or experience.

Earnings: Professional stylists at top agencies are usually well paid and among the best in their field. This trickles all the way down to modestly paid, less experienced stylists still looking to earn a reputation in the field. The salary range for stylists is great—a sought-after stylist can make hundreds of dollars per hour, whereas up-and-comers could earn less than $10 per hour, if they are paid at all.

Fashion Photographer
Job Description: A fashion photographer must make the model and the product or service she is promoting look as appealing as possible. A good fashion photographer has a unique style of shooting and the ability to work with fussy designers, agents, and models.

Education: Photographers often have degrees from art school, although a strong portfolio is what helps a photographer land a job.

Earnings: A beginning fashion photographer might shoot for credits alone. Top-notch photographers bring in several thousand dollars per shoot.

Additional Occupations

Models and those in the modeling industry may interact with the following professionals:
- Hairdressers cut, style, color, wave, or straighten hair as their client wishes; they often consult with clients to determine what look will work best.

- Makeup Artists make up the faces of men and women for photo shoots, TV/film, or in-person appearances.

Models in Nonfiction

Books

- *Advanced Revelations to Plus Size Modeling*, DeLores Pressley and Amie J. Greer. A resource for those looking to get into plus sized modeling.
- *Bettie Page: The Life of a Pin-Up Legend*, Karen Essex and James Swanson. This authorized biography of 1950s model Bettie Page includes a foreword by the famous pinup.
- *Both Sides of the Rainbow*, Tom Christopher and Margie K. Carroll. A young gay man moves to Los Angeles to start a modeling career and spends twenty-four years in a relationship with a famous actor before calling it quits and moving away.
- *How to Become a Successful Commercial Model: The Complete Commercial Modeling Handbook*, Aaron R. Marcus. Practical advice for becoming a commercial (i.e., not fashion) model.
- *Model & Talent 2001: The International Directory of Model and Talent Agencies*, Tricia Blount, ed.
- *The Modeling Life: The One (and Only) Book That Gives You the Inside Story of What the Business Is Like and How You Can Make It*, Donna Rubinstein and Jennifer Kingson Bloom. Anecdotes and advice from the model editor of *Seventeen* magazine.
- *Modelmania: The Working Model's Manual*, Karl Preston.
- *A Model's Primer*, MJ Wilson. Information about how to become a model, written by a photographer.
- *The Professional Model's Handbook: A Comprehensive Guide to Modeling and Related Fields*, Linda A. Balhorn, et al. This includes everything from tips about style to a section dealing with legal forms, meant to educate prospective models.
- *Runway*, Larry Fink.
- *The Truth on Modeling*, Erin Pinckney.
- *The Wilhelmina Guide to Modeling*, Natasha Esch, et al.

Documentaries

- *Catwalk* (1995). Documentary that follows model Christy Tur-lington through fashion shows in Milan, Paris, and New York in the early 1990s.
- *Nico Icon* (1995). A documentary about supermodel-turned-Velvet-Underground-diva Christa Päffgen (also known as Nico).
- *Unzipped* (1995). A behind-the-scenes look at Isaac Mizrahi as he puts together his fall 1994 collection.
- *Wrinkle* (2001). Former models, now in their fifties, gather for a fashion shoot.

Models in Fiction

Books

- *American Star*, Jackie Collins. The unlikely pairing of a small-town beauty turned New York model with a young Italian man from the wrong side of her hometown.
- *Cat's Meow*, Melissa de la Cruz. A romance set against the background of the fashion world.
- *Fashionably Late*, Olivia Goldsmith. This story is set in Man-hattan's fashion industry.
- *Glamorama*, Bret Easton Ellis. A satirical mixture of modeling and terrorism. By the author of *American Psycho* and *Less Than Zero*.
- *Look at Me*, Jennifer Egan. A thirty-five-year-old model's face is so disfigured after a car accident that she is unrecognizable. She must learn to deal with people without getting by on her looks.
- *Miami*, Pat Booth. A glitzy story of a model's rise in Miami.
- *Model Behavior*, Jay McInerney. The author of *Bright Lights, Big City* (which also featured modeling) examines decadence in the modeling industry.
- *Tickled Pink*, Rita Rudner. A novel about two girls' comic misadventures while trying to make it in New York circa 1980. Rudner is a comedienne and the author of the best-selling book *Naked Beneath My Clothes*.

Movies

- *How to Marry a Millionaire* (1953). Three New York models

set out to snag rich, eligible bachelors. With Marilyn Monroe.
- *Darling* (1965). A young model rises from modest origins.
- *Blowup* (1966). A fashion photographer chases young models in this surrealistic film.
- *Lipstick* (1976). A supermodel is raped, and the younger sister takes revenge.
- *Eyes of Laura Mars* (1978). A fashion photographer has premonitions of murders.
- *Looker* (1981). A plastic surgeon gets suspicious when models he has operated on begin to die.
- *The Cover Girl Murders* (1993). One by one, the models at a remote photo shoot turn up dead in this TV movie.
- *Even Cowgirls Get the Blues* (1993). This movie, based on the Tom Robbins novel, includes some modeling background.
- *A Perry Mason Mystery: The Case of the Wicked Wives* (1993). A TV movie in which a photographer is found dead after attempting to produce a fashion shoot with three models who were also his ex-wives. His wife is the main suspect.
- *Prêt-à-Porter (aka Ready to Wear)* (1994). A comedy from writer-director Robert Altman about the Paris fashion scene.
- *Sirens* (1994). A young reverend (Hugh Grant) and his wife experience culture shock when they visit the estate of an eccentric painter and his models.
- *Gia* (1998). The HBO bio of 1970s supermodel Gia Carangi. The screenplay was cowritten by Jay McInerney.

Television
- *That Girl* (1966–1971). A young woman balances acting and modeling ambitions in this sitcom. Currently in syndication.
- *Charlie's Angels* (1976–1981). Three women fight crime undercover, often posing as models.
- *Paper Dolls* (1984). The cutthroat worlds of modeling and cosmetics.
- *thirtysomething* (1987–1991). An excellent drama involving an ad agency. Several story lines involved models and the concept of modeling.
- *Models, Inc.* (1994–1995). A short-lived Aaron Spelling series about a modeling agency.

Web Sites

- Models.com (www.models.com). A Web site for men and women looking to break into the modeling industry. Though much of the site requires registry—for a fee—some news articles and forums are available for free.

- The Insider's Guide to Supermodels and Modeling (www.supermodelguide.com). A Web site devoted to would-be models. Includes information about supermodels currently working in the industry as well as tips about scams and listings of upcoming open calls, etc.

- Hint Fashion Magazine—Chic Happens (www.hintmag.com/chichappens/chichappens.php). An online gossip column focusing on the fashion and modeling industries.

BOOK EXCERPTS

When Philomena looks in the mirror she sees a creature fat and unattractive. This despite the fact that she is a woman whose photographic image is expensively employed to arouse desire in conjunction with certain consumer goods. Or rather, *because* of that fact. Toxic body consciousness being the black lung of her profession. Dressing for the party, she screams that she's bloated and has nothing to wear.

I'm clutching a preparty martini when she makes this declaration. ''You look terrific,'' I say.

She seizes my glass and hurls it at the mirror, shattering both.

—<u>Model Behavior</u>, Jay McInerney

The images his photographer had sent him were clinical in detail. She knew exactly what he wanted, and what he wanted was no surprises. When his client showed up for her live sketching sessions, he wanted to know the architecture of her body as if he'd built it himself. If there was an odd wrinkle in her groin, he wanted the photographer to show it to him. If there was a thickness at her waist, he wanted to see it and he wanted to know how it behaved when she squatted. If her buttocks were uneven, he wanted to know to what degree and how they behaved when she took a step or turned at the waist. If her breasts didn't match, he wanted to know so he could decide what poses presented them to their best advantage.

The more he knew about a subject's anatomy before she showed up for her live sketching sessions, the less time the sessions would require. And the more accomplished he would look at the end of each day when she would inevitably want to see what he had done. He could fudge, but he had to be clever about it. These women knew very well what they looked like, and his flattery had to be subtle enough to avoid outright embarrassment at the fact that what he was drawing was not exactly what he or they were seeing.

—<u>Animosity</u>, David Lindsey

As our little group paused in the doorway I realized that I'd never guessed just how smack-in-the-stomach the collective presence of the top girls in the girl business would be. Now they weren't clacking, one by one, in and out of Loring Model Management, each an individual, as I had come to know them. Now they were banded together in a cloud of heightened awareness of themselves that raised their power to the nth degree. As a group they were plunged into a dense atmosphere of dedicated self-absorption that was deeply knowing and totally privileged, in equal proportions. They were wrapped in the knowledge of their meritocracy, which consisted of the dead-simple fact that at this particular moment in time they were the chosen of the chosen, the anointed. Rules that bound other women had been suspended for them. Their faces, in spite of their youth, carried the weight of so much fantasy that walking into a room filled with top models was ten times more impressive than finding yourself backstage in the presenters' makeup room on Oscar Night.

—<u>Spring Collection</u>, Judith Krantz

CHAPTER 13

Moviemaking

Producer, Director, Scriptwriter, Actor, Talent Agent,
Literary Agent, Reader, Casting Director, Art Director,
Cinematographer/Camera Work, Editor

The Lowdown

Fiction writers love to use characters from Hollywood
for two reasons: (1) writers who work in Hollywood
have a lot of animosity toward the business because of
the way they are treated (venting is cathartic), and (2)
Hollywood is a concentration of all the darkest emotions. Greed, exploitation, desperation, and raw ambition occur in all walks of life, but not with the intensity
and dazzling setting of Hollywood.

Fame and fortune are tremendous lures, so Hollywood stories offer the opportunity to portray innocents
who seek those things and get corrupted by the realities of life. The typical characters include the soulless
producer who seeks nothing but money at the expense
of her relationships; the overbearing director who must
control everyone in his life the way he does the actors
on a set; and the actor who needs adulation in order to
have any self-worth. We might run into these character
types in any business in which there is a lot of money

to be made, but in the Hollywood novel, we have the added glitz of the moviemaking world.

Aside from the issues of greed and ambition, the Hollywood novel offers themes that deal with art vs. reality: What are the effects of art on how we live our lives? When are the influences of art beneficial and when are they manipulative? Is the creation of great art worth the sacrifices one makes in one's personal life?

Job Description

Jobs in the motion picture industry are broken down into two groups: "above the line" and "below the line." These designations come from budgeting a film. Those jobs that are above the line are referred to as talent (including actors, directors, and writers), while those below the line include the craftspersons responsible for making the film (set builders, costume designers, gaffers, etc.). Below-the-line employees are paid a set amount, and therefore it is easier to estimate that budget amount. However, payments for above-the-line employees are negotiable and therefore more difficult to estimate.

Jobs generally relate to one of the three phases of moviemaking: preproduction, production, and postproduction. Preproduction involves planning the movie and includes budgeting, casting, scouting locations, designing sets and costumes, constructing sets, and scheduling. Production involves the actual making of the film. Postproduction involves editing the film and dubbing in sound.

Daily Life

Work Schedule
People working on a movie or television series put in long hours that may begin as early as four or five in the morning and end late at night. Add to that the stress of trying to wrap up films on time and within budget, and you have the intense and sometimes emotionally charged atmosphere of a movie set.

Working Conditions

In general, film production takes place in comfortable surroundings. However, if the film shoots on location, adverse
weather and geographical conditions come into play.

Buzzwords

attached: When talent agrees to direct, produce, and/or act in
a film, they are *attached* to that film. This attachment is often
used to raise money from investors or to convince a studio to
take on the film. This attachment can be legal, through a contract, or informal, through an oral agreement. Contingencies
are common; for example, a famous actor may agree to star in
the film only if he has a say in approving the director.

hyphenates: Directors, producers, and writers who take on
multiple roles in a film (e.g., director-producer, writer-director,
etc.).

indieprod: An independent producer.

packaging: An important element in deal making. A large talent
agency that represents producers, actors, writers, and directors,
try to *package* a film, or offer talent to fill all (or as many as
possible) positions in one big package. This earns the agency
a fee from each of their booked clients and often an additional
bonus from the studio.

paparazzi: Photographers who hound celebrities by taking
photos to sell to tabloids and other publications. Because they
can be aggressive and invade celebrities' privacy, there is often
an adversarial relationship between the paparazzi and their
subjects—and sometimes this leads to violence, as it did with
Sean Penn and with Alec Baldwin.

Pasadena: Slang for passing on (refusing) a project, as in "I'll
take a *Pasadena* on it."

pay or play: Producers anxious to attach a prominent actor to
a project may give them a check (usually 10 percent of the
actor's fee) just to agree to do the film. Even if the film never
gets made (which happens more often than not), the actor
keeps the money. This is a worthwhile investment for the pro-

ducer because having a name actor attached to a project makes it easier to attract financing and other big-name actors.

points: Percentage *points* given to the major participants in a film; a participant will receive a percentage of the money the film makes. Points are sometimes offered in lieu of much up-front money to those making a low-budget film. However, this can be a tricky proposition since most points are tied to a film's profit, and Hollywood bookkeeping is notorious for showing even the highest grossing movies netting a loss. Those with clout make sure their points are attached to the film's gross revenues rather than its profit.

turnaround: When a script commissioned or bought by a studio becomes available for other studios or producers to buy. After years of trying to get a script made into a movie, the studio may decide it's not worth the effort and put it in *turnaround.*

Education

Some jobs require no specialized education, and many people become producers, writers, and even directors by working their way up through a myriad of menial jobs. Even the traditional starting job in the mail room is filled by people with Harvard M.B.A.s, law degrees, and so forth. However, many filmmaker wanna-bes attend film schools such as those at the University of California at Los Angeles or the University of Southern California. Degrees are not necessary for employment, but the knowledge received in such schools can be helpful. In addition, at the major film schools students often make contact with famous filmmakers who might provide opportunities for them in the future. Also, students who eventually make it in the business might be willing to give their fellow students a helping hand.

Job Conflicts

Creative Differences
The main reason filming becomes antagonistic is creative differences: when the director, producer, actors, and/or writer

disagree on the basic elements of the film. For example, the director may want an actor to play a scene dramatically, while the actor thinks it should be played more comically. A producer may ask the writer to cut dialogue or an entire scene that the writer thinks is crucial to the story. This type of collaborative adversity is common in the making of a film, and many believe it helps improve the final product. However, the number of bad films produced gives credence to those who argue that such collaboration can result in a final product that has no vision and is merely a poor copy of a better film. When creative differences become insurmountable, one of the parties probably will quit or be fired.

Development Hell
Movies often start out in development: Someone gets an idea; a writer is hired to turn the idea into a script; the script is offered to various producers, directors, and actors; and actors, producers, and directors agree to be part of the film. But because it often takes so long to round up all the necessary talent, key talent may drop out from the project. This "development hell" can go on for many years before a film finally gets made—if it is ever made. It is not unusual for a studio to invest millions of dollars in developing a project that never results in a movie.

Insecure Talent
The most difficult part of making a living based on talent is the personal insecurity people feel about whether or not (1) they are any good, (2) they deserve success, and (3) their talent will disappear. This insecurity drives many talented people to alcohol, drugs, and other forms of self-abuse. Insecurity may also make talent vulnerable to unscrupulous people who claim to be spiritual advisors then take advantage of their victims.

Ruthlessness and Ambition
There's a lot of money to be made in the movie business, and this attracts many people who want nothing more than to make money. Some say that the real product of Hollywood is

power over others' lives. For those in power, movies are just a necessary evil, a by-product of their game playing.

Lack of Job Security

There's a saying in Hollywood: "You're only as good as your last picture." No matter how famous or hot a person might be, roles in movies headed straight to video are only a matter of time if his last few movies aren't profitable (e.g., William Baldwin). Many television actors have learned the hard way that popularity on TV doesn't always translate to movie popularity (e.g., David Caruso). Top-notch actors, directors, and writers can quickly spiral into oblivion and struggle to find work. This is particularly problematic for those used to an expensive lifestyle.

Celebrity

The prospect of celebrity motivates many to enter the business, but celebrity has its downsides:

1. Celebrities lack privacy as the paparazzi sneak around photographing them at every opportunity. The more private the moment and the worse the celebrity's look, the more a photo is worth to the tabloids.

2. Physical danger is a risk for celebrities and their families. Stalkers are everywhere, breaking into homes (Madonna, David Letterman, George Harrison, etc.) and sometimes threatening their lives (Russell Crowe, Steven Spielberg, etc.). Bodyguards must be ever present for the celebrity and her children to prevent them from being kidnapped.

3. Friendships and romances are hard to form because a celebrity can never be sure if a potential friend or lover is interested in the person or the persona.

Public Perception

Many celebrities feel harnessed to how the public perceives them. An actor's career can rise or fall according to that perception. This may also be true if an actor is identified with a certain type of role. Comic actors (e.g., Tom Hanks, Jack Lemmon, Jim Carrey) often fight for dramatic roles so they won't be typecast for the rest of their career.

Political Interference and Exploitation

Celebrities in the movie business wield a lot of influence in that they can command camera time. Celebrities always have a platform to say whatever they want, but being a famous actor, director, or producer doesn't necessarily make one savvy in politics. Politicians who need more exposure may enlist the support of celebrities, or they may attack Hollywood in order to get more press coverage. For example, witch-hunts aimed at Communists in the 1950s focused on Hollywood more to garner publicity for Sen. Joseph McCarthy than to protect national security. Currently, the issues of violence and sex in television and films often are aimed more at headlines for politicians than protection for citizens.

Ageism, Racism, Sexism

Hollywood is known to show favoritism toward white males, not only on the screen but behind the cameras and in the executive suites. Racial minorities assert that they tend to be limited to stereotypical roles; actresses tend to be relegated to playing "the love interest"; and older actors lament the lack of roles altogether in this business that focuses on the youthful audience. Current lawsuits address these perceived inequities. For example, TV scriptwriters are suing because many TV shows appear to refuse to use writers over the age of fifty, because of a belief that only young writers are hip enough to appeal to the eighteen- to forty-year-old audience that advertisers target. Similar cases are brought by women and people of color. These groups argue that they are less likely to be cast as the main characters of films and that they tend to get paid less than their white, male counterparts.

Unions

All major films are produced under the supervision of labor unions. Actors belong to the Screen Actors Guild (SAG) or the American Federation of Television and Radio Artists (AFTRA), writers belong to the Writers Guild of America (WGA), and directors belong to the Directors Guild of America (DGA). Art directors; cartoonists; editors; costumers; scenic artists; set designers; camera operators; sound technicians; projectionists;

and shipping, booking, and other distribution employees belong to the International Alliance of Theatrical Stage Employees and Motion Picture Machine Operators (IATSE) or the United Scenic Artists Association (USAA). Opera and stage performers, including those in Broadway productions, belong to the Actors Equity Association (AEA). Certain members of the crew may also belong to various other unions. Filmmakers have been complaining for years that the cost of union labor has been driving up the cost of making movies to the point that they must film in other countries or states. On the other hand, recent strike threats by the WGA and SAG might have cost the industry (and California) billions of dollars in lost revenue.

Myths About the Job

Movies Are Shot From Beginning to End, Like a Play
Movie scenes are rarely shot in chronological order. The schedule of shooting is determined by many factors: weather, availability of locations, availability of actors, etc. For example, an actor may be available for shooting for only one month, which means all of her scenes get shot first. An impending storm may necessitate shooting certain outdoor sequences before the storm breaks. In fact, actors in a movie may never actually see each other during filming unless they share scenes.

All Hollywood People Party Most Nights
Hollywood parties are less about having fun than about making and maintaining business contacts. These parties generally are publicized to lure the paparazzi there to snap photos. However, in general, most people who work in Hollywood have families and busy work schedules (when they are working). Those involved in making a movie begin work very early in the morning, so partying all night every night can eventually get them fired. Those who earn a reputation for indulging in drugs eventually find it hard to get work. No one wants to

risk millions of dollars and dozens of careers on someone who isn't reliable.

Anyone Who Makes a Movie or Appears in a TV Series Is Financially Set for Life

This myth is widely held, even by those who aspire to make it. While it's true that someone might be paid a large amount of money for selling a script or acting in a movie, that money has to last a long time because work is so sporadic. A scriptwriter might sell a script for a hundred thousand, but if it is not made into a movie he will find it harder to sell the next one. That hundred grand may have to last him a couple years—and his agent's fee and the taxes might whittle his cut down to about fifty thousand dollars.

The reason famous actors do commercials is that they need the money. Their expenses are often enormous (agents, managers, publicists, bodyguards, drivers, assistants, etc.). Most of the top actors do TV commercials abroad in order to protect their image in the U.S., or they do voice-overs (unseen narrating) for TV commercials to air in the U.S.

Jobs Within the Profession

Producer

Job Description: In general, a producer finds the money to make a movie and takes responsibility for bringing the talent together and overseeing the production from concept through marketing.

To effectively gather talent for a movie, a producer should have many contacts—agents, publishers, and writers—in the industry. Different producers have different styles of overseeing production: Some bully and threaten, some cajole, and some do both. Whatever their technique, producers are under a lot of pressure to meet the conflicting demands of the studios/investors, the directors, and the actors, so they must demonstrate diplomacy and tact.

The various production tasks are handled by different kinds

of producers, including executive producers, line producers, associate producers, and independent producers.

1. An executive producer supervises, either on his own authority (entrepreneur executive producer) or subject to the authority of an employer (employee executive producer), one or more producers on single or multiple productions. This title is merely a formality if the person had little to do with the actual making of the film. This might be the case for investors, owners of the production company, or someone who convinced a big star to be in the movie. Sometimes executive producer credit is given in lieu of more money, especially to writers. Agents of big stars sometimes demand an executive producer credit.

2. Line producers are involved in the daily production, solving problems as they come up. Line producers also develop the budget and try to make sure the production stays within that budget.

3. Associate producers perform production functions delegated and supervised by a producer.

4. Independent producers are a special breed, not unlike wildcat oil drillers of the past. An independent producer is part hustler, convincing people to invest large sums of money; part gambler, risking her career on the next film; and part charmer, persuading actors, writers, and directors to put their own futures on the line.

Following is a list of the typical responsibilities of a producer of a theatrical movie. (A television producer has slightly different responsibilities; see the Web site for the California Occupational Guides at www.calmis.cahwnet.gov/htmlfile/subject/guide.htm).

Development, Preproduction
- Conceive underlying concept of the production or select and secure rights for material (such as a magazine article, novel, or nonfiction book) upon which the production will be based.
- Supervise and oversee the development process, the overall process of developing the concept into a screenplay.

- Secure the initial financing (e.g., studio or independent funding, license fees, loans, etc.).
- Serve as the primary point of contact for the financing entity.
- Supervise the preparation of the preliminary budget.
- Select the director, writer, unit production manager, principal cast, production designer, editor, and cinematographer.
- Approve the final shooting schedule, sign the final budget, and approve and sign the final shooting script.

Production
- Oversee and approve deals for the principal components of the production.
- Supervise the unit production manager.
- Consult in person with the director, the principal cast, and the production designer.
- Select the composer.
- Consult in person on the set design, set dressings, locations and props, visual and mechanical effects, wardrobe, makeup, and hair.
- Manage and approve the weekly cost report.
- Supervise the set, the day-to-day operation of the shooting company, and all talent and craftspeople.
- Supervise on location the operations of the shoot and the performance of talent and craftspeople.
- View the dailies and consult with the director and editor.

Postproduction
- Consult with the editor.
- View and appraise the director's cut.
- Participate in the attainment and approval of the final cut.
- Consult with the composer.
- Supervise the music recording and rerecording sessions.
- Supervise the titles and opticals process.
- Consult on the answer print or edited master, the marketing plan and materials, the plan of distribution and exploitation, the publicity process, and the exploitation of the production in ancillary markets.

Education: No specialized education is required. Producers come from all walks of life: lawyers, doctors, writers, dentists—pretty much anybody who has the rights to a hot property or has the ability to raise money to invest in a film. More important than a degree in film is the ability to organize, to spot talent, and to find material worth producing.

Clothes: Producers dress to suit their tastes and needs. In general, they tend to dress casually, but casual isn't necessarily inexpensive. Producers don expensive clothing perhaps as a matter of taste but mainly to impress those they do business with. This can also extend to the kind of car a producer drives. Who would want to invest millions of dollars with a producer who drives an old car?

Earnings: Producers' earnings vary because they seldom work for a set fee. Instead, a producer receives a percentage of a film's net earnings or ticket sales.

Further Info:
- Association of Independent Feature Film Producers (AIFFP) (www.aiffp.org). Dedicated to the advancement of independent feature films.
- Producers Guild of America (PGA) (www.producersguildonline .com). Web site dedicated to all aspects of producing in movies and television.
- Independent Feature Project (www.ifp.org). Organization committed to the idea that "independent film is an important art form and powerful voice in our society."

Further Reading:
- *A Pound of Flesh: Perilous Tales of How to Produce Movies in Hollywood,* Art Linson. A successful producer recounts his career making many famous movies.
- *Hello, He Lied: And Other Truths From the Hollywood Trenches,* Lynda Rosen Obst. A famed producer gives an insider's view of Hollywood deal making.

Director
Job Description: Directors are usually involved in every aspect of filmmaking, including script discussions, casting, editing,

and sometimes marketing. Some directors even write and produce the film. Directors are in charge of all technical aspects, and they have to make dozens of decisions every day about the minor details (change the buttons on a character's costume) and the major ones (reshoot the ending at a cost of a million dollars). They conduct rehearsals with the actors and approve the costumes, sets, location, lighting, choreography, and music. A director tries to get the most suspense, comedy, or drama out of the script while at the same time eliciting the best possible performances from the actors. Some actors pursue projects with particular directors who are known for drawing out strong (think Academy Award) performances; those directors are referred to as "actors' directors." Other directors are more famous for choreographing explosions and fight scenes.

The duties of a director are sometimes so vast that he takes on an assistant director. The assistant director's duties vary with the director's needs; in general, an assistant director sees to organizing extras, transporting equipment, and arranging for food and accommodations while the film shoots on location. The assistant director may also shoot some of the film's minor scenes.

Education: Film schools are popular starting places for many of the current up-and-coming directors. However, other professionals, such as photographers and commercial directors, may become movie directors.

Aspiring directors can enroll in a training program offered by the DGA.

Clothes: Directors wear whatever is comfortable. Casual clothing is generally preferred due to the long hours of shooting, especially when outdoors.

Earnings: The Directors Guild of America has a pay scale that dictates earnings (for specific amounts see www.dga.org). In 2000, the median annual earnings for directors was $41,030. The middle 50 percent earned between $29,000 and $60,330. The lowest 10 percent earned less than $21,050; the highest 10 percent, more than $87,770. Median annual earnings in the industries employing the largest numbers of producers and directors were as follows:

- Motion picture production and services: $50,280
- Producers, orchestras, and entertainers: $38,820
- Radio and television broadcasting: $34,630

However, not all films are made under union contracts, so payment can vary widely. Also, director's earnings for a film may include points, a certain percentage of the money that the film makes.

Related Note: Many stage directors belong to the Society of Stage Directors and Choreographers (SSDC), and film and television directors belong to the Directors Guild of America (DGA). Earnings of stage directors vary greatly. According to the SSDC, summer theaters offer compensation, including royalties (based on the number of performances), usually ranging from $2,500 to $8,000 for a three- to four-week run. Directing a production at a dinner theater usually pays less than directing one at a summer theater but has greater potential for royalty income. Regional theaters may hire directors for longer periods, and compensation increases accordingly. The highest-paid stage directors work on Broadway and commonly earn $50,000 per production. They also can receive royalties—a negotiated percentage of gross box office receipts—that can exceed the contract fee for long-running box office successes.

Further Info:
- Directors Guild of America (DGA) (www.dga.org). Links and lots of info about being a director.
- Habbycam.com (www.habbycam.com/index.html). This site has a lot of information for those shooting film with digital video.
- Directors Guild—Producer Training Plan
  14724 Ventura Blvd., Suite 775
  Sherman Oaks, CA 91403
  E-mail: trainingprogram@dgptp.org

Further Reading:
- *The Director's Journey: The Creative Collaboration Between Directors, Writers, and Actors*, Mark W. Travis. Details each

step a director takes in developing and directing a script. Focuses on the collaborative nature of the job.

* *DGA Magazine* (www.dga.org/index2.php3?chg=). Provides information, articles, and interviews for professional directors.

Scriptwriter

Job Description: The screenwriter writes the screenplay for a movie—not as simple as it sounds. Sometimes a scriptwriter is hired to write a script based on someone else's idea, which may be nothing more than a sentence ("Two guys steal a car that, unbeknownst to them, has plutonium in it."). Sometimes the script is to be adapted from a novel (*The Silence of the Lambs*), a short story (*In the Bedroom*), a magazine article (*Perfect*), a nonfiction book (*Black Hawk Down*), or even a poem (*Gunga Din*).

The process of writing scripts is painful because writers receive so many suggestions for improvement from so many sources. These suggestions, called notes, come from executives, actors, directors, producers, and even the relatives and lovers of those groups. To make matters worse, the notes often conflict. Nevertheless, the scriptwriter forges ahead, all the while knowing she can be replaced any time at the whim of the producer, director, or actors. A final script may get rewritten fifty times from the time it is greenlighted (given the go-ahead to be made) until the first day of principal photography (when the first frames of film are shot).

Even if the final movie credits show only one or two names for writing, many people probably were involved. It's not unusual for ten or more writers to work on a script. Sometimes only a few pages or even a few lines from a scriptwriter remain in the final script. The efforts of some of the scriptwriters are thrown out altogether.

Many writers make a good living without ever having a script produced. Instead, they work as script doctors, hired to analyze scripts that have already been bought but need work. Some script doctors specialize in comedy, action, dialogue, etc.

The conventional wisdom around Hollywood is that the

scriptwriter is the least powerful member of the filmmaking team. In fact, once a film starts shooting, the writer is generally not welcome on the set unless emergency rewrites are needed. This lack of respect is one issue that the WGA is fighting to rectify.

Hollywood buys the movie rights to many books, but the authors of those books rarely write the screenplays. Why? Good novelists don't always make good screenwriters. While a novel may be 400 pages long, a typical movie script is only about 95 to 120 pages long (each page is roughly equal to one minute of film). Boiling those 400 pages down to 100 pages is a tricky task, and many authors are too protective of their material— unwilling or unable to cut, revise, and perhaps even rethink the story. For example, the Clint Eastwood movie *Absolute Power* is based on a best-selling novel, and the screenplay was written by William Goldman (*Butch Cassidy and the Sundance Kid*, *Marathon Man*, etc.), one of the best and most successful screenwriters in Hollywood and a best-selling novelist himself. He solved the problem of translating a long, complex story to a script by eliminating the novel's main character and elevating a minor character to protagonist status. A script requires that concepts and events be shown and implied rather than discussed. This is an art in itself, one that writers who are brilliant in other genres cannot always master.

Related Note: Television writers on the staff of a series have a little more job security than most other Hollywood writers. However, the demands of writing for a weekly series can take a toll on one's emotions and stamina. Also, it is not uncommon for a staff writer to work on a successful show for several years, get lured away to be the head writer (the writer in charge of the writing staff) of a new show, only to have the new show get cancelled after a few episodes or never even air. That writer may then have trouble getting another job because so many writers are available to fill the jobs. One reason so many writers are willing to take this risk, aside from the hefty paychecks, is the opportunity to create a successful series, which could bring them fame and millions of dollars.

Education: No formal education is required; a scriptwriter just needs a script that someone wants to buy. Many writers do attend film school. Screenwriters, unlike other fiction writers, have to be able to work quickly and take direction. This discipline is also valuable in copywriters and reporters, which is why many screenwriters have such backgrounds. Some scriptwriters have written for educational films or worked in government audiovisual departments.

TV writers also come from all walks of life. Amateurs wishing to break into the business usually write a spec script for an existing TV series then try to get an agent to submit it to the show's producers. Sometimes the writer sends it in herself and it actually gets read. If the script is good or shows tremendous writing ability, it may be purchased, or the writer may be hired for a writing assignment. TV series usually have a staff of writers who work together to write and rewrite scripts. Some writers get their start on a TV show by first working as production assistants (PAs). A PA generally runs errands, such as delivering scripts to the actors. Because PAs are so intimately familiar with the requirements of a particular show's scripts, those staffers may easily adapt to the writing needs of that show.

Clothes: Scriptwriters need not abide by a specific dress code.

Number of Scriptwriters: In one year, aspiring writers might register thirty thousand scripts with the WGA; (this process aims to protect script ideas from being stolen). According to the producers who have to read these scripts, most of them are terrible and have no hope of ever being made into movies. Then again, with only four hundred to five hundred scripts being made annually in Hollywood, the odds aren't good even for a brilliant script.

The proliferation of books and community college classes on scriptwriting—as well as the potential for fame, fortune, and hobnobbing with celebrities—lures a lot of people to try their hand at scriptwriting. Most never finish a script, and those that do finish and register a script often can't find an agent who will represent it. Nevertheless, every year some unknown waitress or cook or mail carrier comes out of nowhere and sells her script for a lot of money—and suddenly another ten thousand scriptwriters are hard at work at their PCs.

Earnings: The WGA sets a detailed and complex scale for payments to scriptwriters (for specific amounts see www.wga .org/producers_index.html). However, not all films are made under union contracts, so writers' earnings can widely vary.

Further Info:

- Writers Guild of America, West (www.wga.org) and Writers Guild of America, East (www.wgae.org). The WGA site provides a list of many other screenwriters' professional associations.
- ScriptCrawler.net (www.scriptcrawler.net/). You can find TV, movie, and radio scripts here.

Further Reading:

- *Adventures in the Screen Trade* and *Which Lie Did I Tell?*, William Goldman. Both books are invaluable for understanding the profession of screenwriting.
- *Monster*, John Gregory Dunne. An excellent account of Dunne and his wife-co-writer Joan Didion's surreal experiences as screenwriters of *Up Close & Personal.*
- *The Writer Got Screwed (but Didn't Have To): A Guide to the Legal and Business Practices of Writing for the Entertainment Industry*, Brooke Wharton. An excellent guide to the legalities of being a writer.
- *Scenario.* A magazine that features several complete screenplays in each issue.
- *Creative Screenwriting* (www.creativescreenwriting.com). A magazine that offers interviews with professional screenwriters.
- *Written By.* The official magazine of the WGA.
- *Screentalk* (www.screentalk.org). An international magazine of screenwriting with interviews and instructional articles.

Actor

Note: *Actor* is now generally used to refer to both males and females. Many females prefer this term to *actress.*

Job Description: An actor's job is to portray a character. An actor can be hired for a lead or starring role, a supporting role, or an extra role. An extra is a person you see in the background and has no speaking lines (actors who have lines get paid more money). Lead roles usually go to actors with some box office draw. Most of the time, a major star doesn't have to audition for a part; a script is sent to him in hopes that he'll agree to act in it. Sometimes a major star who wishes to change how she is perceived by the public will ask to audition for a part that she might not otherwise have been considered for.

Once the major roles have been cast, usually by agreement of the director and producer, the other roles are cast. A casting director is usually hired, he proposes certain actors for certain parts, and the director and producer have the final say as to who gets cast.

Actors approach their craft in all kinds of ways. Some so immerse themselves in a part that they are completely different in each role (e.g., Meryl Streep, Cate Blanchett, Guy Pierce). Others tend to rely on their own personality traits to define every character they play. In fact, the audience goes to see them precisely because they want to see that personality again and again. When such actors try to flex their acting ability by playing roles too far outside the box, the audiences stay away.

Actors may arrive at the set at four or five in the morning and stay there until eight or nine at night. They may have to endure hours of makeup (e.g., Rebecca Romijn-Stamos in *X-Men*). They may face hours of boredom when there is nothing for them to do—perhaps a shot is being set up which requires the lights to be arranged, the cameras to be positioned, and the extras to be instructed. (This is one reason many actors have the fancy trailers one reads about so often. They have a place to wait and things to occupy that time.) During this time, the stars' stand-ins are used. The stand-ins literally stand in the place where the star will be, so the lighting can be arranged properly. When the scene is ready to shoot, the actor may have to do the scene more than once. Some directors, such as Clint Eastwood, do only a few takes of a scene then move on. Others, such as Stanley Kubrick, shoot the same scene dozens of times. This can be exhausting, both physically and creatively, for actors, and tempers can flare on a particularly taxing shoot.

The average actor does not have a trailer, a trainer, or any other special perks. She goes on countless auditions and sits in a waiting room with dozens of other actors seeking the same part. They read some lines for the casting director, director, and producer (the panel may vary) and are dismissed with a "Nice job. We'll be in touch."

To become a movie extra, one must usually be listed by a casting agency, such as Central Casting, a no-fee agency that supplies extras to the major movie studios in Hollywood. Applicants are accepted only when the number of persons of a particular type on the list—for example, athletic young women, old men, or small children—falls below the foreseeable need. In recent years, only a very small proportion of applicants has succeeded in being listed.

Education: No specific degree is required for acting. Some successful actors have studied extensively at famous acting schools; others have had no formal training at all. However, many believe a natural acting ability can be honed and perfected by attending acting school or participating in acting workshops. Most colleges and universities have acting programs, and some even offer a focus in acting for the screen, which is very different than acting for the stage. Over five hundred colleges and universities offer bachelor's, master's, and doctoral degrees in dramatic and theater arts.

Some experience in any of the following is helpful: modeling, singing, dancing, performing in commercials, and performing in regional theater or summer stock.

Clothes: While acting, an actor wears the designated wardrobe.

Earnings: As of 2001, SAG and AFTRA actors with speaking parts earn a minimum daily rate of $636 or a rate of $2,206 for a five-day week. Actors also receive contributions to their health and pension plans and additional compensation for reruns and foreign telecasts of the productions in which they appear. (For a detailed schedule of payments, go to www.sag.com.) According to Actors' Equity Association (Equity), the minimum weekly salary for actors in Broadway productions as of 2001 was $1,252. Since 2000, actors in Off-Broadway theaters received minimums ranging from $440 to $551 a week, depending on the seating capacity of the theater. Regional theaters that operate under an Equity agreement pay actors $500 to $728 per week. For touring productions, actors receive an additional $106 per day for living expenses ($112 per day in larger, higher-cost cities). According to Equity, fewer than 15 percent of its dues-paying members actually worked during any given week during 2000. Median earnings for actors in the theater able to find employment in 2000 were less than $10,000.

Annual income is generally low because of the sporadic nature of the work. The Actors' Equity Association reports that in any given week only about 15 percent of its members are employed. During a year, only half of the membership will receive any pay at all for performing. The median annual earnings for actors in all mediums in 2000 was $25,920. The middle 50 percent earned between $16,950 and $59,769. The lowest 10 percent earned less than $12,700, and the highest 10 percent earned more than $93,620. Median annual earnings in the industries employing the largest numbers of actors were as follows:

- Motion picture production and services: $54,440
- Producers, orchestras, and entertainers: $28,310
- Miscellaneous amusement and recreation services: $13,500

The average income that SAG members earn from acting, less than $5,000 a year, is low because employment is erratic. Therefore, most actors must supplement their incomes by holding jobs in other fields.

However, an actor is paid according to drawing power at the box office. Therefore, stars such as Julia Roberts, Harrison Ford, and Arnold Schwarzenegger can earn $20 million or more per movie—such earnings are reserved for a very few actors. Even those who earn that $20 million take hits for taxes, the agent's 10 to 20 percent, a manager's 10 to 20 percent, possibly another percentage for a lawyer (sometimes the manager might also be a lawyer), and a publicist. Of the nearly 100,000 SAG members, only about 50 might be considered stars.

The amount of money an actor earns is usually related to the final budget of the film. If a major star wants to do a smaller film he may willingly take less money. Most actors do not earn enough to make a living. In fact, a favorite Hollywood joke is

Young Man: "I'm an actor."
Other Guy: "At what restaurant?"

Further Info:
- Screen Actors Guild. Represents actors working in television and motion pictures.
- Actors' Equity Association
  165 W. Forty-sixth St.
  New York, NY 10036
  www.actorsequity.org
  Represents stage actors.
- American Federation of Television and Radio Artists
  4340 East-West Hwy., Suite 204
  Bethesda, MD 20814
  The ActorSource Homepage(www.actorsource.com/). Information for new and veteran actors.

Further Reading:
- *If Chins Could Kill: Confessions of a B Movie Actor*, Bruce Campbell. This star of *Armies of Darkness* and the *Xena: Warrior Princess* TV series discusses his career.
- *How to Be a Working Actor: An Insider's Guide to Finding Jobs in Theater, Film, and Television*, Mari Lyn Henry and Lynne Rogers.
- *You Can Work On-Camera!: Acting in Commercials and Corporate Films*, John Leslie Wolfe and Brenna McDonough. Provides much-needed training for actors aspiring to work in a range of media, including television commercials, corporate films, and video communications.

Talent Agent, Literary Agent

Job Description: A talent agent represents most of the "above the line" people associated with making a film. Producers, directors, writers, and actors all have at least one agent. Because agents often specialize in a specific medium (television, movies, theater, books), several agents may be needed. Agents help find jobs for their clients, negotiate employment contracts, and generally guide their clients' careers. To that end, an agent spends her day reading scripts, interacting with clients and potential clients, and making and maintaining industry contacts.

There are several large Hollywood agencies, such as the William Morris Agency, but the majority are smaller houses, sometimes with only a few employees. Typically, these smaller houses employ one or two licensed agents and several interns who act as readers.

Small agencies commonly complain that they discover unknown talent and nurture those people's careers to the breakthrough to the big bucks, only to be dumped in favor of larger, glitzier agencies.

Agents can have close personal relationships with their clients—after all, the clients place their futures in their agents' hands. They can become close friends and confidants. On the other hand, business is business, and a client who doesn't think the agent is doing whatever he can to promote the client's career will fire him, close friend or not.

Scriptwriters often complain that getting an agent is harder than selling a script. This can be true: Because of the number of scripts submitted, not just from professional scriptwriters but also from wanna-bes everywhere, Hollywood is constantly awash with thousands of scripts. A hierarchy has been established so the bad scripts get filtered out and the higher-ups see only those with real potential. Agents are one filter in this hierarchy, which is why major studios rarely read a script not submitted through an agent.

The top agents are elite in Hollywood, making multimillion-dollar deals and demanding producer credits on films they're associated with. Some have aspirations of becoming producers, and several have gone on to make movies.

Education: No specific education is required, though most agents have a college education and started out by apprenticing at an agency. A recent trend in Hollywood is the proliferation of lawyer-agents who offer the bonus of legal expertise in negotiating contracts. Agents must be licensed by the state.

Clothes and Tools: Because an agent spends so much time on the phone, a hands-free headset is essential.

Earnings: An agent generally takes 10 to 20 percent of a client's earnings. However, some powerful agents also insist on a producer credit, for which they receive a separate amount.

Professional Associations:
- The Association of Authors' Representatives, Inc. (AAR) is a not-for-profit organization of independent literary and dramatic agents.
  P.O. Box 237201, Ansonia Station
  New York, NY 10003
  www.aar-online.org/

Further Info:
- Writers Guild of America, West (www.wga.org). Offers a list of agents.
- Screen Actors Guild (http://216.10.108.26/agents/). Offers a list of franchised agents.

Further Reading:
- *2002 Guide to Literary Agents (Guide to Literary Agents)*, Rachel Vater.
- *Writer's Guide to Book Editors, Publishers, and Literary Agents, 2002–2003: Who They Are! What They Want! And How to Win Them Over!*, Jeff Herman.
- *Literary Agents: What They Do, How They Do It, and How to Find and Work With the Right One for You, Revised and Expanded*, Michael Larsen.
- *The Publishers Weekly*. Covers the publishing industry and gives information about book deals and Hollywood deals involving books.

Reader

Job Description: Readers are the backbone of the movie industry, despite the fact that they are on a lower rung of the career ladder. This is a starting point for many who wish to work their way up within a production company or talent agency. A reader reads a script then writes coverage, which describes the plot and includes the reader's opinion of the script, particularly as to whether the film merits pursuing. Bad coverage from a reader can immediately kill a script's chances because that coverage can stay with a script as it moves to various production companies or studios. Ironically, the reader who assassinates a script is not likely to be highly trained or even especially literate in movies (hence the universal rejection by readers of the script for *Casablanca* when it was recently submitted to various studios under a different name).

This is a temporary position, often filled by part-timers, many of whom are students. Readers either get promoted up from this job or pushed out. It's not a career.

Education: No specific education is required, but most readers come from a college background, usually with a major in English, film, or theater.

Earnings: Readers who are interns receive no pay other than the experience they can then note on a resume. Other readers are paid per script covered; the rate usually ranges from $25 to $100 per script, though it can be higher.

Casting Director

Job Description: The casting director reads a script then brainstorms with a director over what types of actors are needed. She holds auditions or assembles actors she's familiar with. To prevent offering just the same pool of actors, she has to constantly search for new talent. This involves scouting regional and college theaters.

Education: No specific education is required, but a casting director can benefit from a degree in communications, radio, TV and film, or even acting. Even with a degree, however, one still may have to work without pay as a casting intern or volunteer to get experience.

Earnings: Depending upon the film's budget, the casting director earns between $40,000 and $200,000 per film.

Professional Associations:
- Casting Society of America (CSA) (www.castingsociety.com/). An organization of professional casting directors from films, television, and theater.

Further Info:
- Future Casting 2000 (www.futurecasting2000.com/newsletter
.htm). A newsletter with excellent articles about the business.
- Casting Managers.com (http://castingmanagers.com). A Web
site for professional casting directors.
- *The Casting Director*, Bea Silvern, Light Lab Productions, and
Chip Taylor Communications, producers. Selecting the right
person for the right acting role is an important behind-the-
scenes task, and this video recording gives viewers valuable
insights. Also, this program offers viewers the chance to learn
firsthand the entire process of how actors and actresses work
with a casting director.

Further Reading:
- *The Back Stage Guide to Casting Directors*, Hettie Lynne
Hurtes. This book provides invaluable information for the
established casting director as well as the person interested
in becoming a casting director.
- *Film Producers, Studios, Agents, and Casting Directors
Guide*, 6th ed., David M. Kipen, ed.

Art Director
Job Description: The art director designs sets in order to create
the appropriate mood for movies and other productions. They
supervise the people involved in creating these sets, including
illustrators, scenic designers, model makers, carpenters, painters, electricians, laborers, set decorators, costume designers,
and makeup and hairstyling artists. Some art directors have
used the position to gain entry into directing and producing.
Art directors often work in movies, television, and theater.

Education: Art direction courses are offered at many colleges
and universities. These students usually get hands-on experience by designing and building sets for school productions.

Clothes: Casual clothing is appropriate for art directors.

Cinematographer/Camera Work
Job Description: A cinematographer composes camera shots
that capture the mood, tone, or inflection the director wants.

Cinematographers don't usually run the cameras; instead they plan the appropriate shots and then coordinate the filming.

The camera operators run the cameras. They use television, video, or motion picture cameras to shoot a wide range of subjects, including motion pictures, television series, studio programs, news and sporting events, music videos, documentaries, and training sessions. Videographers specialize in filming on videotape and work mostly for independent television stations, local affiliates, large cable and television networks, or small independent production companies. Studio camera operators work in a broadcast studio and usually videotape from a fixed position their subjects. News camera operators, also called electronic news gathering (ENG) operators, are part of a reporting team and generally work in the field. ENG operators may need to edit raw footage in the field and transmit it to a television affiliate for broadcast.

Camera operators in entry-level jobs set up lights, cameras, and other equipment. They may also be permitted to do minor camera adjustments or offer suggestions concerning what subject matter to capture. Camera operators in the film and television industries usually are hired for projects based on recommendations from individuals such as producers, directors of photography, and camera assistants whom they have worked with or through interviews with producers.

A camera operator needs a sharp eye, artistic inclination, and hand-eye coordination. They also need the strength to hold a camera for extended periods.

Self-employed camera operators must know how to submit bids, write contracts, get permission to shoot at locations that generally are not open to the public, obtain releases to use video images of people, price their services, secure copyright protection for their work, and keep financial records.

Camera operators and editors may become directors of photography for movie studios, advertising agencies, or television programs. Some teach at technical schools, film schools, or universities.

Assistant camera operators are responsible for the care, transportation, and setup of the cameras. They operate the slate and slapstick, which are now electronic.

The director of photography plans the lighting needs. This is more important than the average moviegoer may realize. Some actors are so self-conscious about lighting—it can make one look significantly younger or older—that they use their own lighting experts whenever they are photographed.

Gaffers are technicians who set up lighting according to the direction of the director of photography.

The best boy grip assists the gaffer.

A boom operator holds a long pole that has a microphone on the end. The microphone is extended to be as close to an actor as possible without getting into the shot.

Education: For cinematographers and camera operators, a formal education is becoming more desirable, along with apprenticeship training. A solid technical understanding of camera operation is essential. Camera operators go through on-the-job training or complete formal postsecondary training at vocational schools, colleges, universities, or photographic institutes. Formal education may be required for some positions. Many universities and community colleges, vocational and technical institutes, and private trade schools offer courses in camera operation and videography. Basic courses cover equipment, processes, and techniques.

Earnings: Median annual earnings for television, video, and motion picture camera operators were $27,870 in 2000. The middle 50 percent earned between $19,230 and $44,150. The lowest 10 percent earned less than $14,130, and the highest 10 percent earned more than $63,690. Median annual earnings for camera operators were $31,560 in motion picture production and services and $23,470 in radio and television broadcasting. In general, the cinematographer earns between $1,000 and $25,000 per week during filming.

Further Info:
- The International Alliance of Theatrical Stage Employees (IATSE)
  1430 Broadway, 20th Floor
  New York, NY 10018
  Phone: (212) 730-1170
  www.iatse.lm.com

- American Society of Cinematographers (www.cinematograph er.com). A global community for cinematographers that contains information on film festivals, new tools, resources, and more.
- Society of Operating Cameramen
  P.O. Box 2006
  Toluca Lake, CA 91610
  Phone: (818) 382-7070
  www.soc.org

Further Reading:
- *The Five C's of Cinematography: Motion Picture Filming Techniques*, Joseph V. Mascelli.
- *Practical Cinematography*, Paul Wheeler.

Editor

Job Description: The editor arranges all the shot film to make the most powerful movie possible. Many more hours of film are shot than are ever seen in a movie, because each scene is shot from different angles or with different acting interpretations. Also, scenes are shot out of sequence, meaning, for example, the ending may be shot first. The editor tries to capture the tone of each scene by selecting the best angle, close-up, etc., and he works to put together footage that reveals the best combination of photography, performance, consistency, and timing. Timing is a key element in editing, because different genres require different kinds of timing. For example, comic scenes were cut from the original cut of *Butch Cassidy and the Sundance Kid* after preview audiences laughed too much at certain scenes. The filmmakers felt that the wrong tone was being conveyed. In particular scenes, a comic moment that might get a big laugh from an audience needs to have some buffer space after it so the audience doesn't laugh over any important dialogue. Editing is a specialized skill in that a good editor can heighten the impact of a scene while a bad editor can destroy it altogether.

Generally, the editor works closely with the director (and many directors started out as editors). In addition, editors work with sound effects editors to determine the movie's sound requirements—which are fulfilled by recording any specific sounds needed or getting them from a sound effects library—and incorporate the sound track into the appropriate places in the film.

Increasing numbers of movie and television productions are edited on computer editing equipment, which most newer filmmakers insist on using. Many feature films are still edited in the traditional way on viewing devices known as Moviolas or flatbed editing machines, but this too is changing. Traditionally, editors run strips of film through these machines at various speeds. They mark frames where a particular shot or piece of sound is to begin or end. After the scenes are edited, assistant editors use a splicer to join separate strips of film. The sequences are then ready for viewing. Computer editing uses personal computers and special software to rearrange film sequences. The television industry does much of its work on videotape rather than film. Videotape editing requires special training on the electronic equipment used in the editing process.

Assistant editors also prepare work for editors, ordering whatever is needed, maintaining schedules, arranging screenings for the directors and producers, supervising apprentices, and providing necessary general support to film editors.

Film editors do most of their work in cutting rooms, projection rooms, and on shooting stages. Modern cutting rooms usually have space for three or four editing benches, viewing machines, and film bins. Deadlines and high production costs bring a lot of pressure on editors, who work on average forty to sixty hours per week.

Los Angeles, where major television shows and motion pictures are produced, hosts most of the editing jobs; some of these jobs are in the San Francisco Bay area and larger metropolitan areas. In Los Angeles employment is often seasonal (the peak hiring period in television is from July through February). Editors who work on educational or industrial films generally don't experience seasonal fluctuations in employment.

Education: An editor generally has a formal education as well as apprenticeship training. Editors often start out as editing room assistants.

Number of Editors: There are approximately 3,690 film editors in the U.S.

Earnings: Median annual earnings for film and video editors were $34,160 in 2000. The middle 50 percent earned between $24,800 and $52,000. The lowest 10 percent earned less than $18,970, and the highest 10 percent earned more than $71,280. Median annual earnings were $36,770 for film editors in motion picture production and services, the industry employing the largest numbers of film and video editors. In 1997, California film editors earned an average of $23.48 per hour and a median wage of $22.98 per hour. Pay rates in films are a little higher than rates in television because they require different degrees of skill. However, because of the nature of the film business, an editor may work only a few weeks a year. Most editors work on a freelance basis. Editors receive up to four times their hourly rate when they work more than twelve consecutive hours on weekends and holidays.

Professional Associations: Most film editors belong to IATSE, while editors in the television industry are affiliated with the National Association of Broadcast Employees and Technicians (NABET), the International Brotherhood of Electrical Workers (IBEW), or are covered by an industrial union agreement.
- American Cinema Editors
  100 Universal City Plaza, Building 2282, Room 234
  Universal City, CA 91608
  www.ace-filmeditors.org
  e-mail: amercinema@earthlink.net
- Motion Picture Editors Guild of the International Alliance of Theatrical Stage Employees (www.editorsguild.com). To contact IATSE Local 700, call (800) 705-8700.
  - West Coast Office
    7715 Sunset Blvd., Suite 200
    Hollywood, CA 90046
    Phone: (323) 876-4770
    Fax: (323) 876-0861
  - East Coast Office
    165 W. Forty-sixth St., Suite 900

New York, NY 10036
Phone: (212) 302-0700
Fax: (212) 302-1091

- National Association of Broadcast Employees and Technicians (NABET)
  433 Natoma St., Suite 220
  San Francisco, CA 94103
  Phone: (415) 398-3160
  www.nabet51.org
- National Association of Broadcasters
  1771 N St., NW
  Washington, DC 20036
  Phone: (202) 429-5300
  www.nab.org
- International Brotherhood of Electrical Workers (IBEW)
  1125 Fifteenth St., NW
  Washington, DC 20005
  Phone: (202) 833-7000
  www.ibew.org

Further Info:
- The Writers Guild of America (www.wga.org) offers a list of agents.

Further Reading:
- *The Film Editing Room Handbook: How to Manage the Near Chaos of the Cutting Room*, Norman Hollyn.
- *Technique of Film Editing*, Karel Reisz and Gavin Millar.
- *Guide to Post-production for TV and Film: Managing the Process*, Barbara Clark and Susan J. Spohr.
- *On Film Editing: An Introduction to the Art of Film Construction*, Edward Dmytryk.
- *When the Shooting Stops, the Cutting Begins: A Film Editor's Story*, Ralph Rosenblum and Robert Karen, Ph.D.

Additional Occupations

The credits at the end of a film can give you an idea of all the people involved in producing one film. The number of people involved is often directly proportional to the budget:

the bigger the budget, the higher the number of people. Small-budget films and documentaries are often shot with a small crew. Following are a few of these other positions:

- cartoonist
- costume designer
- location scout
- manager
- musical director
- scenic artist
- set designer
- sound technician
- stunt coordinator

Most employment in this industry is centered around Los Angeles and New York City. Studios are also located in Florida, Texas, and North Carolina. Because it's cheaper to shoot in Canada, many movies are shot there, with Toronto doubling for Los Angeles and other U.S. cities. Most opportunities in television production are in Los Angeles, New York City, Chicago, and Atlanta. Employers for the above positions include the following:

- movie studios
- advertising agencies
- industries for industrial documentaries
- recording companies for music videos

Exact numbers of jobs are difficult to establish because so many people in the industry are freelancers, contract workers, or part-timers. As of 1998, there were 270,000 wage and salary jobs in motion picture production and distribution. Seven major studios produce most of the feature films in the U.S. However, there are also many smaller independent production companies that produce movies. Most motion picture and distribution companies employ fewer than ten workers.

Moviemakers in Nonfiction

Books
Thousands of books deal with the film industry; the following titles are a small taste to get you started.

- *All You Need to Know About the Movie and T.V. Business,* Gail Resnik and Scott Trost. A guide by two entertainment attorneys about jobs in the business.
- *Breaking & Entering: Land Your First Job in Film Production,* April Fitzsimmons. Extensive description of the day-to-day workings on a movie set as well as valuable information for how to pursue a career in one of the many areas of filmmaking.
- *How to Make It in Hollywood: All the Right Moves,* Linda Buzzell. Linda Buzzell, a renowned psychotherapist and career counselor, explains Hollywood jobs, and how to get hired and advance in them.

Documentaries
- "Our Hollywood Education" (1992). Interviews with various people in the business.
- *American Movie* (1999). A disturbing and fascinating account of a man obsessed with making his own low-budget movies.
- *Project Greenlight* (2001). An HBO documentary series that follows a first-time director shooting from his own script. Lots of insight to the complications a director faces.

Moviemakers in Fiction

This is territory well mined, particularly by many disillusioned screenwriters who thumb their noses at terrible people they've encountered in Hollywood. This is just a sampling of the many works that have chronicled Hollywood, and the audiences' appetite for more will certainly be satisfied.

Books
- *Children of Light,* Robert Stone. A literary novel about the dark underbelly of modern Hollywood.
- *The Day of the Locust,* Nathanael West. This dark novel about 1930s Hollywood was made into the 1975 movie.
- *Force Majeure,* Bruce Wagner. A Hollywood novel by a professional screenwriter.
- *Hollywood Wives,* Jackie Collins. A glitzy story of the "sexca-

pades" of Hollywood wives.
- *The Player*, Michael Tolkin. Screenwriter (*The Rapture*) Tolkin gives an insider's account of greed and ambition in Hollywood.
- *Postcards From the Edge*, Carrie Fisher. A comic, yet edgy, account of life in Hollywood's fast lane. Fisher is an actress (*Star Wars*) and acclaimed scriptwriter. This novel was made into a movie starring Meryl Streep.
- *Somebody's Darling*, Larry McMurtry. This acclaimed novelist details the life of a fictional female director and her personal struggles.
- *What Makes Sammy Run?*, Budd Schulberg. Perhaps the best Hollywood novel ever written, this story captures the ruthless ambition that drives so many in the business.

Movies
- *Valley of the Dolls* (1967). A movie about a group of women affected by show business. Based on the famous glitz novel.
- *Medium Cool* (1969). A compelling account of a TV cameraman who prefers the distance from people that viewing life through a camera gives him.
- *Day for Night* (1973). An excellent François Truffaut film about the troubles a director has filming a love story. French.
- *Network* (1976). A scathing satire about television programming and network news.
- *Hooper* (1978). Burt Reynolds portrays a stuntman in this film that shows lots of details about movie stunts.
- *The Stunt Man* (1980). A black comedy with depth set in the world of filmmaking and stunts.
- *Modern Romance* (1981). An Albert Brooks film in which he plays a film editor with romance problems. Has an interesting scene showing how an editor works.
- *Sweet Liberty* (1986). A solid Alan Alda film about the havoc created when Hollywood comes to a small town to make a movie. (See David Mamet's *State and Main* [2000] for a similar plot concept.)
- *Mistress* (1992). This picture follows a washed-up writer and the compromises he must make to raise the money to make his own film.

- *The Player* (1992). Veteran director Robert Altman's satiric drama about the shallowness of Hollywood filmmakers.
- *I'll Do Anything* (1994). A struggling actor (Nick Nolte) raises a young daughter whose fame eclipses his own. Includes a great monologue about acting.
- *Get Shorty* (1995). Based on the Elmore Leonard novel, this comic film is about a loan shark (John Travolta) who comes to Hollywood and ends up making movies.
- *Search and Destroy* (1995). Adapted from a play, this film satirizes Hollywood types in search of spiritual fulfillment.
- *Bowfinger* (1999). A hilarious story of an indie producer loser (Steve Martin) making a low-budget film by exploiting a star's twin brother (Eddie Murphy).

Television

- *Action* (1999). A satiric sitcom about the treachery of show business.
- *Beggers and Choosers* (1999–2001). A Showtime original series that satirically depicts the struggles at a television network.

Web Sites

These sites offer general information.

- **Academy of Motion Picture Arts and Sciences (www.oscars .org).** The Academy does more than just produce the Academy Awards.

- **Sundance Institute (www.sundance.org).** Information about this haven run by actor-producer-director Robert Redford for independent filmmakers.

- **IATSE Local 695 (www.695.com).** Local 695 represents sound technicians, videotape engineers, and television broadcast engineers.

- **UniqueFilms.com (www.uniquefilms.com).** This commercial Web site for filmmakers also offers many links related to various aspects of moviemaking.

- **Independent Feature Project (www.ifp.org).** Information on independent films and the independent film industry.

- **The Internet Movie Database (www.imdb.com).** The best site for information about specific movies.

- **Variety.com (www.variety.com).** The latest news about the business of making movies and television shows.

- **Film-Makers.com (www.film-makers.com/).** An online starting point for filmmakers.

- **Vocational Information Center (http://vocationalinformati oncenter.freeservers.com).** Excellent descriptions of film making jobs include lots of details.

BOOK EXCERPTS

''You have to understand, it's a very difficult job. I see people all day long. My phone rings a hundred times a day. Take all the stories that are presented to the studio, either in pitches, as scripts, or as books and magazine articles that get covered, and we are talking about seventy thousand stories a year.''

The door opened. Griffin got out. The short-haired man stayed with him, watching him. The hallway was quiet.

''I don't know how I can make it up to you. I'm sorry that I hurt people's feelings along the way. I'm trying to be better, I really am. But you're going too far. It's an incredibly difficult business. You can have great ideas, you can have all the talent in the world, but you have to get lucky.

And no one has the formula for luck. The only consolation to this is that you get

---

lucky, you look different, and then it gets easier.''

—The Player, Michael Tolkin

＊

As we descended into the smoky, rushing L.A. dusk, with the reptilian coil of freeways rippling like golden boas underneath us, I momentarily stopped believing in my own fantasy. Maybe I was not going to die suddenly. Maybe I was just going to get old.

Going to New York had been a mistake. Lots of people go away for a week and come home and step right back into their lives. That was the normally normal way. Having once been normal, I had even done it that way myself; but not this time. My life had no more permanence than a movie set. Turn your back for two minutes and someone would hitch it to a tractor and pull it to another part of the lot. It was a collapsible, storefront life, because it was without hope, the brick and mortar of any life.

—Somebody's Darling, Larry McMurtry

＊

Then I got nostalgic. I was always a soft guy, and I said:
Sure, kid, and remember, don't say ain't.
This was too much for Sammy. He didn't like it. He didn't like to be reminded. There are

two kinds of big shots: those who tell as
many people as they can that they started
out as newsboys at two dollars and peanuts
a week, and those who take every step as if
it were the only level they knew, those who
drive ahead in high speed and never bother
to look back to see where they've been. I
began to have a strong hunch that Sammy fell
roughly into the latter category, only more
so.

—What Makes Sammy Run?, Budd Schulberg

CHAPTER 14

Political Sciences

President, Member of the House of Representatives, Senator, Congressional Aide or Staffer, Lobbyist, Political Scientist, Political Cartoonist

The Lowdown

No profession seems to embody the concept of absolute power like that of politician does. Power implies that momentous decisions must be made, though not all politicians are worthy of erecting statues. The policy of national security seems to permit a lot of nasty deeds to go undiscovered or unpunished. In fact, the world of politics requires readers to constantly review their own moral stance. Readers might say lying is wrong, but they forgive lying by politicians if it's done in the national interest. But who decides what the national interest is? And what happens when a politician's career is intertwined with the national interest? Readers think murder is wrong, yet politicians might permit murder if it protects national security. For example, undercover operatives paid by the CIA to infiltrate terrorist cells are sometimes demanded by the terrorists to demonstrate loyalty to the cell by killing an innocent person. In order to uncover information that might prevent hundreds from dying, an operative has to execute an innocent person. Politicians sometimes have the responsibility of making decisions in these catch-22s.

This means the writer using politicians as characters has the opportunity to explore plots that have high stakes and hard-hitting themes. In addition, the writer can explore the various types of people who wish to be politicians, from the dedicated public servant to the power-hungry egotist anxious to find a place in history books rather than the hearts of the people.

Job Description

The politician survives in his post, a position of elected power, by continually seeking and winning reelection. Politicians inhabit all levels of government from the White House to Congress to the state assembly to city hall. Their basic mantra is the same: to serve the interests of the country (or state or city, etc.) and their constituents better than their opposition can. Politicians never work alone. Aggressively competitive, politicians rely heavily on the backing of political parties, as well as the fund-raising machinery that can help them get elected and enact their vision of government's role. In addition, they rely on a support system of campaign staff, media representatives, paid consultants, and financial advisors.

Politicians can introduce and vote on bills that are often rooted in deep convictions, such as campaign finance reform, health care reform, or national defense issues. Developing, nurturing, and seeing the implementation of one's own bill can be deeply satisfying. Serving constituents' interests, heading a successful reelection campaign, and working one's way up the political ladder boost a politician's self-image and enable them to use their elected power to make a difference. In addition, politicians' titles purchase a large number of perks from hobnobbing with the political and cultural elite to riding aboard Air Force One.

If reelection is seen as the reward for a previous term of good representation, then a successful politician is an often reelected one. Being a politician, regardless of one's level in government, requires a desire to represent and serve the public. In addition, a politician needs to have incredible stamina and energy to make it through arduous working hours and the disappointments of stalled or failed political agendas. An ability to clearly communicate and a personable character go far in ensuring a politician's success. A politician and a politician's staff must be able to raise an incredible amount of money to finance a future campaign. Fund-raising skills are therefore another hallmark of a successful politician. Other attributes the successful politician has include negotiation skills, little fear of compromise, and an openness to constituents' points of view.

Salary

A member of Congress makes in excess of $140,000 a year, with senators and members of the House of Representatives receiving the same amount, in accordance with the Constitution. Often, though, a politician's salary represents a pay cut compared to what she made prior to being elected. Staff members make anywhere from $116,000 for a chief of staff to $22,500 for a staff assistant. The salaries of state legislators vary greatly from state to state, with an average salary of $30,000 per year. For 1990–91, New Hampshire legislators earned only $200 a year, while New York paid its legislators $115,000. Some states don't offer a salary, instead paying between $10 and $75 per day of service for legislators in session. Many state legislators, therefore, hold other jobs. Governors earn between $35,000 and $85,000 annually and almost always live in a state-financed official residence.

Benefits

Federal politicians benefit from health insurance and federal retirement plans, and they have access to health club facilities. Current and past presidents and their families also receive Secret Service protection.

Expenses

Politicians usually receive an account to cover new staff and office expenses. A limited number of trips to and from a congressperson's home state are also paid for.

Daily Life

Work Schedule

Contrary to what we see in political cartoons, a politician doesn't spend half the day relaxing in a leather chair and smoking cigars. Most politicians begin work early each day, and may work late into the evening, putting in more than eighty hours of work per week. When on Capitol Hill, a politician begins the workday by going through the day's itinerary with his staff. He meets with other politicians, lobbyists, and constituents and spends a large part of the day in committees and hearings. Reading staff summaries and reports on pending legislation also consumes much of a politician's available time. Debating and voting on legislation are integral in a politician's day, and communicating with the press before and after the passage or defeat of a piece of legislation is also common. Putting in appearances at rallies, dedications, and fund-raising events can extend a politician's working hours. During a campaign, politicians may embark on whirlwind tours, hopping from place to place and meeting at rallies and events. The daily schedules during these months include strategy sessions and extensive press interviews.

Dressing the Part

While Congress is in session, the adopted standard of dress is business formal. While on the campaign trail, politicians may exchange their suits for jeans and rolled-up shirtsleeves as they try to appeal to the average voter.

Keys to the Kingdom

Politicians have access to the Capitol building as well as nearby federal office buildings. Members of Congress may also use private subway lines that run under Capitol Hill. The original portions were installed in 1909, and the updated system allows politicians to easily access nearby Rayburn House, as well as the offices in the Russell, Dirksen, and Hart buildings.

Tools of the Trade

A politician's most important tool is her persuasive ability in meetings, on the House or Senate floor, and in the media. In addition to speaking persuasively, a politician—and his staff—must be able to present clear, orderly written communication, in the form of letters, proposed bills, or statements on the bills of other members of Congress. A politician's primary tool is the phone, which she uses to talk to her constituents, her staff, lobbyists, the press, and other politicians.

Elbow Rubbing

A member of Congress meets with a number of professionals during the course of the day. These may be other congresspeople, staff members, aides, lobbyists, and news reporters and moderators. During the course of a reelection campaign, additional professionals cross a politician's path daily, including consultants, media staff, financial advisors, logistics personnel, press liaisons, and constituents.

Buzzwords

access: Face-to-face time with a politician. Given to lobbyists in exchange for contributions.

the ask: Naming a price for political access.

bait: Interested parties are given unique access (or *bait*), e.g., a round of golf with a congressman, to a politician in exchange for a contribution.

bundling: A collection of checks from members of a corporation. Given to a candidate to circumvent political contribution laws barring direct giving by a corporation.

maintenance: Caring for large financial contributors.

menu: A price list for various levels of political access.

republicrat: A lobbyist with no specific political party interest. Often a donor to the current power holders.

the zips: The zip codes of the most generous campaign contributors.

Education

While there aren't any formal education requirements for becoming a politician, most candidates hold at least a bachelor's degree, often in history, law, economics, finance, political science, urban affairs, or business administration. A background in marketing and public relations gives a potential politician a leg up, as does confidence in public speaking and debating. Many politicians, particularly in Washington, DC, have a law background. While a law degree certainly gives a politician a strong foundation as to the history, workings, and repercussions of laws, being a lawyer also means a politician is likely to find work should he lose an election or retire from politics.

Job Conflicts

Profession and Family

Especially at the local level, a life in the political arena offers little job security. Even the most successful politicians are at the mercy of the will of the voters and must bear the strain of a political loss. While in office, politicians may struggle with personal beliefs that are in opposition to those of her political party. The enormous sums of money required to run a campaign may necessitate the acceptance of lobbying funds—and with them the pressure of appeasing contributors if future legislation doesn't fall in their favor. Due to long hours and frequent travel, politicians often lack the time and energy for the kind of personal and family life they wish they could enjoy. Campaigns and terms in office can take their toll on family members as well: They find themselves displaced, under intense media scrutiny, and under familial obligation to let their lives be dictated by another's political career.

Too Much Exposure

Being a politician means being continuously in the public eye. Any disparaging comment or gaffe can be filmed, photographed, and played on the evening news. Like actors, politicians lack a sense of privacy and anonymity and lose a degree of freedom. The past can also be a specter for any politician in the intrusive glare of the limelight.

Forever Fund-Raising

It's not cheap being a politician. Even on the local level, vast amounts of money are needed to finance a campaign, the expenses of which range from staff salaries to logistical support to advertising and media time. The self-made millionaire may not find the fund-raising task to be as daunting as other politicians do, but even the richest politician needs assistance with U.S. Senate races now costing upwards of $63 million and U.S. House campaigns at $6 million. In 2000, the total spent on Senate campaigns in the State of New York was $91 million, with $11.5 million spent by candidates vying for one seat in the House of Representatives. These numbers pale in comparison to presidential campaigns. In 2000, George W. Bush raised and spent $185 million to Al Gore's $120 million. Considering the relative brevity of political terms, any elected politician wanting to serve more than once needs to begin raising funds for the next election as soon as he takes office. The groups who contribute the most include, in order of donation amounts, lawyers and law firms, retirees, health professionals, the real estate industry, securities companies, insurance companies, banks, unions, and political action committees (PACs).

Myths About the Job

Politicians Take Direction From Public Opinion Polls

Many people believe that a politician will alter her stance on an issue based on the results of public opinion polls. However, recent studies show that most politicians don't rely on or even conduct polls. Most politicians discount polling as imprecise and of little value. Instead, they formulate their positions on issues based on their personal beliefs and those they share with their political parties. When it comes to gauging public opinion, most politicians pay attention to the constituents in their home districts, through face-to-face meetings, incoming mail, and phone conversations.

Lobbyists Control Politicians

While it's true that politicians and political parties receive enormous amounts of money to help finance their campaigns, pandering to the highest bidder can be the surest way to fall under media scrutiny. If a politician's personal convictions and the needs of his electorate appear to be overruled by outside contributors, his election bid may prove difficult. While some lobbying money may be directed to particular politicians, much of it is donated to political parties. In addition, contributors often fund both candidates in an election as a step toward support from the election winner.

All Politicians Are Wealthy

True, you won't find many poor senators or members of the House, but politicians on Capitol Hill make up only a small fraction of the politicians in the U.S. Some politicians working in state assemblies may receive generous benefits, but many other politicians are paid almost nothing at all. Considering the many politicians working at the city and county level, wealth is hardly ubiquitous. Even at the federal level, it's safe to say that few become involved in politics for immediate financial gain. Many, in fact, take pay cuts. Wealth to be received from politics is more likely to come from postterm book contracts and speaking engagements.

Jobs Within the Profession

President

Job Description: The president is the nation's chief executive, enforcing and upholding the Constitution and laws of the U.S. The president appoints a cabinet to deal with domestic and foreign affairs, and he appoints federal judges, ambassadors, diplomats, and Supreme Court justices. In addition, the president has veto and pardon power, and he is the commander in chief of the armed forces. A presidential candidate must be at least thirty-five years old and a born U.S. citizen. The candidate must have resided in the U.S. for at least fourteen years and, if elected, is limited to two four-year terms. Presidential campaigns are kicked off at least a year before an election, and campaign offices are set up in every state.

Education: While there's no formal education requirement, a solid background and extensive experience serve a president well.

Earnings: $400,000 a year.

Further Info:
- GovSpot (www.govspot.com/executive). Provides information on the government's executive branch.

Member of the House of Representatives

Job Description: Members of the House of Representatives work for their constituents' interests. These congresspeople originate all revenue and tax bills. They serve two-year terms and are limited to one-hour debates on the floor. To be elected to the 435-seat House of Representatives, a candidate must be at least twenty-five years old, a resident of the state in which they are running, and a U.S. citizen for at least seven years.

Earnings: $140,000 a year.

Further Info:
- GovSpot (www.govspot.com/legislative). Provides information on the House of Representatives.

Senator

Job Description: A senator represents in Congress the interests of her home state. Senators have approval power for presidential appointees and are allowed to filibuster, or delay, legislation by talking for hours or days on end. Requirements include being thirty years of age, having been a U.S. citizen for nine years, and being a resident of the state from which they are elected. Senators serve six-year terms, and one-third of the one hundred senate seats are up for election every two years. Ninety percent of senatorial incumbents get reelected.

Earnings: $140,000 a year.

Further Info:
- GovSpot (www.govspot.com/legislative). Provides information on the Senate.
- Congressional Management Foundation
  513 Capital Court NE, Suite 300
  Washington, DC 20002
- Democratic National Committee
  430 South Capital St. SE
  Washington, DC 20003
- Republican National Committee
  310 First St. SE
  Washington, DC 20003

Congressional Aide or Staffer

Job Description: Congressional aides write and review letters and press releases as well as handle constituent correspondence and inquiries. They express and represent a politician's views in all communication and may speak for their employers when the elected officials are unavailable. Aides alert the media to important and favorable news about a representative or senator. Aides also monitor the news and media for reactions and stories and coordinate schedules.

Further Info:
- *Get a Job On Capitol Hill,* Stephanie Vance.
  (See www.fabjob.com/congress.asp?affiliate=232.)

Lobbyist

Job Description: A lobbyist can be an individual constituent who writes to his representative or a professional, paid by organizations, to garner favor with government officials. Lobbyists provide persuasive information, pressure, or enticements to reinforce or sway a politician's point of view and vote. Lobbyists often work for more than one interest. The largest lobbying efforts are conducted by business, labor, farming, and education organizations, including the American Medical Association, the American Bar Association, the National Rifle Association, and the National Wildlife Federation. Lobbyists' work hours must fit with politicians' schedules. While some restrictions mandate that an official must be out of office for a certain period of time before becoming a lobbyist, members of Congress are not subject to any such rule. Lobbyists who have formerly been officials or politicians in government will have an easier time gaining access to congressional members and staff.

Education: Knowledge of the workings of government, as well as a background in the subject matter of one's clients, are important for lobbyists.

Earnings: The amount lobbyists can make depends entirely on whom they represent and the success of their efforts.

Further Info:
- People's Lobby
  3456 W. Olympic Blvd.
  Los Angeles, CA 90019
- Women's Lobby
  201 Massachusetts Ave. NE
  Washington, DC 20002

Further Reading:
- *How to Lobby Congress: A Guide for the Citizen Lobbyist,* Donald deKieffer.

Political Scientist

Job Description: Political scientists study current and past political systems at all levels of government. They act as consultants to political parties, media organizations, politicians, and federal agencies. Political scientists may analyze election results, predict the outcome of political events, survey public opinion, and study the actions of political decisions, especially in the courts.

Education: Political scientists hold a minimum of a bachelor's degree in political science.

Earnings: Political scientists earned a median income of $81,000 in 2000.

Further Info:
- National Association of Schools of Public Affairs and Administration

1120 G St. NW, Suite 730
Washington, DC 20005
(www.naspaa.org)

Political Cartoonist

Job Description: Nearly as old as politics itself, political cartoonists caricaturize, satirize, mock, or support individuals, countries, corporations, or issues. The political cartoonist is the rarest breed among cartoonists. Most have a background in politics and history and work in metropolitan areas.

Education: A political cartoonist may have attended art school or studied cartooning. Political cartoonists must stay constantly abreast of current events and developments.

Further Info:
- Political Cartoons and Cartoonists (www.boondocksnet.com/gallery/pc_intro.html). Edited by Jim Zwick, this site covers the history of political cartoons.

Additional Occupations

Other professionals who play an important part in the running of government include

- campaign finance director
- chief of staff
- clerk
- communications director
- governor
- mayor
- office manager
- policy analyst
- press assistant
- press secretary
- school board member
- staff assistant
- state legislator

Employers for the above positions include the following:

- congressional office
- governor's office
- local, state, and national campaigns
- state legislative branch

Politicians in Nonfiction

Books
- *Campaign Strategies and Message Design: A Practitioner's Guide From Start to Finish*, Mary Anne Moffitt. Methods for communicating a winning campaign message.
- *Hardball: How Politics Is Played, Told by One Who Knows the Game*, Christopher Matthews. The inside scoop on the political game and the experts in the field.
- *How to Run for Local Office: A Complete Step-by-Step Guide That Will Take You Through the Entire Process of Running and Winning a Local Election*, Robert J. Thomas. An exhaustive guide for the new politician.
- *The Polished Politician: The Political Candidate's Personal Handbook*, Lillian Brown. Tips for the aspiring politician.
- *Winning Political Campaigns: A Comprehensive Guide to Electoral Success*, William S. Bike. Winning moves to use to get into office.

Politicians in Fiction

Books
- *Full Disclosure*, William Safire. A president is disabled during an assassination attempt.
- *In the Lake of the Woods*, Tim O'Brien. Life after a failed senate reelection campaign.
- *Primary Colors*. A fictionalized account of President Clinton's first bid for the White House. Made into a movie starring John Travolta.
- *The Running Mate*, Joe Klein. A senator loses an election and revisits Vietnam.

- *The Woody*, Peter Lefcourt. A senator struggles to be reelected.

Movies

- *Mr. Smith Goes to Washington* (1939). A young naive senator battles a corrupt Congress.
- *All the King's Men* (1949). A fictional account of Senator Huey Long of Louisiana. Also a novel.
- *Advise and Consent* (1962). A candidate for secretary of state faces troubles in a senate investigation.
- *The Candidate* (1972). Depicts a tainted U.S. Senate race in California.
- *All the President's Men* (1976). An account of Woodward and Bernstein's investigative journalism on Watergate.
- *The Seduction of Joe Tynan* (1979). A young senator faces moral dilemmas.
- *The Distinguished Gentleman* (1992). A con man becomes a politician.
- *Speechless* (1994). Political speechwriters fall in love.
- *City Hall* (1996). Behind-the-scenes politics involving the New York City mayor (Al Pacino).
- *Wag the Dog* (1997). A satire about a presidential sex scandal.

Television

- *Spin City* (1996–). A sitcom about life in the New York mayor's office.
- *The West Wing* (1999–). A compelling drama about the president and his White House staff.

Web Sites

- Google Web Directory (http://directory.google.com/Top/Regional/North_America/United_States/Government/Elections/). A categorized index of local and national elections, campaigns, and candidates.

- Congress Merge (www.congressmerge.com/onlinedb/schedule.htm). Current congressional schedules.

- Yahoo! Index of Political Parties and Groups (http://dir.yah oo.com/Government/U_S__Government/Politics/Parties/. Links to the active political parties in the United States.

BOOK EXCERPTS

Barton Nilson, a senior senator and former governor of Wisconsin, was going nowhere as a prairie populist—he was traveling the state in an RV, camping out instead of staying at hotels, and offering Franklin Roosevelt's jobs program (forestry, road-building) to out-of-work computer jockeys. He seemed ancient at sixty-two—slower, less hungry; it was a valedictory campaign. He had a great head of hair—silver, parted in the middle: perfect prairie-populist hair. He gave grand, juicy speeches in a voice made for crystal radio sets—a dry, crackly, distant, American voice.

—Primary Colors

We shook hands. . . . I've seen him do it two million times now, but I couldn't tell you *how* he does it, the right-handed part of it. . . . He is a genius with [the other hand]. He might put it on your elbow, or up by your biceps: these are basic, reflexive moves. He is interested in you. He is honored to meet you. . . . He'll share a laugh or a secret then—a light secret, not a real one—flattering you with the illusion of conspiracy.

—Primary Colors

[The president] stopped halfway up the stairs and sat on the landing. Good house, he thought; not a palace, not a museum, and not, as some Presidents called it, ''a big white jail.'' Ericson was sitting in its approximate center, with two floors above and below him, the East and West wings stretching out on either side. Most of the other trappings of office were ego-satisfying—the motorcades, the plane, Camp David, the Marine Band, the cocoon of aides and guards—but the House had what none of those had: the ability to give its occupant a historic sense of place.

—Full Disclosure, William Safire

''Senator, let's review your situation,'' Richardson continued. ''You are at forty-one, two points behind among likelies—still within the margin of error. A responsible journalist, if such a creature could be found, would call the race a dead heat. And he would be wrong. Why? Because you're the incumbent. An incumbent below fifty is in the twilight zone. An incumbent below forty-five should start thinking about which industry group might hire him as a lobbyist if he loses. The rule of thumb is, seventy-five percent of undecideds will go against the incumbent.''

—The Running Mate, Joe Klein

Again, John Wade won big, by more than 60,000 votes, then spent the next four years cutting ribbons. Predictably, the lieutenant governorship was a do-nothing job, worse than tedious, but from the beginning he viewed it as little more than a stop along the way. He ran errands, paid attention to his party work, kept his face in the papers. If a Kiwanis club up in Duluth needed a luncheon speaker, he'd make the drive, tell a few jokes over chicken fricassee and give off a winner's golden glow.

—In the Lake of the Woods, Tim O'Brien

The steam room in the Senate Health Facility, as it was now officially called instead of the more familiar Senate Gym, was the type of place where you could lose a pound or two of excess water weight while you were traveling for support on a piece of legislation. In the midst of the wet steam, partisan politics were replaced by a sort of bonhomie that was fostered, perhaps, by the humbling sight of the naked middle-aged male body devoid of any type of sartorial or cosmetic embellishment. It was difficult to posture with your belly hanging out.

—The Woody, Peter Lefcourt

CHAPTER 15

Sex Industry

Prostitute, Exotic Dancer, Stripper, Phone Sex Operator, Web Camera Model, Porn Star

The Lowdown

Perhaps it says something about American's attitude toward prostitution that nearly every major actress in Hollywood has played a hooker at some point in her career. Some commentators attribute this phenomenon to America's immaturity about the realities of sex, making us judgmental and embarrassed about sexual topics that other countries take in stride. Because of this, prostitutes and pimps as characters offer many advantages to a writer:

1. Readers are interested in sex, so submerging them into a world of illicit and kinky sex arouses prurient interest.

2. Because prostitution is illegal, the stakes are high and other illegal activities can be brought in, including drugs, assault, police corruption, and murder.

3. Exploring the motivation of a prostitute allows the writer to delve into issues of need versus morality, as well as the hypocrisy of a society that condemns prostitution but plows billions of dollars into it a year.

4. The needs of the men and women who frequent prostitutes can be used to build morally complex characters.

5. Thematically, prostitution provides an opportunity to probe, on a symbolic level, the concept of physical needs versus spiritual needs.

6. The settings of the world of illicit sex—brothels, motels, alleys, sex shops—are intriguing, colorful backdrops for various types of stories.

Job Description

The sex industry encompasses a wide range of professions, both legal and illegal, including a host of auxiliary professions in publishing and video production. From call girls to porn stars, from phone sex operators to strippers, women and men in the sex industry make a living through some use of their bodies. Whether speaking in a sultry voice, giving sexual massages, or renting out their bodies, workers compete in an industry that can be competitive, difficult, dangerous, and surprisingly unprofitable.

Except for certain areas in Nevada, prostitutes work outside the tax system and, as a result, do not accumulate credit toward benefits such as Social Security and Medicare. In addition, whether working for pimps or as independent contractors, they are not entitled to health insurance. Street prostitutes with pimps tend to turn over all earnings to the pimps in exchange for their material needs. Those working in a bordello or other establishment have to pay a cut to the house. Being outside the system, prostitutes experience the high cost of uninsured medical treatment, especially for frequent checkups, tests for sexually transmitted diseases (STDs), and prescription drugs.

Daily Life

Work Schedule

A typical street prostitute with a pimp might work all night and into the early morning, stopping to hand over earnings during the course of the work schedule. The number of clients varies depending on the prostitute and the area, though ten or more customers a night wouldn't be uncommon. A street prostitute also may have to lure the customers and assure her clients that she isn't an undercover cop—sometimes by flashing. Generally, few undercover cops would flash clients as part of their job. There's no 100 percent assurance that a street prostitute who flashes isn't an undercover cop, however. High-class escorts, a step above those found in the yellow pages, have the fewest number of clients per evening but charge the highest rates.

Dressing the Part
The uniform of street prostitution is characterized by skimpy clothing, even in the coldest climates. Bordello workers may lounge in nightwear, dispensing with even the token modesty of street prostitution. On the other hand, sex workers employed within front businesses, like massage parlors and escort services, often wear professional clothing since they do not reveal sexual services unless asked or tipped.

Keys to the Kingdom
Prostitutes in bordellos and massage parlors have access to the facilities of their places of business. Depending on whether they are incall (working out of their own house) or outcall (going to the client's home) prostitutes, some may use their own homes for business.

Tools of the Trade
In addition to their own bodies, some prostitutes, especially those in bordellos, use sex toys to provide services. These toys range from dildos to sadomasochist ("S&M") equipment and vary depending on a prostitute's inclinations, the clients' tastes, and the size of the clients' pocketbooks.

Elbow Rubbing
Among most professions, prostitutes experience the broadest cross section of clients. Their customers come from every profession, social class, and marital status. Prostitutes working the

streets also are in contact with their colleagues and perhaps a pimp. Workers in massage parlors that offer sex may encounter clients with legitimate muscular complaints. Prostitutes in bordellos may interact with attendant staff such as housekeepers, bar staff, and owners.

An illegal activity in every state but Nevada (and there legal only away from big cities and in bordello settings), prostitution brings with it the threat of arrest. Prostitutes, especially those working the streets, have run-ins with law enforcement officials ranging from the arresting officer to a sentencing judge.

Slang Titles
- Call Girl
- Escort
- Ho
- Hooker
- Streetwalker

Buzzwords

ATM: Men in a stripper's audience.

bareback blow job or *French without:* Oral sex without a condom.

bitch: A pimp's term for his prostitutes.

checking trap: Pimping.

dating: Seeing a prostitute.

French: Oral sex.

fresh turnout: A new prostitute.

full service: Intercourse.

Greek: Anal sex.

half and half: Oral sex and intercourse.

incall: A prostitute working out of her own place.

knockin': The loss or gain of one of a pimp's prostitutes.

mack: A pimp.

on the track: On the job.

outcall: A prostitute who visits the customer's place.

square, boyfriend-girlfriend: A person from the nonprostitution, nonpimping culture.

track: An area of prostitution.

the turnout: The process of a person becoming a prostitute, usually through a pimp.

Job Conflicts

Lack of an Out
Prostitutes can find themselves in conflict with and trapped by abusive pimps. Prostitutes may face criminal prosecution if they are caught, and the resulting criminal record can hinder their efforts to secure legitimate employment.

Burnout
Eventually, successful retirement or age, violence, or drug abuse concludes a prostitute's career. However, because of the material benefits and schedule flexibility that prostitution affords some practitioners, few leave for lesser paying work. One study shows that the ultimate sign of burnout, attempted suicide, has been considered by 75 percent of call girls and 42 percent of brothel workers, vs. 61 percent of nonprostitutes.

Violence on the Job
While violence is prevalent in prostitution, the degree of abuse varies according to working conditions. Physical abuse for street prostitutes comes from clients and sometimes the police, though many streetwalkers face psychological and physical abuse by their pimps. Brothel prostitutes, working in a controlled environment, may experience violence less often than women in domestic situations.

Myths About the Job

Prostitutes Make Good Money

There's no doubt that prostitution is a highly lucrative business, but most prostitutes don't keep most of the money that exchanges hands. The true wealth lies in the hands of pimps, bordellos, and escort service management. While an attractive, motivated prostitute may make well over a thousand dollars a night, much, if not all, of that money may go directly to a pimp. In addition, cash flow is unsteady due to various factors. The supply of prostitution usually rises just before welfare checks are disbursed, when those not usually drawn to prostitution find themselves needing extra cash and competing with full-time prostitutes. Police pressure and presence can limit the prostitution trade. While the income may seem high, earnings drop significantly as a prostitute ages. The inherent risks of violence, substance abuse, an arrest record, and disease impact a prostitute later in life, offsetting any short-term financial gain.

Most Prostitutes Would Rather Be in a Different Profession

While few prostitutes enter the business for any reason other than financial need, few would leave for a lesser paying profession. Prostitutes set their own hours, make money without paying taxes, and work without worrying about a slowing business climate. In addition, those who are employed in legal establishments, such as Nevada's bordellos, work in relative safety and charge rates which would be difficult to attain in another profession.

Prostitution Is the Leading Spreader of Disease

While a prostitute who engages in unprotected sex will spread disease, many prostitutes insist on using condoms to protect themselves and their livelihood. According to the U.S. Department of Health, 30 to 35 percent of sexually transmitted disease in the U.S. occurs among teenagers. Only 3 to 5 percent of sexually transmitted disease occurs through prostitution.

Jobs Within the Profession

Prostitute

Job Description: As the world's oldest profession, prostitution has had time to diversify beyond streetwalkers and call girls. Some of the current incarnations include workers in massage parlors and escort services, and even prostitutes employed in legal brothels, such as the Nevada "ranches." Although the work requirements for prostitutes may be similar, prostitutes with pimps, workers in massage parlors, and prostitutes in a bordello have very different on-the-job experiences. Prostitutes with pimps typically receive none of the proceeds of their work directly. Instead, they hand over 100 percent of their earnings to the pimps who, in turn, supply them with material needs, such as an apartment, food, clothing, medicine, and sometimes drugs. Prostitutes in legal bordellos get a percentage of their earnings docked by the house, but they earn much more than streetwalkers and do so in a relatively safe and secure setting. Workers in massage parlors offering sex services usually receive payment for sexual services in the form of tips. These services are initiated by customers; however the workers limit the range of sex services they provide.

Most prostitutes are in the business for one simple reason: money. A prostitute's greatest motivation is to earn and keep the kind of money that would be difficult to earn in a legitimate position. Success depends on a number of factors, among them the type of prostitution they're engaged in, their physical attractiveness, and their location. The most successful prostitutes are attractive women working for high-class escort services in large cities. Prostitutes in legal bordellos can earn large sums, but they miss out on the benefits of being wined and dined as a precursor to sex—and they operate strictly within the unpopulated boonies of Nevada. Those who perhaps work the hardest—streetwalkers—make very little money and suffer the most abuse, from both customers and pimps.

A successful prostitute enjoys the ability to control the amount she works, and she benefits from the flexibility that comes with being an independent contractor. This flexibility allows a prostitute to earn decent money and still have the time to raise a child, care for someone with an illness, or—if leaving the profession is a goal—prepare for another occupation. In addition, prostitutes may be able to cultivate a group of clients who enjoy their services, so they can have a degree of job satisfaction, job security, and even safety.

Earnings: The take-home pay of a prostitute varies widely based on a number of factors, including place of business (street, massage parlor, bordello) and any management, i.e., a pimp. Prostitutes with a pimp receive no direct money from their work, while other prostitutes suffer a much less severe cut. How much a prostitute can earn is also based on the prostitute's location, looks, age, repertoire of sexual acts, and the amount of work over a given period. A street prostitute or massage worker may charge the following amounts:

- Oral sex: $30–$50
- Intercourse: $50–$70
- Half and half: $50–$100
- Anal sex: $70–$150

Call girls may typically take in somewhere between $75 and $1,500 an hour, or in the range of $75,000 a year and up, with half going to the house. Prostitutes in bordellos, after the house's take, may approach $100,000 a year or more in earnings.

Number of Prostitutes: According to the National Task Force on Prostitution, about 1 percent of women in the U.S.—over one million people—have been prostitutes. In a large city with massage parlors, call girls, and escort services, only 10 to 20 percent of prostitutes may work the streets. In small cities and towns, this percentage may be as high as 50 percent. Prostitutes come from every background, though arrest data doesn't accurately reflect who prostitutes are. Street work makes up only 20 percent of prostitution but accounts for 85 to 90 percent of all arrests. In addition, a higher number of nonwhite prostitutes are arrested despite being a minority. Finally, 20 to 30 percent of prostitutes in big cities may be men, and in some cities, such as San Francisco, transgender workers account for up to 25 percent of the female statistic.

Further Info:
- COYOTE (Call Off Your Old Tired Ethics) is a prostitutes' rights organization.
  2269 Chestnut St., #452
  San Francisco, CA 94123
- COYOTE
  1626 Wilcox Ave., #580
  Los Angeles, CA 90028
- Sex Workers Alliance of Vancouver
  P.O. Box 3075
  Vancouver, BC V6B 3X6
  Canada
- Sex Workers Outreach Project
  P.O. Box 1354
  Strawberry Hills, NSW 2012
  Australia

Exotic Dancer, Stripper

Job Description: Exotic dancers and strippers may get started in this profession by being noticed by a strip club manager during amateur night. Most dancers and strippers are hired as independent contractors and earn their living through tips. As independent contractors, they are ineligible for unemployment benefits, workers compensation, and other benefits. Many clubs also require payment of up to 50 percent of a stripper's earnings. Some strippers may have a quota which, if not met, becomes a debt to the strip club. Some clubs impose fines for everything from being late to missing work because of illness. Though outwardly against the rules, strippers may engage in sex with club owners or guests to pay off debts or in exchange for better and more lucrative working hours. Sex between strippers and patrons is not typical, though having to compete with other strippers for tips may lead to more overt acts. Private dances include everything short of sexual intercourse. In general, dancers and strippers are vulnerable to alcohol abuse because of their work setting: Customers offer free drinks to strippers, and some house policies forbid turning down a drink from a patron.

Further Info:
- The Exotic Dancer Page (www.exclusivetvlnet.com/dancer/ home.htm). Links and resources for exotic dancers.

Phone Sex Operator, Web Camera Model

Job Description: Unlike strippers, phone sex operators and Web camera models work from home or a business closed to the public. They communicate with clients through a dedicated phone number and/or an Internet connection and Web camera. Many phone sex and Web camera companies require their workers to solicit customers in online chat rooms.

Earnings: Income depends on the length of time a client can be kept on the phone or online. Clients are charged between $2 and $4 per minute, while workers earn about half of that. Phone sex operators and Web camera models can earn up to $600 a week.

Further Reading:
- *Diary of a Phone Sex "Mistress,"* Gary Anthony.

Porn Star

Job Description: Porn stars make a living by starring in adult films, which require modest acting skills and large amounts of real or simulated sex with other actors. Female stars are paid more than men and may be on contract with a production company. The majority of work is in Los Angeles, where most production companies are located. The length of one's career in adult films can be limited by age. Actors are tested monthly for sexually transmitted diseases.

Earnings: Porn stars are paid approximately $500 per sex scene, sometimes less. Successful stars may be paid several thousand dollars per movie.

Further Reading:
- *1, 2, 3, Be a Porn Star: A Step-by-Step Guide to the Adult Sex Industry*, Ana Loria.

Additional Occupations

Some professions in the sex industry are decidedly seedy, but the industry also requires its share of professionals to handle money, promotion, and management. Some of these include

- accountant
- brothel manager
- graphic artist
- massage parlor manager
- photographer
- pimp
- strip club owner
- videographer
- Web site programmer

Employers for the above positions include the following:

- adult film production company
- adult magazine
- adult Web site
- brothel
- strip club

Sex Industry Workers in Nonfiction

Books
- *Brothel: Mustang Ranch and Its Women*, Alexa Albert. The inner workings of a legal brothel in Nevada.
- *Common Women: Prostitution and Sexuality in Medieval England*, Ruth Mazo Karras. An examination of prostitution in the Middle Ages.
- *Good Girls/Bad Girls: Feminists and Sex Trade Workers Face to Face*, Laurie Bell, ed. Descriptions of prostitutes' working conditions.
- *Mayflower Madam: The Secret Life of Sydney Biddle Barrows*, Sydney Biddle Barrows. The story of an escort service and why men use them.
- *1, 2, 3, Be a Porn Star: A Step-by-Step Guide to the Adult Sex Industry*, Ana Loria. A guide to working in adult films.

- *Tricks and Treats: Sex Workers Write About Their Clients*, Matt Bernstein Sycamore, ed. Detailed accounts of escorts' lives and clients from an inside perspective.
- *Turning Pro: A Guide to Sex Work for the Ambitious and the Intrigued*, Magdalene Meretrix. A guide for starting out as a sex worker, from phone sex to exotic dancing.

Documentaries
- *American Pimp* (2000). The world of pimping and prostitution through the eyes of pimps.
- *Live Nude Girls Unite* (2000). A documentary about a strippers' and exotic dancers' union.

Sex Industry Workers in Fiction

Books
- *Bone House*, Betsy Tobin. Examines how a prostitute and her death affects a seventeenth-century rural village in England.
- *The Diary of a Manhattan Call Girl*, Tracy Quan. A semiautobiographical novel based on the author's experience as a call girl.
- *Keeper of the House*, Rebecca T. Godwin. A story of a 1930s brothel in South Carolina, from the point of view of a housekeeping staff member.
- *Maggie, a Girl of the Streets*, Stephen Crane. A slum girl's descent into prostitution.
- *Moll Flanders*, Daniel Defoe. A classic tale of a prostitute.
- *Nowhere to Hide*, James Elliott. A call girl witnesses murder and gets protection.
- *Storyville*, Lois Battle. Depicts legal prostitution at the turn of the nineteenth century in the Storyville district of New Orleans.

Movies
- *Belle de Jour* (1967). A married woman begins working in a brothel.
- *Midnight Cowboy* (1969). Male prostitution in New York City.
- *Klute* (1971). A call girl is stalked.

- *Risky Business* (1983). A suburban teenager (Tom Cruise) steps into the world of call girls and pimps.
- *Street Smart* (1987). An intense drama about a magazine writer who investigates the world of pimps.
- *Pretty Woman* (1990). A romantic comedy about a john and a hooker (Julia Roberts) falling in love.
- *Johns* (1996). Male prostitution in Los Angeles.
- *Boogie Nights* (1997). A portrayal of the pornography industry in the 1970s and 1980s.
- *Claire Dolan* (1998). A call girl leaves her pimp to start a different life.
- *Dangerous Beauty* (1998). Prostitution in the sixteenth century.

Web Sites

- **Prostitutes' Education Network** (www.bayswan.org/penet.html). Contains articles, papers, statistics, and links related to prostitution.

- **World Sex Guide** (www.worldsexguide.org). Johns' points of view of prostitutes and prostitution.

- **About.com: Sexuality** (http://sexuality.about.com/health/sexuality/library/weekly/aa031797.htm?rnk=r1&terms=prostitution). Newsletter addressing prostitution-related issues.

- **BlackStockings** (www.blackstockings-seattle.com). A discussion site about and for sex industry workers.

- **AdultStaffing** (www.adultstaffing.com/). Job boards for sex industry workers, including salaries and job requirements.

- **Stripper Power** (http://stripperpower.com/hustle.shtml). Links to stripping resources.

BOOK EXCERPTS

I do not know when she began to trade her body, or how it happened, or indeed whether she had planned it so. Only that it seemed both right and natural. As a child, I used to play outside her cottage. Men came and went, and always they were cheerful. When I asked my mother why Dora had so many visitors, she told me that the house was a shop, selling things that people liked but did not need. . . . I came to think of her house as a sort of tavern, where men could come and gorge like kings, and feel contented.

—Bone House, Betsy Tobin

How they stand it, jumping in bed with any old man's got the money and inclination, I ain't know. In between changing linens, I now and again catch sight of customers. They every kind of man you can think of—saw one so fat he had slits for eyes, fingers like wild hog sausages, following close behind tiny Chantal, who's leading him off to her outback room. . . . They're loud and sometimes mean, I hear Chantal and Bess talk about that, how sometime they treat them so rough . . . All night long, those girls traipse back and forth between parlor and rooms, with me right behind, tearing off sheets, making up beds.

—Keeper of the House, Rebecca T. Godwin

Darla . . . made up names for different kinds
of tricks, put them in groups, said it kinda
helped you know what to expect, gave you
something to think about while you're waiting for it to be over. Quick trick, that was
one—like one of them scared-to-death cher-
ries we get sometime, else one of them old
ones, skin hangs on them like a bad set of
long johns—that's what Darla used to say.
You know the ones—sometime can't even wait
till they get inside, groaning while they're
walking behind you—seem like they ain't been
touched by human hands for years. Wham-bam-
thankyou-mammers, she called them. . . . Then
she had other ones—hick trick for rubes,
slick trick—them fancy ones, think they know
stuff. Lick trick. Called that Irish boy,
Sean, from the paper mill, mick trick. And
then there's sick tricks, now we get every
once in a while. Scary ones.

—Keeper of the House, Rebecca T. Godwin

Mollie couldn't believe her luck. She'd
been ready to take anything, but this was
the sort of girl you recruited once in a
lifetime. . . . her father had probably
knocked her about, she'd run away with some
john who'd popped her cherry and left her
flat. . . . She took Kate into the bathroom,
told her to undress, and ran a tub for her.
Turning around after scattering a generous
amount of bath salts into the water, she saw

Kate sitting naked on the chair and exclaimed, ''Oh, dearie, you sittin' on a gold mine!'' The girl's body was as beautiful as her face. Once she was dolled up, she'd be the toast of the District.

While Kate bathed and washed her hair, Mollie gave her usual lecture, explaining the cost of ''board'' and the cut she'd take on the customers. She opened the cabinet and showed her the douches and preventatives. . . .

There were certain positions, squeezes, and feigned cries of pleasure that could bring a man off fast. You shouldn't take off your clothes unless the customer was an overnighter. There were ways of protecting your breasts and face if it looked as though the customer were going to get rough.

—<u>Storyville</u>, Lois Battle

Index

F

Fashion photographer, 230
Fast Copy, 158-159
Federal Bureau of
    Investigation (FBI)
  agent, 169-170
  Web site, 177
Fiction
  advertising, 24-25
  architecture, 45
  clorgy, 60 70
  dentistry, 106-107
  firefighting, 142
  journalism, 156-157
  law enforcement, 176-177
  lawyer, 90
  life sciences, 197
  medical sciences, 218-219
  modeling, 232-233
  moviemaking, 270-272
  political sciences, 288-289
  sex industry, 304-305
  teaching, 125-127
Film-Makers.com, 273
FindLaw, Web site, 92
Fire chief, 141-142
Fire Department, City of New
    York, Web site, 143
Fire dispatcher, 140-141
Fire investigator, 137-139
Firefighting, 132-133
  daily life, 134-135
  education, 135
  fiction and nonfiction, 142
  job conflicts, 136-137
  job description, 133-134

  jobs within profession,
    137-142
  myths, 137
  Web sites, 143
Firehouse.com, 143
Forensic dentist, 105
Forty Words for Sorrow, 179
Fountainhead, The, 46-47
Fourth Angel, The, 143
Full Disclosure, 291

G

Gerritsen, Tess, 223
Getting Straight, 28-29,
    130-131
Godwin, Rebecca T.,
    306-307
Golden Age, The, 158
Googlc Web Directory,
    political sciences, 289
Graphic designer, 17-18
Grass, Günter, 108
Greene, Graham, 71
Grisham, John, 94

H

Harmful Intent, 220
Haruf, Kent, 129
Harvest, 222-223
Hint Fashion Magazine, Web
    site, 234
Homes, A.M., 145
Homosexuality, in clergy, 54
Hostile Witness, 93
Hudson, Jeffrey, 223

I

IATSE Local 695, Web site, 272

Illustrated Architecture Dictionary, Web site, 46

In the Lake of the Woods, 292

Independent contractor, advertising, 20-21

Independent Feature Project, Web site, 273

In-house advertising department, 7

Inner-City School Teacher Blues, Web site, 128

INS agent, 173-174

Insider's Guide to Supermodels and Modeling, The, Web site, 234

Institute for the Study of American Religion, Web site, 70

Interior designer, 40-41

Intern architect, 38

Internet Movie Database, The, Web site, 273

Internet Resources for Family Physicians, Web site, 219

Isaacs, Susan, 109

J

Jenkins, Dan, 159

Job conflicts
advertising, 11-12
architecture, 35-36

clergy, 53-55
dentistry, 101-102
firefighting, 136-137
journalism, 149-150
law enforcement, 166
lawyer, 82-83
life sciences, 185-187
medical sciences, 209-210
modeling, 226-227
moviemaking, 240-244
political sciences, 281-282
sex industry, 297
teaching, 116-117

Job description
actor, 254-256
advertising, 6-8
account executive, 21
creative director, 14-15
director, 13-14
animal behaviorist, 191-192
animal caretaker, 192-193
architecture, 31-32
architect, 37
drafter, 38-39
arson investigator, 137-138
art director, 15, 262
artist's model, 229
ATF agent, 171-172
attorney. *See* Lawyer
bailiff, 88
biochemist, 194
biologist, 189-190
botanist, 194-195
building contractor, 40
cantor, 64
casting director, 261

K

More Of The Best Books For Writers!

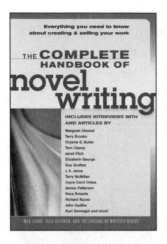

The Complete Handbook of Novel Writing—Here's your ticket to an extraordinary gathering of best-selling authors and publishing insiders. Their advice and experience will help you turn those ideas, notes and half-finished manuscripts into a finely polished novel that's ready to sell! You'll also find interviews with some of the world's finest writers, including Margaret Atwood, Tom Clancy, Sue Grafton, Nora Roberts and more.

ISBN 1-58297-159-5 ✶ paperback ✶
400 pages ✶ #10825-K

Lessons from a Lifetime of Writing—Best-selling author David Morrell distills more than 30 years of writing and publishing experience into this single masterwork of advice and instruction. With unique insights that illuminate the craft and business of writing, he examines everything from motivation and focus to the building blocks of good fiction: plot, character, dialogue, description and more.

ISBN 1-58297-143-9 ✶ hardcover ✶
256 pages ✶ #10808-K

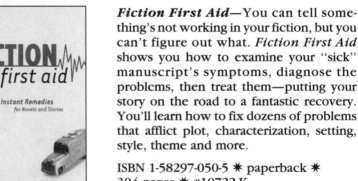

Fiction First Aid—You can tell something's not working in your fiction, but you can't figure out what. *Fiction First Aid* shows you how to examine your "sick" manuscript's symptoms, diagnose the problems, then treat them—putting your story on the road to a fantastic recovery. You'll learn how to fix dozens of problems that afflict plot, characterization, setting, style, theme and more.

ISBN 1-58297-050-5 ✶ paperback ✶
304 pages ✶ #10722-K

45 Master Characters—Make your characters and their stories more compelling, complex and original than ever before. This book explores the most common male and female archetypes—the mythic, cross-cultural models from which all characters originate—and shows you how to use them as foundations for your own unique characters. Examples culled from literature, television and film illustrate just how memorable and effective these archetypes can be.

ISBN 1-58297-069-6 ✳ hardcover ✳ 256 pages ✳ 10752-K

The Pocket Muse—This wonderful book is your key to finding inspiration when and where you want it. Hundreds of thought-provoking prompts, exercises and illustrations help you get started writing, overcome writer's block, develop a writing habit, and think more creatively. You'll find all the inspiration you need to create a story and think about how you write in new and surprising ways.

ISBN 1-58297-142-0 ✳ hardcover ✳ 256 pages ✳ #10806-K

The Writer's Idea Book—This is the guide writers reach for time after time to jump start their creativity and develop ideas. Four distinctive sections, each geared toward a different stage of writing, offer dozens of unique approaches to "freeing the muse." In all, you'll find more than 400 idea-generating prompts guaranteed to get your writing started on the right foot, or back on track!

ISBN 1-58297-179-X ✳ paperback ✳ 272 pages ✳ #10841-K

Agents, Editors, and You—Here's your ticket to the world of publishing—a once-in-a-lifetime roundup of the editors and agents that can turn your manuscript into money. Through interviews and articles, they'll teach you how to navigate the publishing landscape like an insider. You'll learn what editors and agents are looking for, what an agent really does, how to write a stand-out book proposal and more!

ISBN 1-58297-152-8 ✳ paperback ✳ 256 pages ✳ #10817-K

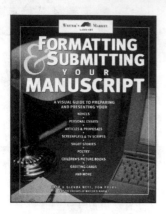

Formatting & Submitting Your Manuscript—Increase your odds of getting published! *Formatting & Submitting Your Manuscript* makes it easy by featuring full-size examples of how to present your manuscript. Covering every part of the manuscript submission package—from query letters and proposals to synopses and follow-up correspondence—this guide shows you the dos and don'ts for creating a persuasive and professional first impression.

ISBN 0-89879-921-X ✷ paperback ✷ 248 pages ✷ #10618-K

Get Organized, Get Published—This lively, inspirational and browsable book provides tips for living the writer's life simply and efficiently. You'll find page after page of useful advice, covering everything from organizing your desk to tracking submissions. By following this advice, you'll generate more ideas, complete more projects, and systematically submit your work to editors and agents.

ISBN 1-58297-003-3 ✷ hardcover ✷ 240 pages ✷ #10689-K

Guerrilla Marketing for Writers—Packed with proven insights and advice, *Guerrilla Marketing for Writers* details 100 "classified secrets" that will help you sell your work before and after it's published. This wide range of weapons—practical low-cost and no-cost marketing techniques—will help you design a powerful strategy for strengthening your proposals, promoting your books and maximizing your sales.

ISBN 0-89879-983-X ✷ hardcover ✷ 292 pages ✷ #10667-K

These books and other fine Writer's Digest titles are available from your local bookstore, online supplier or by calling 1-800-448-0915.